REMINISCENCES OF MANCHESTER
FIFTY YEARS AGO

The Development of Industrial Society Series

J. T. Slugg

REMINISCENCES OF MANCHESTER FIFTY YEARS AGO

IRISH UNIVERSITY PRESS
Shannon   Ireland

First edition Manchester and London 1881

This I U P reprint is a photolithographic facsimile of the first edition and is unabridged, retaining the original printer's imprint.

© *1971 Irish University Press Shannon Ireland*

All forms of micropublishing
© *Irish University Microforms Shannon Ireland*

ISBN 0 7165 1771 X

T M MacGlinchey Publisher

Irish University Press Shannon Ireland

PRINTED IN THE REPUBLIC OF IRELAND BY
ROBERT HOGG PRINTER TO IRISH UNIVERSITY PRESS

The Development of Industrial Society Series

This series comprises reprints of contemporary documents and commentaries on the social, political and economic upheavals in nineteenth-century England.

England, as the first industrial nation, was also the first country to experience the tremendous social and cultural impact consequent on the alienation of people in industrialized countries from their rural ancestry. The Industrial Revolution which had begun to intensify in the mid-eighteenth century, spread swiftly from England to Europe and America. Its effects have been far-reaching: the growth of cities with their urgent social and physical problems; greater social mobility; mass education; increasingly complex administration requirements in both local and central government; the growth of democracy and the development of new theories in economics; agricultural reform and the transformation of a way of life.

While it would be pretentious to claim for a series such as this an in-depth coverage of all these aspects of the new society, the works selected range in content from *The Hungry Forties* (1904), a collection of letters by ordinary working people describing their living conditions and the effects of mechanization on their day-to-day lives, to such analytical studies as Leone Levi's *History of British Commerce* (1880) and *Wages and Earnings of the Working Classes* (1885); M. T. Sadler's *The Law of Population* (1830); John Wade's radical documentation of government corruption, *The Extraordinary Black Book* (1831); C. Edward Lester's trenchant social investigation, *The Glory and Shame of England* (1866); and many other influential books and pamphlets.

The editor's intention has been to make available important contemporary accounts, studies and records, written or compiled by men and women of integrity and scholarship whose reactions to the growth of a new kind of society are valid touchstones for today's reader. Each title (and the particular edition used) has been chosen on a twofold basis (1) its intrinsic worth as a record or commentary, and (2) its contribution to the development of an industrial society. It is hoped that this collection will help to increase our understanding of a people and an epoch.

The Editor
Irish University Press

REMINISCENCES

OF

MANCHESTER

FIFTY YEARS AGO.

BY

J. T. SLUGG, F.R.A.S.,

AUTHOR OF "THE STARS AND THE TELESCOPE,"
AND "INTRODUCTION TO OBSERVATIONAL ASTRONOMY."

MANCHESTER:
J. E. CORNISH, 33, PICCADILLY, AND 16, ST. ANN'S SQUARE.

LONDON: SIMPKIN, MARSHALL, & Co.

1881.

PREFACE.

THE present volume of Reminiscences is intended to convey an approximate idea of the Manchester of Fifty Years Ago—of its outward aspect, its trade, customs, manners, and society, and its form of government some years before it obtained its Charter of Incorporation, and long before it attained to the dignity of a city.

If justification were needed for its publication, it will be found in the wide interest which its contents excited as they appeared in the columns of the *Manchester City News*. Such a step as their appearance in book form was the farthest thing imaginable from the mind of the author when he sent his first chapter to the editor of that journal, his expectation then being that all he had to say would be completed in some half-dozen or dozen chapters. As he proceeded, however, his work grew under his hand, a result which was fostered by a classification of the subjects.

The area covered by the numerous topics handled being large, it was impossible to avoid an occasional mistake. These errors were pointed out in most cases by correspondents of the *City News*, and also privately. In the present volume such corrections have been adopted, and a most careful revision has been made of the contents. The author wishes to draw attention to the fact that the period to which these Reminiscences refers is that which is indicated in the title. Many aged persons who remember well-known characters living in Manchester fifty-five or sixty years ago have been disappointed at not finding their names mentioned, and have erroneously spoken of the absence of such names as omissions.

Many portions have been re-written, and a considerable quantity of new matter has been added. To those gentlemen who have kindly furnished information and corrections, the author tenders his sincere thanks. Their names are too numerous to mention, and to single any out would be invidious.

J. T. S.

Chorlton-cum-Hardy,
  January, 1881.

CONTENTS.

CHAPTER.			PAGE.
I.	STREETS AND BRIDGES.		1
II.	WHOLESALE FIRMS		17
III.	CALICO PRINTERS.		27
IV.	BLEACHERS, DRYSALTERS, AND HOOKERS-IN .		41
V.	DOCTORS		47
VI.	DRUGGISTS.		60
VII.	BOOKSELLERS.		77
VIII.	SUNDRY TRADERS, ENGINEERS, AND PROFESSORS		91
IX.	NOTABLE PERSONS.		105
X.	PLACES OF WORSHIP—CHURCH OF ENGLAND .		115
XI.	Do.	INDEPENDENT CHAPELS .	128
XII.	Do.	WESLEYAN METHODIST CHAPELS	147
XIII.	Do.	UNITARIAN CHAPELS .	170
XIV.	Do.	VARIOUS .	181
XV.	LAWYERS AND MAGISTRATES		195
XVI.	THE POST OFFICE.		202
XVII.	STAGE COACHING DAYS		209
XVIII.	TRAVEL AND GOODS CARRIAGE BY ROAD AND CANAL		219
XIX.	OPENING OF THE RAILWAY TO LIVERPOOL .		227
XX.	GOVERNMENT OF TOWN : CURIOUS OFFICIALS .		235
XXI.	GAS, WATER, AND HACKNEY COACHES		242
XXII.	MEDICAL AND OTHER CHARITABLE INSTITUTIONS		247
XXIII.	LITERARY, SCIENTIFIC, AND OTHER SOCIETIES .		260
XXIV.	NEWSPAPERS		276
XXV.	BUILDING CLUBS		292
XXVI.	MUSIC, PAGANINI, AND MALIBRAN .		297
XXVII.	PUBLIC AMUSEMENTS		307
XXVIII.	DRESS AND CONCLUSION		316
	APPENDIX		323
	OBITUARY .		333

REMINISCENCES OF MANCHESTER

FIFTY YEARS AGO.

———◆———

CHAPTER I.

THE STREETS AND BRIDGES.

IT was on the afternoon of a certain Monday in March, 1829, that I was driven to Manchester in his gig by the father of the late Mr. John Robinson Kay, formerly a director of the Lancashire and Yorkshire Railway, who lived at Longholme, near Bacup, where my father, who was a Wesleyan minister, then was stationed. Having lived in Manchester ever since, I propose to furnish some reminiscences of the Manchester of that period.

Mr. Kay was a manufacturer of cloth, both by steam power and hand loom, and always attended the Manchester market on a Tuesday. A very different thing it was then for a country manufacturer to attend the Tuesday's market from what it is now. With what ease and comfort, by the aid of a first-class carriage and an express train, he is now transported to Manchester, going and returning the same

day, even to and from places as distant as Blackburn and
Burnley.   Then, if a manufacturer lived fifteen or twenty
miles from Manchester, he generally came on the Monday
previously, frequently driving his own conveyance, and put
up at some inn—there were not many "hotels" in those
days—the name of which was given in the "Directory,"
as well as the address of his place of business in town.
Accordingly, in that for 1829, we find, under the head of
"Country Manufacturers," "Kay, Thomas, calico manufacturer, Longholme, 3, Walton's Buildings, Tues., White
Lion, Hanging Ditch."   This is a sample of most other
entries under that head, though here and there one may be
found having only the place of business named.

After Mr. Kay had put his horse up at the White Lion,
he conducted me to my future home, No. 21, Market
Street.   The same shop is now numbered 41, inasmuch as
the streets were not then numbered on the sensible plan at
present adopted, viz., the even numbers on one side and
the odd on the other.   Market Street was numbered, for
instance, from the first shop on the left-hand side going up—
which was then, and till very lately, that of Clark, cutler—
consecutively to the last shop on the same side, which was
occupied by R. and J. Gleave, booksellers, and was numbered 61 ; then crossing over the top of Market Street, 62
was the Royal Hotel and New Bridgewater Arms, kept by
Henry Charles Lacey, which had been removed from the
corner of High Street a few years previously ; and the last
shop on the left-hand side going down was 108, occupied
by Mr. Prince, a grocer, who made a princely fortune, and
from whom Prince's Court was named.   Prince's Court

existed till the last enlargement of the Exchange, which
now covers the site. A few weeks after my coming to Manchester, I was taken to the office of Messrs. Atkinson and
Birch, in Norfolk Street, then one of the leading firms of
solicitors, and bound an apprentice to W. Dentith and Co.,
wholesale and retail druggists. One of my fellow-apprentices
was the youngest son of the celebrated Dr. Warren, and
brother of the late Samuel Warren, recorder of Hull, and
author of the " Diary of a Late Physician," and " Ten
Thousand a Year." Warren's brother Edward was an artist
of some promise.

About ten or twelve years before the time I speak of a
special Act of Parliament had empowered certain commissioners to widen and improve Market Street. This had
been nearly completed but not entirely ; there were two old
piles of buildings still left standing. One was that which
occupied the site of the front part of the present Exchange,
and which when pulled down was succeeded by the ever-
memorable Newall's Buildings (No. 1). Mr. Newall, who
was a grocer, was then living, his shop being the first in the
old building going up the street. In the alteration Market
Street had been raised at the lower end and lowered at the
middle part. Consequently the floor of Newall's shop was
lower than the level of the street, and to enter it you had
to descend by a step. The next shop to this was Shaw's, a
saddler ; then came a florist and seedsman, whose nursery
was in Cheetwood. Next was Charles Lovatt, the well-
known tobacconist. By the way, there were then only
twenty-three tobacconists in the whole of Manchester and
Salford. To-day, to show how society has in one respect

made a retrograde movement, I may mention that the last
"Directory" contains the names of nearly 500.   Of course
some allowance must be made for increase of population,
but will that account for all this difference?   The last place
of business in this old pile was the Peacock Coach Office,
kept by Mr. John Knowles, the father of the late proprietor
of the Theatre Royal, who also carried on the business of a
coal merchant at Ducie Street, Piccadilly.   It was from this
office that the afterwards popular London coach the Peveril
of the Peak started, it then being only a two-horse one.

The other pile of old buildings stood nearly opposite
Spring Gardens, on the site now occupied by the shop of
Messrs. Woolley and the adjacent ones.   The street here
having been considerably lowered, the footpath on that
side was on a sort of bank, which separated the carriage way
from the path.   Singular to say, there was also a coach
office in this old pile, the Swan, kept by Weatherald and
Webster—(the latter gentleman was a Quaker)—from which
the Red Rover used to start.   Next to it was the shop of
Mr. Hargreaves, then one of the oldest druggists in Manchester; and hereabouts was the place of business for a
time of Old Weatherley, the bookseller.   A little higher up
was Cunliffes, Brooks, and Co.'s Bank ; and near it was the
warehouse of Mr. Emmanuel Mendel, father of Mr. Sam
Mendel, a rope, twine, and pitch-paper manufacturer, his
house being in Brazennose Street.   A little higher up again
was the Palace Inn, which stood back, having a good open
space in front, and being a large brick house having a double
flight of steps at the front door.   It is well known that in
1745 Mr. Dickensen lived and entertained Prince Charles

here. John, the head waiter for many years, was widely known. He afterwards kept the King's Arms, at the bottom of King Street, his name being Pownall.

The time prescribed by the Act of Parliament for effecting the improvement of Market Street was limited, I believe, to twelve years. When it had transpired, there was one more alteration to be effected and which was consequently not made for many years after. The next shop to the inn at the corner of Palace Street, occupied by Mr. John Roberts, the stationer, projected a little beyond the line of the street, and has only been pulled down at a recent date, having been the subject of litigation between Mr. James Cheetham, the last occupier, and the Corporation. The office of the *Guardian* newspaper, published by Messrs. Taylor and Garnett, was on the opposite side of the street, nearer Brown Street. Neither Corporation Street nor New Brown Street had then any existence, whilst a portion of Cross Street running from Chapel Walks to Market Street, then known as Pool Fold, was a narrow and somewhat dingy street. In it was the office of Hannibal Becker and Co., large oil of vitriol manufacturers. Mr. Becker was an ancestor of a well-known member of the Manchester School Board. The first shop on the right hand near where the Exchange steps now stand, was that of Patison, a confectioner; next was a tavern called the Rifleman; and next the book shop of Ann Hopps, the wife of James Hopps, who was the brother of John, a well-known bookseller. The shop was entered by a flight of steps, and Mrs. Hopps lodged with Morris, a chimney sweeper, who lived farther on in the same street.

Of course we should hardly expect that any one who was in business fifty years ago in Market Street would be found there to-day. In the case of the Messrs. Darbyshire, the business is still carried on by the sons, whom I well remember as youths. A few other names are still perpetuated—though the owners have long since passed away—in Lynch and Jewsbury, the druggists, Mr. Daniel Lynch being a leading man amongst the Freemasons of that day. The celebrated James Everett, the Wesleyan minister, at that time kept a stationer's shop about ten doors above Clark's. He was originally a Wesleyan minister, but on account of a throat affection went into business, and afterwards re-entered the ministry. The next shop was that of the fashionable hatter of that day, Mr. Mountcastle, whose appearance was rather remarkable, being very good looking, always unusually well dressed, and wearing a scrupulously white neckerchief. At that time there was a very heavy duty on all kinds of glass, and as a consequence not a single shop-window contained any plate glass, but shop windows were composed of small squares of ordinary crown glass. The first shop which made a venture in that line was one very near Mr. Mountcastle's, I think a milliner's, and called Chantilly House. This was before the duty was taken off. There were two windows, and in the centre of each was inserted a brass frame about two feet long and one and a half broad, holding a sheet of plate glass. It used to be said that the two cost more than £30. If the object of the proprietor was to cause a little sensation I am sure he was gratified, for everybody went to see these "large" squares of plate glass.

The next building to the Bridgewater Arms coach office was the warehouse of H. Bannerman and Sons ; and not far from this was the office of Mr. David Holt, generally known as Quaker Holt, a cotton spinner, who was reputed to be the best carver at a public dinner-table in Manchester. He was one of the commissioners for the widening of Market Street. Nearly opposite to Dentiths' was the Norwich Union Fire Office, having a statue of Justice blindfolded over the door. The Talbot Inn, which was pulled down a few years since, was then standing at the corner of the street now called West Mosley Street ; and a little lower down was the Mosley Arms, afterwards removed to Piccadilly. Turning out of Market Street into Brown Street, next to the Commercial Inn, were the Shambles, since converted into the Post Office ; and over was the Manor Court Room, where the Court Leet was held, where the boroughreeve and constables were elected, and where the "Court of Requests" was held. The Court, which had only jurisdiction to the amount of forty shillings, was presided over by commissioners, of whom the chairman was a barrister named Hill, whilst his colleagues were laymen, as in a Court of Quarter Sessions.

The left-hand side of Piccadilly going from Market Street consisted principally of shops, a few private houses, and offices. Amongst the shops was that of Mr. Joseph Kidson, a tailor, which remains yet in the hands of his son. The supply of water was then in the hands of the Manchester and Salford Waterworks Company, and it was here they had their offices. Near to them was that of the well-known John Law, a solicitor, who was very popular as an advocate in the police court, his opponent generally being another solicitor, Edward Foulkes. Opposite the end of Portland Street were two good houses, in one of which Mr. John Roberts the stationer lived, the other being occupied by Mr. James Bloor, one of the principal pawnbrokers, whose business was conducted at the back of his premises in Back Piccadilly, the front presenting all the appearance of a private house. Mr. Bloor now resides at Southport, a hale and hearty old man nearly eighty years of age, and he told me lately that having been born in that house he resided there for seventy-two years. Will not this fact bear out what Mr. Turner the surgeon used to say as to the mistaken views of those people who are so fond of talking of the unhealthiness of Manchester? Mr. Turner lived for the greater part of his life in the heart of Manchester, and after spending many of his last years in Mosley Street, died at a good old age. I am tempted to add my own testimony to the effect that at a most important period of my life, when being developed from a boy into a man, I lived eight years in Market Street, and had not a day's illness during the whole time.

Instead of the magnificent hotel which now stands at the corner of Portland Street, there existed two or three large brick houses, known as Portland Place. In the first of them dwelt Mr. Thomas Houldsworth, who lived to be one of the oldest members of Parliament, representing successively Pontefract, Newton, and North Notts. "Houldsworth's Factory," in Little Lever Street, was well known all over Manchester. He was very popular amongst his employés, as well as amongst the inhabitants generally, and was a liberal supporter of the races, keeping a stud of racehorses his jockeys always wearing green and gold. The next house was occupied by Mr. Robert Ogden, cotton spinner; and the next by the two partners in the firm of Hargreaves and Dugdale, calico printers, whose warehouse was in Marsden's Square.

The Infirmary was a plain brick building, without the two wings, which have been added to it since; the lunatic asylum, which had a lower elevation, being an extension of the main building. In front was the sheet of water known as the Infirmary Pond, separated from the footpath by palisading. At the Infirmary gates stood the public baths, the income arising from them being appropriated to the support of the Infirmary. The charge for a cold bath to non subscribers was 1s.; to subscribers of half-a-guinea, 10d.; and to those of a guinea, 9d. The price of a vapour bath was 5s.; of a vapour and hot bath when used together, 6s.; and of the shampooing bath, 7s. They were under the superintendence of Mr. William Galor, who was succeeded by Mr. John Haworth, for many years a councillor for St. George's Ward, and now a resident of Southport, in the enjoyment of excellent health at the age of seventy-six.

Perhaps there is no street which has been so completely metamorphosed in the course of fifty years as Mosley Street. I do not mean as to its shape and size, for they are not altered, but as to its character. Could one of its old residents see to-day its warehouses lining each side and the immense stream of traffic pouring constantly through it, he would be astonished. Fifty years ago it was a quiet, orderly, genteel street, the abode of some of the *élite* of Manchester.

Here were the residences of the Rev. Dr. Calvert, warden of the Collegiate Church, Daniel Grant, Sam Brooks, David Bannerman, Thomas Worthington, Leo Schuster, S. L. Behrens, John Frederick Foster, the Stipendiary Magistrate, and several of the leading medical men. The Portico was there, as also the Royal Institution, which had been recently built, at a cost of £26,000. The Assembly Room, opposite the Portico, was a plain brick building; whilst on the other side of Charlotte Street, but on the same side of Mosley Street, was the chapel where Dr. M'Call was preaching to large congregations every Sunday. Higher up the street was the Unitarian Chapel, where the Rev. J. J. Tayler officiated. I well remember a hue and cry that one Sunday morning Daniel Grant's house had been robbed whilst the inmates were at church. The large warehouses in Parker Street, behind the Infirmary, had then no existence, whilst George Street and Faulkner Street contained principally private residences. In fact, I cannot remember that there was a single warehouse in either of these streets, Mosley Street, Portland Street, Peter Street, Oxford Road, or Dickenson Street, except that in the latter street was Pickford's canal warehouse, an arm of the canal reaching into the warehouse, where the boats were loaded with goods for London. It is an extraordinary circumstance that whilst so many buildings in this street and neighbourhood which existed fifty years ago have been destroyed to make way for the erection of large and substantial warehouses on their site, there is nearly opposite to the former site of Pickford's warehouse a row of small cottages which were there at the time I speak of, and which are standing yet.

Peter Street, which now has its Free Trade Hall, Concert Hall, Theatre, and other public buildings, contained nothing of the kind fifty years ago. Both the Theatre Royal and "Concert Rooms" were in Fountain Street, the former occupying a site between York Street and Charlotte Street, on which the warehouse of Daniel Lee and Co. now stands; whilst music was not then honoured by being domiciled in a separate building, but had apartments next door to the churchwardens' office and nearly opposite the theatre. The large space of ground known as St. Peter's Field, on which the building erected for a museum with others now stand, and on which the great meeting of 60,000 persons was held which ended so disastrously, in 1819, was still unoccupied by buildings. A large meeting of, it was said, 40,000 or 50,000 persons was held on it shortly after the time of which I am writing for some political purpose.

Oxford Road was pretty much then as it is now, except that of course the traffic was much less; no railway bridge crossed it, there were fewer shops and more private houses, and a little beyond Tuer Street, the houses were large and detached, the homes of the wealthy. Here were the residences of Richard Potter, afterwards M.P. for Wigan; William Entwistle, once M.P. for South Lancashire; the Rev. Dr. M'Call, James Wood, the founder of the firm of Wood and Westhead; and John Fernley, who before he died presented such a magnificent gift to the Wesleyan Connexion, in the shape of a large and handsome chapel, day and Sunday schools, a school for ministers' daughters, and a minister's house at Southport. Mr. Jeremiah Garnett, one of the proprietors of the *Manchester Guardian*, lived in one of the houses which have since been converted into shops opposite to the east side of All Saints' Church, known then as Grosvenor Place.

Chorlton-upon-Medlock was then known as Chorlton Row. The Stretford Road was not made, and the townships of Hulme and Moss Side consisted mainly of fields. What houses and shops there were in Hulme were chiefly in Chester Road and the neighbourhood. Jackson's Lane contained thirty or forty houses at the Chester Road end, and then became a winding country lane extending in the direction of Greenheys. I remember taking a walk one Sunday afternoon soon after I came to Manchester, and turning out of Oxford Road into a street which I think was Boundary Street, when I soon got into the fields, and by following a footpath at last found myself in Jackson Street, near to Chester Road.

For more than forty years no alteration was made in Deansgate itself of any importance ; so that the Deansgate of fifty years ago was very like that of ten years ago. The names of some streets turning out of Deansgate have been altered, whilst one or two new streets have been made, and others have disappeared. Cupid's Alley has been changed into Atkinson Street, and Parliament Street into Hardman Street, the latter street being in such bad repute it was thought best to obliterate the name. Neither John Dalton Street nor Lower King Street existed at that time. At the corner of Bridge Street and Deansgate were commodious meat shambles, and behind them the pork shambles. Where now is the beginning of Lower King Street was an open space, known as the Star Yard, leading to the stables behind

the Star Hotel. At the other corner of the yard was the
Star Coach Office. The inn was kept by Mr. Thomas
Yates. He was about the last gentleman in Manchester
who wore that peculiar appendage of hair hanging down the
back, known as a queue. Mrs. Yates survived him, and
continued the business to the time of her death, when she
was succeeded by her daughter, Miss Ann Yates, in whose
hands it still remains. Mrs. Yates, who was a tall handsome
lady, appeared at the first Fancy Dress Ball in 1828,
dressed as an " Old English Lady," attracting considerable
attention from her fine representation of the character.

King Street, from Deansgate to Cross Street, has not
undergone any important alteration. The part opposite the
Old Town Hall has been widened. St. Ann's Street,
leading from the Square into Deansgate, only extended as
far as Back Square, the remainder of the way consisting of
a very narrow street, known as Toll Lane, so called, I
suppose, from the fact that it being originally the principal
entrance to Acres Fair, held in the Square, toll was there
demanded on the cattle passing through.

One of the most important alterations ever made in
Manchester was the opening out of Victoria Street and the
making of the road past the Cathedral to its junction with
Strangeways, together with the building of Victoria Bridge,
an improvement be it remembered designed and completed
without the assistance of the Corporation, for it then had
no existence. Most persons are aware that what is now
Victoria Street was formerly Smithy Door. The entrance
to it from Market Street was like a narrow isthmus passing
between the projecting corners of two buildings opposite

each other, the space between the curbstones being only
sufficient to allow a vehicle to pass with scarcely an inch to
spare. The width of the footpath was proportionate, so that
it was dangerous for a person to attempt to pass through at
the same time as a vehicle. The right-hand building was
the Unicorn Inn, kept by Joseph Challender, at which the
celebrated club known as " John Shaw's " a few years afterwards used to meet. The other end of Smithy Door
opened into a street which was a continuation of Cateaton
Street, and was joined to the bridge which there spanned
the Irwell. This was a very narrow structure and had a
much greater declivity than has the present bridge. It was
known as the " Old Bridge," and the street which joined
Cateaton Street with it, and which blocked up that end of
Smithy Door, was " Old Bridge Street." The footpath
which now separates the Cathedral yard from the Mitre
Hotel was continued round the yard on the river side, just
as it is yet on the other side. Between this footpath and
the high rocky bank of the river were a few shops and two
or three taverns, of which I remember the Blackamoor's
Head was one and the inevitable Ring-o'-Bells another.
The fine open space in which the statue of Cromwell now
stands had then no existence. Foot passengers could get
into Strangeways by means of the footpath, but carriages
had to go round by Hanging Ditch and Fennel Street. So
also in going to Cheetham Hill, a foot passenger would
have to take the right-hand footpath of the churchyard and
proceed through Long Millgate to Ducie Bridge; whilst a
vehicle would have to get into Millgate by Hanging Ditch
and Fennel Street.

Manchester was then encircled by a number of toll-bars, at some of which foot passengers had to pay toll for crossing a bridge. There was a toll-bar on Ducie Bridge; one in Strangeways, not far from Strangeways Hall, which was then standing; one at Longsight, one on Broughton Bridge, one on Blackfriars Bridge, one in Regent Road, one in Stretford Road after it was formed, one at Pendleton, and I think others. I remember the case of a medical man who wanted to see a patient that lived just through the Strangeways bar, and who left his gig waiting whilst he walked through to see his patient and back. He was summoned by the keeper of the bar before the magistrates and had to pay the toll.

The bridges connecting Salford with Manchester were the iron bridge leading from Strangeways to Greengate, the Old Bridge, Blackfriars, New Bailey, and Regent Road. Like the Old Bridge, the New Bailey one has been replaced with a handsome structure, more suited to the increasing traffic passing over it. The little chain bridge, as it was called, in Lower Broughton, was then in existence, for I remember the circumstance that very shortly after I came to Manchester, a number of soldiers of the rifle corps which was then stationed here, and who wore a green uniform, were crossing the bridge, when, in consequence of the uniformity of their step, the chains gave way, and a number of them were precipitated into the river, without any fatal result, though with some serious injury to a few. Had they broken the regularity of their step, and crossed the bridge in non-military fashion, I suppose the misfortune would not have happened. A singular circumstance connected with the accident was, that the bridge was erected by the father-in-law of the officer in command of the men, and who lived at the castellated mansion close by, called Castle Irwell.

To return to the central part of the town, the streets in which the principal Manchester warehouses were to be found, were High Street, Cannon Street, Marsden Square, Church Street, and the smaller streets running out of these. There was not then, or for some years after, a single warehouse in Manchester making any pretensions to architectural effect, either in the home or shipping trade. Not only were the buildings in which the latter were carried on very plain structures, but they were to be found mostly in retired situations, such as Back George Street, Mulberry Street, Queen Street, and Back Mosley Street.

CHAPTER II.

WHOLESALE FIRMS.

I REMARKED, in the last chapter, that fifty years ago the principal warehouses were to be found in High Street, Cannon Street, and the neighbourhood. The first warehouse in High Street, on the right, turning out of Market Street, was that of Wood and Wales. The senior partner was the same gentleman, I believe, who in after years took a great interest in the passing of the act which prevents boys climbing chimneys to sweep them, and was so active in seeing its provisions carried out. The next warehouse was that of Butterworth and Brooks, calico printers, and a little further was the warehouse of Leese, Kershaw, and Callender, then one of the leading houses in the general home trade. Joe Leese, as I have heard him familiarly called, lived at the Polygon, Ardwick. James Kershaw, as is generally known, became M.P. for Stockport. He was a prominent member of the Congregationalist body. The third partner was William Romaine Callender, father of the late member for Manchester, who resided in Plymouth Grove. Mr. Callender was also a Congregationalist. A few doors further was the firm of Wood and Westhead. Both gentlemen were leading members of the Wesleyan body,

Mr. James Wood being a popular local preacher. His son, Dr. Peter Wood, was one of the physicians to the Infirmary for some years, until his retirement to Southport, where he died a few years since. Mr. Edward Westhead, his partner, lived in Cavendish Street, at the large house near the corner of Cambridge Street, behind which there was then a large garden. His eldest son, Joshua Procter Westhead, was M.P. for York for some years. He inherited the Lea Castle estates, in Warwickshire, from his uncle, Captain Brown, whose name he assumed under the form of Brown-Westhead.

Right amongst the surrounding warehouses in High Street was the office of Mr. Capes, the auctioneer, father of the late senior partner in the firm of Capes, Dunn, and Co., whom I remember very well at that time as a clerk in the office of Gardner, Harter, and Co., drysalters, Chapel Walks. Near to this was the warehouse of Mr. Thomas Worthington, whose house was in Mosley Street, but who afterwards resided at Sharston Hall, in Cheshire. On the opposite side of the street was that of William Maclure and Sons. Mr. Maclure lived at Tipping Street, Ardwick, and was the father, I believe, of a gentleman well known amongst us. Mr. George Royle Chappell's warehouse was near to this. He was an active member of the Wesleyan body, and resided in Nelson Street, Oxford Road. When he went to reside there first—shewing the then insecurity of the roads outside the town—and was detained late at the warehouse, he used to secure a place on a London coach which started at about nine or ten o'clock at night and went through Oxford Road and Wilmslow. The Sun Fire Office ought to be honourably mentioned as having so long and so bravely resisted the ambitious tendency to change, which has led some insurance offices to seek success more by dependence upon outside show than upon substantial merit. The "Sun Fire Office: Robert Duck, agent," was No. 1, High Street, in 1811 (how long before I cannot say); it was so in 1829; it was still there under the same agency in 1848; and there in 1876 under another agency. At last I find it has yielded to the march of events, and is there no longer. All honour to the Sun Fire Office.

In Marsden Square was the warehouse of William Allen and Brothers, who removed afterwards to High Street. Mr. Allen was the father of Mr. William Shepperd Allen, the present M.P. for Newcastle-under-Lyme. Here also were Pickford's Van Office, and the Savings Bank under the management of Mr. Gibson. A few years previously, Mr. Thomas Price, a fustian manufacturer, whose warehouse was in the square, had been left alone in his office during the dinner hour, and was found by his clerk lying on the floor dead, having been brutally murdered. His warehouseman was suspected of the crime and tried at Lancaster, but the evidence not being strong enough to convict him, he was acquitted. Here also was the warehouse of Mr. Hugh Greaves, father of the late George Greaves, the surgeon, of Stretford Road, who died a few years since of blood poisoning, in consequence of pricking his hand during an operation.

In Cannon Street, Messrs. Wright and Lee had their place of business, the firm afterwards becoming that of Daniel Lee and Co. Near to this was the warehouse of

Mr. Absalom Watkin, father of Sir Edward; and lower down that of Francis Marris, Son, and Jackson, becoming afterwards Edward and John Jackson, of York Street, and the bank of Scholes, Tetlow, and Co. At the lower end of the street, on the Market Street side, was the warehouse of Potters and Norris. The "Potters" consisted of the two brothers, Thomas and Richard. The latter became M.P. for Wigan, whilst the former was the first Mayor of Manchester, and was knighted. He was the father of the late Sir John Potter, and of Mr. Thomas Bayley Potter, M.P. for Rochdale. His residence was at Buile Hill, Pendleton. I well remember him driving to business in a plain one-horse open vehicle, with his two sons, then very young men, and arriving soon after eight every morning at the Market Street end of Cromford Court, which was close to Mr. Dentith's shop, where they alighted and walked through Cromford Court to Cannon Street. One of the most popular Churchmen in Manchester fifty years ago was Mr. Benjamin Braidley, a merchant, whose warehouse was in New Cannon Street, his house being in Lever Street. He was several times chosen boroughreeve, and two or three times was a candidate for the honour of representing Manchester in Parliament, but without success. In the same street was the warehouse of Broadhurst, Henson, and Broadhurst, a well-known firm. On its dissolution Mr. Broadhurst obtained the appointment of Borough Treasurer under the Corporation. The warehouse of Fletcher, Burd, and Wood was then in Friday Street. The firm was afterwards changed to Samuel Fletcher, Son, and Co., and the business removed to one of the large warehouses in Parker Street.

Mr. Samuel Fletcher was one of the foremost members amongst the Congregationalists, and no man was ever more deservedly and more generally respected. His residence was in Oxford Road. His partner, Mr. Burd, on the establishment of the Corporation, became Alderman Burd.

The late Mr. John Slagg's warehouse was a door or two from Market Street, in Pall Mall, and being near to Mr. Dentith's shop, I well remember him when comparatively a young man. In the course of time the word "company" was added to the name of the firm, but the same warehouse has been occupied by the firm till nearly the present time. Mr. Thomas Slagg, his father, at that time kept the Clarendon Inn, in Oxford Road, behind which, in 1824, was a well-frequented bowling green. He died wealthy, leaving behind him another son, Thomas, who has resided at Lytham* some years, and a daughter who married Mr. Briggs, a manufacturer at Blackburn.

Besides the streets which have been named, there were several smaller warehouses in Fountain Street and Spring Gardens. Instead of the palatial warehouse built by Messrs. J. and S. Watts in Portland Street, at the time I speak of they occupied a shop in Deansgate, nearly opposite the present Barton Arcade, where they carried on the drapery business. Their business was afterwards removed, first to a fine warehouse in New Brown Street, when that street was opened out; then to a larger one in Fountain Street, behind the present Manchester and Liverpool Bank; and afterwards to their present one in Portland Street.

---

* He has died since these lines first appeared in print.

One of the oldest and most prosperous wholesale houses in Manchester is that of John and Nathaniel Philips and Co., of Church Street, the firm having been in existence more than eighty years. Originally they had a mill in Salford, and afterwards a warehouse in Somerset Street, Garside Street. Their name appears in the Directory of 1811, as merchants and tape manufacturers, and in 1829 they still occupied the premises in Somerset Street, but shortly after removed to Church Street. Mr. Mark Philips, who was four times returned as M.P. for Manchester (once in opposition to Mr. W. E. Gladstone, then a Conservative candidate), was a member of the firm. Another house in Church Street deserves mention, inasmuch as the history of the rise and progress of the firm of John, James, and George Cooper may be taken as a type of the history of scores of other houses who have been successful in the Manchester trade. Fifty years ago Mr. John Cooper, who migrated from a village near Leek, was a draper in Oldham Street, having converted a private house into a shop. At first his speciality was mourning, but shortly after he bought a small manufactory at Dunstable, and began the wholesale straw-bonnet trade, in rooms over the Oldham Street shop. After a time he was joined by the two brothers, when they extended their premises backwards along Church Street, and afterwards acquired the premises now occupied by them, and I suppose are now one of the best known houses in the kingdom.

Our energetic and venerable fellow-townsman, Mr. John Rylands, was then a young man in partnership with his father in New High Street, in a warehouse which still forms

a part of the extensive premises occupied by the Company
bearing his name. So that the motto of the Eccles-cake
maker might truly be written over their door, "Never
Removed," though it should be added, "But Greatly
Extended!" The firm was then Rylands and Sons, and
they employed a number of handloom weavers in the manufacture of checks. There is a characteristic anecdote told
of young John Rylands by an old man who is now employed
in carting coals at Altrincham. It would appear that it was
a practice with some of the weavers to damp the "cut," as
it was called, before bringing it to the employer, I presume
for the purpose of making it weigh heavier. When this
carter was a lad his mother used to weave for Rylands and
Sons, and she occasionally sent her son with the cut. It
was young John's business to receive the work and examine
it. On the lad's bringing a cut one day the following conversation took place :—

"Now, my lad, I want you to tell me something. If
you'll tell me the truth I'll give you a penny."

"Ay, my mother tells me allus to tell t' truth."

"Very well ; what did your mother do to this cut before
she gave it you ?"

"Hoo did nowt, nobbut just weet it a bit."

"Robert (to the cashier), give this lad a penny."

A neighbour, who had also brought some work in, over-
hearing the conversation, and getting home before the lad,
told his mother what had been said. Whereupon the good
woman prepared to give her son a good thrashing on his
return, but he made such a piteous appeal to her to the
effect that she " had allus towd him to tell t' truth," that he

quite disarmed her wrath.   As usual, the anecdote remains
unfinished, and we are not told what young Mr. John did.

The firm of Carlton, Walker, and Co., has been one of
high repute.   Fifty years ago Mr. James Carlton was in
business alone as a muslin manufacturer, at 13, New High
Street, his residence then being in Strangeways; but shortly
afterwards he removed to Irwell House, Lower Broughton,
where he continued to reside for many years.   There has
perhaps not been a Manchester merchant whose character
for honour and integrity stood higher than James Carlton's.
Very quiet and undemonstrative, he was the true Christian
gentleman, and was a prominent member of the Congregationalist body.   Shortly after the time referred to he left the
warehouse in New High Street, and founded the firm of
Carlton, Walker, and Lewis, in whose service my only
brother died, the new warehouse being in Mosley Street,
and still in the occupation of George Walker and Co.

In those days the small easy neckties now worn by
gentlemen were unknown, and the neck was generally encased either in a deep stiff stock which buckled behind, or
in a large silk handkerchief, inside which was a very deep
stiffener, a specimen of which may be seen in the portrait of
Baron Stockmar, given in the first volume of Theodore
Martin's " Life of the Prince Consort."   One of the principal
manufacturers of this class of goods was Frederick Ramsden,
who first had a shop in Deansgate.   His trade having greatly
enlarged, shortly after New Brown Street was opened out he
took a warehouse in it, and entered into the general trade;
when my brother (having served an apprenticeship with Mr.
Peter Drummond, a large draper, in Deansgate, and father

of Dr. Drummond, of Higher Broughton) entered Ramsden's service, and after a while travelled for him. After being with him six years he entered into an engagement with Carlton, Walker, and Lewis, and having travelled for them one year he came home to die, at the early age of twenty-seven. There used to be a little tale told of one of their travellers, a Welshman, which, as a good joke, is worth repeating. There is a certain class of goods known as jaconets, and which, I am told, are glazed calicoes used for lining the sleeves of coats, &c., and were sent out on wooden rollers. When these goods were first introduced, the firm in question did a large trade in them. The Welshman once visited a draper in the principality, and in describing the big trade his firm was doing in this class of goods, he gravely assured his customer that such was the demand for them that they had been obliged to buy a large forest in America in order to provide wood for the rollers.

Amongst packers and makers-up, I may be allowed to mention the London firm of Wheelton, Brewer, and Buckland, which opened a branch in Manchester very shortly after the time of which I am writing, under the management of Mr. John Brewer. Their place of business was the New Market Hall, opposite the end of Strutt Street, near the *City News* office. Though an old building it had been substantially built and contained a large room on the ground floor, which was flagged as though it had once been a market-hall. I see it is now replaced by a more modern structure. Mr. Wheelton was sheriff of London at the time of the collision between the Court of Queen's Bench and the House of Commons in connection with the trial of

Stockdale v. Hansard. Stockdale was a publisher of a certain class of literature, and had been attacked by some member in his place in the House of Commons. His speech was in due course printed by Hansard, against whom Stockdale brought an action in the Queen's Bench for libel. It was decided that although the member was privileged in what he said, Hansard was not in his publication of it, and Stockdale obtained a verdict. It was the sheriff's place to levy execution, which by his officers he did. Great excitement prevailed in the House because of this supposed infringement of the liberties of Parliament, and, after Wheelton had been summoned to the bar of the House to explain his conduct, Parliament avenged itself by lodging the poor sheriff in the Tower, where he remained for about a week, when he was liberated.

CHAPTER III.

CALICO PRINTERS.

FIFTY years ago all the ingenuity of a Chancellor of the Exchequer was employed, not in discovering how he could relieve the burden of taxation, but how many ways there were into the pocket of the British taxpayer. As a consequence we cannot be surprised that not only were newspapers and advertisements heavily taxed, but soap, leather, glass, and many other articles of general consumption, amongst them being printed calicoes, which paid a duty of 3½d. per square yard. I well remember how the tab ends of prints used to bear certain numbers and hieroglyphics which had been impressed on them by the exciseman. Of course there was a heavy penalty for either buying or selling a piece of print without such marks. Every printworks was under the supervision of an exciseman, who used to visit the place at certain times to levy the duty and impress the pieces with his stamp. Tales were rife as to excisemen visiting various printworks for this purpose, and sometimes being so well plied with liquor as to lose self-control, when their stamp would be borrowed for a short time, and used pretty freely in stamping hundreds of pieces, which were consequently admitted into the market duty-free.

I have mentioned that the second warehouse on the right-hand side of High Street, was that of Butterworth and Brooks, calico printers, whose works were at the other side of Bury. When a boy, I accompanied my father over the works, and remember being allowed to enter a room which we were told very few persons were allowed to enter, inasmuch as a new process of engraving copper rollers was carried on in it. This was by working a small steel roller, which had the pattern engraved on it, on a large copper one, by means of a press, the hard steel cutting the pattern on the softer copper, and the process being many times repeated till the whole surface of the copper roller was covered with the pattern.

The second partner in the firm was the well-known John Brooks, whose residence was then in Lever Street, and who was the brother of Samuel Brooks, the banker. How different in some things were the two men. Both successful in business, the one took an active interest in public affairs, the other but little, if any. The banker's name would be occasionally found on a committee, but he seldom appeared on the platform, and I cannot remember him once making a speech on any public question. When Brunel, the great engineer, and the builder of the Great Eastern, whilst playing with his children on one occasion, unfortunately swallowed half a sovereign, which stuck in the gullet, remaining there two or three days, during which there was considerable public excitement about it, it is said that John Brooks remarked to a friend, "They should send for our Sam, for if anybody can get it, he can." John Brooks was a great friend of Mr. Benjamin Braidley, the well-known

Conservative, and though a Conservative himself, he came out nobly during the Anti-Corn-Law agitation, distinguishing himself as well by his energetic opposition to the Corn Law as by his munificent support of the funds required to carry on the agitation. When the last supreme effort was made to effect a breach in the walls of protection, and at a large and enthusiastic meeting of merchants and manufacturers, held in the Town Hall, it was resolved to raise a fund of £250,000, John Brooks, with twenty-two others, put down his name for £1,000. He was a worthy coadjutor for some years of Richard Cobden, John Bright, George Wilson, and other pioneers in the early days of the agitation. He made no pretensions to oratory. His speeches were brief, quaint, witty, and sensible, interspersed with a few sentences in the Lancashire dialect, and always to the point. I have a vivid recollection of attending one of the earliest meetings of the Anti-Corn-Law agitation, held in the first Free Trade Hall (the present one being the third), at which John Bright spoke before he was M.P., and John Brooks. The audience had to stand; there were no seats. The room was not more than half full, and the rain was dripping through the roof here and there. There was a little sympathy and a little enthusiasm, the tide was just beginning to turn; but I often contrast that meeting with the last occasion on which John Bright spoke on the same spot.

Another large firm of calico printers whose warehouse was also in High Street, but higher up on the opposite side, was that of Fort Brothers, their works being at Oaken-shaw, near Accrington. Their principal manager at the warehouse was Mr. Fred. Brooks, a well-known musical man, living at Prestwich. He played the organ at Prestwich Church, and in consequence came a good deal in contact with the Earl of Wilton, who took considerable interest in him. Like many other musical men, he was careless as to his health, and was cut off in his prime. I well remember a short time before his death hearing him express his regret, and his determination to turn over a new leaf. Another large firm was that of Ainsworth, Sykes, and Co., whose works were at Clitheroe, their warehouse being in Cannon Street. Some years after they took some works at Garratt, near to Brook Street. The firm of John Dugdale and Brothers, who 50 years ago were calico printers, still carry on business as merchants. Their warehouse was in Cannon Street, and their works near Burnley. Mr. John Dugdale resided at Richmond Hill, Greengate. No one who passes along Greengate to Broughton Bridge to-day could suppose that two or three comfortable and respectable large de-tached houses existed on the left-hand side in that locality fifty years ago. Such, however, was the case, Mr. Lockett, the well-known engraver to calico printers, occupying the next house to Mr. Dugdale's. In 1835 Mr. Dugdale was induced to become a candidate for the representation of Salford in Parliament, in opposition to Mr. Joseph Brotherton. During my apprenticeship Dentith sold his retail business to Horatio Miller, a gentleman from London, to whom I was turned over. Miller became intimate with Dugdale, and I was induced to join Mr. John Hadfield, a solicitor, in canvassing for Dugdale. Of course we were un-successful. I think this was my first and last time of undertaking such a task. Some time during the election, Dugdale, who was a blunt, plain-speaking Lancashire man, was chaffed by an elector as to his wealth, when he replied, "Ay, I fairly stink o' brass." For many years after he was known in Salford as " Owd Stink o' Brass." He afterwards left Richmond Hill, and went to reside at a pleasantly-situated house on the bank of the Irwell, near to Eccles. In 1834, he purchased for £7,500 the old Union Clubhouse, at the Infirmary end of Mosley Street, on the left-hand side going down, next to Mr. Daniel Grant's house. He was an intimate friend of Sam Brooks, the banker. Many are the tales which were told of the little friendly tricks they played on one another ; as, for instance, that Sam Brooks, having a pony to sell, informed Dugdale that a pony was to be sold by auction at the Star Yard, and suggested to him that he should buy it. The latter, supposing he was to buy it for the banker, did so, paying a good price for it. On going to the bank and seeing Mr. Brooks, he said, " Well, Sam, I've bought thee that pony," when he was informed that he had misunderstood the suggestion, which was that he should buy it for himself, but that he (Brooks) knew the pony very well, it having once belonged to him, and he was sure that John Dugdale would be pleased with his bargain.

I suppose that everybody has heard of Hoyle's prints and Hoyle's printworks. Whether or not their prints were as popular fifty years ago as they have been more recently I cannot say. I find the firm has been in existence the greater part of a century, if not quite a century. In 1811 the works of Thomas Hoyle and Son were where they are to-day, the warehouse being in Watling Street, and Mr. Thomas

Hoyle's residence at Ardwick. Fifty years ago the ware-house was in Friday Street, next door to Fletcher, Burd, and Wood's, and Mr. Hoyle's house at Mayfield, near the works, which one may easily imagine was a more airy and a pleasanter situation than at present. Another well-known printworks was Barge's, at Broughton Bridge, the firm being John Barge and Co., and their warehouse being in Peel Street. Mr. Tom Barge, one of the partners, was well-known, and resided in Roman Street, Stony Knolls. Mr. John Fildes, once M.P. for Grimsby, was a cashier in their service. The works of Lomas and Bradbury were in the neighbourhood, the entrance to them being on the left-hand side of Strangeways, going towards Broughton. Mr. Lomas was the inventor of a method of printing calicoes on both sides alike.

In 1829 the firm of Edmund and Robert Peel, calico printers, had their warehouse in Watling Street, at the corner of Friday Street. They were successors—though not the immediate successors—of the first Sir Robert Peel, who began business about 1770, when only twenty years of age, and who married the daughter of Mr. Yates, who subsequently became his partner. In 1811 their warehouse was in Peel Street, the firm then being Peel, Yates, Halliwell and Co., the street being named no doubt after Mr. Peel; whilst the last-named partner gave the name to Halliwell Lane, Cheetham Hill, he having built the first two or three large houses on the right, in one of which he lived. More than forty-five years ago I learnt from an old gentleman, who was formerly a draper in Hull, that when he first came to Manchester to buy goods, Peel's warehouse was approached by an avenue of trees. The cart was in the habit of bringing a load of prints on three mornings in the week—Tuesdays, Thursdays, and Saturdays—from the works. The warehouse doors were not opened till nine o'clock, by which time the prints were all arranged in the saleroom. A crowd of drapers was generally waiting for the doors to be opened, when they would rush upstairs to the saleroom, and a scramble for prints would ensue, each draper making a pile on the floor of such prints as he had chosen, and waiting for the entering clerk coming round to look them over and enter them. What a contrast with the state of things to-day! No wonder that the first Sir Robert Peel is said to have died worth £2,500,000, and that the firm of Peel, Yates, and Halliwell used to pay £40,000 annually to the excise for duty on printed goods.

Many firms entitled themselves calico printers who were not really such, but who either purchased patterns from a pattern designer or employed their own designer. They bought calico, had it bleached, and forwarded it to some printworks to be printed with their own design. Others, again, who both on their invoices and their signboards called themselves calico printers, were merely dealers in prints. I rather think the firm of Robert Turner, jun., and Co., who fifty years ago had a warehouse next to that of Wood and Westhead, in High Street, and who were entitled calico printers, were amongst the first-named. I have mentioned that on the site of the Queen's Hotel there stood three or four large brick houses, in one of which Mr. Houldsworth, M.P., lived. The door of the corner house was in Piccadilly, and in it Mr. Robert Turner resided. He kept a stud of racehorses as well as Mr. Houldsworth, and was the brother of Mr. William Turner, of Pot Shrigley, the father of the young lady who was abducted from school by Edward Gibbon Wakefield. Robert Turner, of Piccadilly, followed Wakefield and Miss Turner to France and brought her home again. It was clearly proved on the trial that there had been no cohabitation, and she afterwards became the wife of Mr. Legh, of Lyme. Her father was reputed to be immensely wealthy, but at his death this was proved to be an error.

Four or five doors from Turner's warehouse was that of a very large and respectable firm of calico printers, whose works were at Rhodes, near Middleton—that of Daniel Burton and Sons. They began business somewhere about the beginning of the present century, but have ceased to exist more than thirty years. Mr. Daniel Burton was the father of the late Dr. Burton, the founder and rector of All Saints' Church, who was at the beginning of his career a Methodist preacher, the other members of the family being also devoted Wesleyans. Daniel Burton had three other sons, John, George, and James Daniel. Fifty years ago, John was the factotum of the trustees of Oldham Street Chapel and George became a Wesleyan local preacher. At the time when rioting was so fashionable amongst the working classes, there was once a riot at the Rhodes Printworks, when one of the sons despatched a messenger to Manchester for the assistance of the cavalry. Accordingly a troop of Scotch Greys galloped over and quelled the riot. A few Sundays after, in the little Wesleyan Chapel, on the preacher reading his text, " What must I do to be saved?" a shrill voice from one of the congregation answered the question by exclaiming, " Send for th' Scotch Greys."

The firm of Charles and Edmund Potter and Co. began their business rather more than fifty years ago, their warehouse being then in Fountain Street and their works at Dinting, near Glossop. Though Charles has only been dead a few years the name of the firm was changed to that of Edmund Potter and Co. many years ago, and still exists at the present day. Edmund at that time lived with his mother in Oxford Road, a little this side of All Saints' Church, but on the opposite side and near to Dr. Burton, the rector. As is well known, he was M.P. for Carlisle for some years. Besides those printworks in the immediate vicinity of Manchester already named, may be mentioned those of Hedley, Atkinson, and Co., at Broughton Grove, behind the present Grove Inn, Higher Broughton, which was not then built. The works of Otho Hulme and Sons were at Spring Vale, their warehouse being at the lower end of Cannon Street, near to that of Potters and Norris.

Nearly opposite to it was the warehouse of William Grant and Brothers, I suppose the best-known firm of calico printers which Manchester ever produced. They were in business at the beginning of the century as merchants, but afterwards became calico printers, their works being at Ramsbottom. At one time William Grant resided in Lever Street, but afterwards lived near the works. Fifty years ago the firm consisted of William and Daniel, the latter residing in the fourth house on the left-hand side of Mosley Street going down. He went to live there about the year 1815, and

resided in that street till his death, long after other residents
had been driven away and wholesale places of business had
taken almost entire possession of the street. In 1848 he was
living lower down the street, having moved to another house
a little past the warehouse occupied by the late firm of
Carlton, Walker, and Co. In less than twenty years the
character of the street had completely changed, so that
Daniel Grant's house was the only private residence remaining in it, if we except those of two or three medical
men at the lower end of the street, and which of course
cannot be spoken of as private residences. He died at a
good old age; and, in addition to those I have already
named, he affords another instance of the longevity enjoyed
by many who have lived for many years in the very heart of
Manchester.

I never saw William Grant but once; but as Mr. Miller
had occasional business transactions with the firm, I sometimes saw and had opportunities of speaking to Daniel. It
is said that Charles Dickens in his description of the
Cheeryble Brothers in *Nicholas Nickleby*, has attempted to
pourtray the members of the firm of William Grant and
Brother. If so, as it regards their generosity, benevolence,
and goodness of heart, I consider he has drawn a true
picture, but all the rest is mere caricature. From what I
remember of Daniel Grant I should say he was anything
but loquacious, and was rather reserved and dignified in his
manner, though condescending, considerate, and very kind
to all he had to do with. I well remember how proud I
was one morning when, my master having learnt that they
were wanting concentrated lime juice at the works, he sent

me to the warehouse to see Daniel Grant and make him an offer of some. To my delight he ordered about a hundred pounds worth. In giving me the order he wasted no words, and yet he did it so kindly that I have never forgotten the circumstance. In later years he used to arrive at his warehouse about ten or eleven o'clock, and usually came in his carriage. By the time of his arrival a number of poor people had gathered at the warehouse door awaiting his arrival. When his carriage drew up they would divide into two lines, forming an avenue from the carriage to the warehouse door through which he passed. If he did not distribute his alms to them himself he would send a clerk out to them, and I believe they seldom went away unrelieved.

The process of impressing cotton fabrics with a pattern in colours was not confined to calico, but was extended to cotton velvets. The material mostly used as a pigment was chrome yellow, of which, I remember, we used to sell a great deal to the firm of Jackson, Watson, and Greg, whose warehouse was in the neighbourhood of Watling Street. A large trade was done in these printed velvets, though what became of them, whether they were used for coats and waistcoats in the agricultural districts, or were exported, I cannot say. At the time when the Anti-Corn-Law agitation was at its height, and a suspicion lurked in the minds of many, especially amongst the supporters of Protection, that Sir Robert Peel was undergoing a process of conversion, and was about to bring in a measure of free trade in corn, and whilst the country was anxiously awaiting some sign from him, Mr. Charles Ramsay, of Ancoats Vale, printed a

pattern consisting of an ear of corn with the stalk and a
flowing blade or leaf.   On this blade was printed the word
" FREE."   He forwarded a piece of it to Sir Robert Peel,
asking his acceptance of it as a piece of printed cotton
velvet, but without drawing his attention particularly to the
nature of the design.   Sir Robert, of course, gracefully
accepted it, and thanked the donor.   In a very short time
a paragraph went the round of the papers describing the
pattern, and reporting Sir Robert's acceptance of it.   Infer-
ences were drawn, and the Protectionist party were up in
arms, but the storm was instantly quelled by Peel's returning the piece to the donor with an explanatory note.
I have in my possession a small portion of this piece of
printed velvet which was the cause of so much commotion,
which I had given to me at the time, and have religiously
preserved ever since.

In travelling from Buxton to Manchester, after passing
New Mills, a beautiful valley on the right opens to our
view, and in it a cluster of white buildings is seen.   These
are the Strines Printworks.   The Strines Printing Company
have occupied a prominent position in Manchester for
many years.   Fifty years ago their warehouse was in Mulberry Street, Deansgate, which was then a very nondescript
sort of street.   The Roman Catholic Chapel was there,
having since undergone considerable architectural improvement in its external appearance.   Attached to it were the
residences of the Revs. Henry Gillow, Daniel Hearne, and
John Billington.   The street was then as narrow as it is
now, but nearly all the old buildings having been replaced by
modern warehouses (one of which is the large handsome

block erected by Mr. John Heywood), it has lost its dingy character and put on a brighter aspect. It then contained, besides the warehouse of the Strines Printing Company, five others, several private dwellings, and the tap of the Hope public-house. One of these houses was the residence of Mr. Addison, a silk mercer and haberdasher, of King Street; one was occupied by Mr. James Parry, a portrait painter; one by a tailor, and another by a dressmaker; whilst one or two, it was whispered, were houses of questionable repute.

Mr. James Bury has supplied the following account of other large firms of calico printers. Messrs. John Whitehead and Sons had their works at Breightmet, near Bolton. Their warehouse was nearly opposite Grant's, and like it, was one of the old family residences of which the street was then composed, and having only a few years before a row of trees facing the dwellings along each side of the street. John Whitehead was a crofter or bleacher at Levenshulme, but towards the close of the last century he began calico printing at Breightmet, and lived at Ainsworth Hall. Early in the present century the business devolved on his three sons, John, James, and Thomas. The latter lived at Bank House, Bolton; whilst James lived in Piccadilly, in one of the two houses now the Mosley Arms Hotel; Whitehead's doorway and hall being now Boyd's, the stationer's shop. A sister, Miss Mary Whitehead, lived in her own house in Mosley Street, at the corner of York Street, her neighbour at the other end of the row being Daniel Grant. Common report pictured these two for man and wife, a picture which it need hardly be said was never realized. The lady bought an estate at Burnage, and there built a mansion which she named Brook Flat. Subsequent to her death, it was called Burnage Hall, and was lately rented by Mr. Samuel Watts. Another daughter, Miss Sally Whitehead, married an attorney of Manchester named Redhead.

James Whitehead was the holder of original £100 shares in the Old Quay Company, which were, years after his death, sold for several times their original value. He was one of the directors of the company. One of the pleasures of the directors was to take a day's voyage down the river to Warrington, dining on board their own boat. There is still on the river a flat named "The Whitehead."

The firm was very successful and amassed great wealth, one pattern alone, called the "Bird's-eye," realizing upwards of thirty thousand pounds. It was a circle with two lines, one blue and the other white, on a chocolate ground. It became as famous as Tommy Hoyle and Son's "lilacs," and there was scarcely a village dame in the kingdom who did not feel proud of her "bird's-eye" print gown. Of all the great wealth of this family of the Whiteheads only Burnage Hall Estate is held by a Whitehead, a widow, the remainder being taken by females to others or dissipated.

Another firm was Samuel Matley and Sons, whose warehouse was the first door in New High Street from Tib Street, now the entrance to Rylands and Son's. The family lived in Mosley Street, now John L. Kennedy and Co., No. 47. One of the sons, "Sam," was a Manchester "buck," a fine, handsome, gay young fellow.

CHAPTER IV.

BLEACHERS, DRYSALTERS, AND HOOKERS-IN.

THERE were several large bleachworks in the neighbourhood of Manchester, amongst which might be
named those of the Bealeys, at Radcliffe, near Bury, and
the Ainsworths, at Halliwell, Bolton.   The ancient name
for a bleacher was a "whitster," and the business seems to
be as old as the cotton trade.   There are not many firms,
either manufacturing or otherwise, which are in full operation to-day, and can look back to an uninterruptedly
prosperous career of at least one hundred and thirty years,
through father, grandfather, great-grandfather, and great-
great-grandfather.   The large and flourishing bleaching
concern of Richard Bealey and Co., at Radcliffe, however,
is in this proud position.   The first lease of land and buildings for their bleachworks is dated May 26, 1750, and re-
cites the previous occupation of the lessees.   The conveyance is from James Marsden to William Bealey, Richard
Bealey, and Joseph Bealey, since which time they or
their descendants have constantly occupied the works as
"whitsters."   Joseph was the second son of William, and
was the great-grandfather of the present head of the
firm.   Joseph's son Richard succeeded to the business in

partnership with his brother Ralph, their warehouse being in Bank Street, and, in accordance with a custom referred to previously, their inn was the White Horse, Hanging Ditch.

In 1811 Richard was in partnership with his son Adam, as Richard Bealey and Son, their warehouse being in New Cannon Street. Richard died in 1817, and was succeeded by Adam, who did not live many years after. He had married a Chester lady, whose sister became the wife of the Rev. Dr. Warren. She survived her husband many years, and carried on the business in her own name as " Mary Bealey." In 1829, the time these notices specially refer to, her warehouse was in Birchin Lane. Both she and her husband were strongly attached to the Wesleyan cause. Amongst that body few ladies have been as widely known, and as deservedly respected, on account of her noble deeds and many virtues, as Mrs. Mary Bealey. Her daughter married the well-known Wesleyan lawyer, Mr. Percival Bunting, who retired from Manchester to London a few years ago. Her eldest son, Richard, is now at the head of the firm, and is a county magistrate. I believe there is a probability of the business being perpetuated in the family many years longer; and one cannot but wish for the family as long and as prosperous a career in the future as they have enjoyed in the past.

Having spoken of calico printers and bleachers, it is not possible to avoid a passing glance at the Drysalters, the interests of the two being so united. They were an active and intelligent class. What a flutter they used to be in on Tuesday, Thursday, and Saturday mornings, when the printers' carts arrived each with a load of

prints, and with requisitions for certain drugs and dry-
salteries wanted at the works, to be sent back in the
carts. Like the busy bee gathering honey from every
opening flower, they were quite as busy going from
door to door of the print warehouses, showing samples,
giving quotations, and gathering orders. The most prominent figure of that busy band was the late William
Benjamin Watkins, afterwards Mr. Alderman Watkins, who
with his robust frame was to be seen on these occasions
trudging about with quick, firm step, dressed in buckskin
knee breeches and top boots. By some of us juveniles (and
I fear by others too) he was irreverently designated "Buckskin Billy."

Poor Gregson, the author of "Gimcrackiana," has hit off
what I have described :—

> Dear drysalters ! who on accustomed round
> Each Tuesday, Thursday, Saturday are found,
> Skipping up warehouse steps with action smart :
> "Good morning, sir ! Pray have you had a cart ?
> Is there aught wanting for the works to-day ?
> Promptest attention shall our porters pay.
> Our drugs are excellent, and you well know
> That at this time they are extremely low."

I know not whether the institution of "hooking-in" still
exists, or whether, owing to the march of civilization, it has
been abolished. Fifty years ago it was in a very flourishing
condition. Hookers-in abounded at every street corner.
In the days when there were no railways, and men had to
use the more tedious mode of travelling by stage coach, a
journey to Manchester and back was a more formidable
affair. Country drapers from distant places could not then

run over to Manchester, buy goods, and return in a day. Hence they came here seldomer, but stayed longer and bought more largely at once. Living then in Market Street, I had opportunities of seeing the hookers-in swarm about the doors of the Thatched House Tavern, the White Bear, and similar inns every morning, besieging the head waiters, who were pretty well fee'd, with the view of ascertaining who had arrived over night. Many were the tales which were told of them. One was that an old and a young stager in different lines were talking together at the warehouse door of the latter, when a gentleman passed, on which the old stager said to the other: "That is Mr. So-and-so, from Leicester; he is a large buyer in your way." Away went the young one after the gentleman, and presenting his card, begged him to turn in and look round, with the assurance that they had some goods very cheap which would exactly suit him. He did his work so well that there was no resistance, and Mr. So-and-so followed to see the stock. Casting his eye round the first room, he quickly assured the salesman that there was nothing in that room in his line. So with the next, and so with the next. At last the question was put to him, "What line is yours?" "Oh," replied he, "I am David Bellhouse, the timber merchant." One well-known gentleman of this class was Mr. Joseph Scott, familiarly known as Joe Scott. He was a smart, well-dressed man, with a dash of the aristocrat in his appearance. I have heard it stated that he was once sent to London by his employers on a special mission, which only required his presence there for a day or so. He went to an ordinary inn and announced himself as "Lord ———." Shortly after

the waiter pointed him out to another gentleman as
"Lord ———," when he was much astonished by the
reply, "That! ———; why, that's Joe Scott, of Manchester."
It used to be said that the firm of William Grant and
Brothers was the first to employ hookers-in, and the first to
give up the use of them.

Mr. Thomas Brittain has contributed the following re-
miniscence of hookers-in :—" My connection with the Manchester trade from 1831 to 1845 brought me frequently in
contact with the 'hookers-in,' as they were familiarly called,
and I knew many of them personally. They were known
to each other pretty generally by nicknames. One of the
most successful of them was a Mr. Peel, who was known as
Sir Robert Peel. Another, a Mr. Lewis, was reported to
have made an attempt on his own life; he was named
Sudden Death ever afterwards. Previous to this one of the
hookers-in had obtained the name of Murder—I cannot
remember why—and another the name of Battle; so that
amongst this interesting fraternity there were 'Battle,
Murder, and Sudden Death.'

"The more successful of the hookers-in obtained excellent remuneration for their services. One of them was said
to receive a thousand a year, and I am inclined to believe
it. They were not a long-lived race, for the daily discharge
of their duties brought them into continual connection with
the hotels, where they had to treat their clients; and then
by a kind of commercial necessity, they were compelled to
drink more than was good for them. I have a lingering
respect for the fraternity. Amongst them were many
excellent fellows, but it is not to be regretted that railways

and other changes in business life have caused the hookers-
in (as I formerly knew them) to become things of the past."

Before quitting those subjects which are more immediately connected with the Manchester trade, it may
be well to remark that at the time I speak of it was
customary to lock up the warehouse during the dinner
hour; keeping it open was the exception, not the rule.
Then the circumference was nearer the centre, Manchester
had not spread itself out as it has done since, and the
homes of the employés were nearer the scenes of their
labour.   There were few who did not go home to dinner,
and hence there were hardly any restaurants such as now
abound on every hand.   There was no Saturday half-
holiday, and both master and man made much longer
hours than is now the practice.   In busy times it was no
unusual thing to be at business till ten or eleven o'clock,
and even twelve, on Saturday nights as well as other nights.

CHAPTER V.

DOCTORS.

IN 1829 there were twenty-two physicians practising in Manchester, and 104 surgeons, making a total of 126 medical men. It is not possible now to divide them into two distinct classes, as was the case formerly. Then, medical etiquette prohibited a physician performing a surgical operation, however trivial. The physician was quite distinct from the surgeon. At present there are in Manchester 270 medical men, many of whom, though, possessing the title of M.D. are practising as surgeons. I calculate there are 30 gentlemen who are pure physicians, 158 who are pure surgeons, and 82 who, though they have the title of M.D. (conferred by a Scotch or Irish college), practice as surgeons. Four of the physicians of half a century ago were in practice at the latter end of the last century, namely, Dr. Banks, who then lived in Market Street, removing afterwards to George Street; Dr. Michael Ward, who resided in King Street, and afterwards in Downing Street; Dr. Mitchell, living in Piccadilly; and Dr. S. A. Bardsley, uncle of the late Dr. James L. Bardsley. The former of the two was residing in Chatham Street, Piccadilly, in 1794,

and continued to do so till about 1827. The elder
Bardsley eventually gave up the house in Chatham Street
to his nephew, who began practice some years before,
and the uncle retired to Ardwick Green. The late Dr.
J. L. Bardsley received the honour of knighthood about
twenty-five years ago, and eventually went to reside in
Greenheys, but retained the house in Chatham Street for
consulting rooms to the time of his retirement. At the
beginning of the present century, what is now the lower end
of Mosley Street, from Bond Street to St. Peter's church,
was called Dawson Street, and in it Dr. Hull lived, who in
1829, was one of the leading physicians in Manchester.
Dr. Edward Holme, F.R.S., was a vice-president of the
Literary and Philosophical Society, and lived in King
Street, and Dr. Davenport Hulme, who was one of the
physicians to the Infirmary, lived in Mosley Street, both of
them enjoying a large practice.

It is impossible to call to remembrance the medical men
who were in practice in Manchester half a century since
without being struck with the fact of the longevity of many
of them, notwithstanding that they lived in the very heart
of Manchester during a great part of their lives, as in the
case of the late Mr. Turner, proving, as I think, that our
good city is not the unhealthy place some people would
represent it to be. The elder Bardsley lived to be a very
old man. I well remember him as a slender, tall, old
gentleman, with his head bent forward in walking ; whilst
Sir James was far advanced in life when he was called away.
The same observation is true with respect to the others I
have named—Drs. Hull, Davenport Hulme, Holme,

Banks, Mitchell, Ward, and to two other leading physicians of that day, Drs. Lyons and Jarrold. In a former notice I mentioned the case of Mr. Bloor, now of Southport, who lived seventy-two years in one house in Piccadilly. The next house but one to his was the residence of Mr. John Windsor, F.L.S., an old and much-respected surgeon. He began practice in the same house in 1815, and after living there fifty-three years, died in 1868, in his eighty-second year. He was a native of Settle-in-Craven, and the author of " Flora Cravoniensis," to which the *Athenæum* lately referred in complimentary terms. In the early part of his life he was a member of the Society of Friends, and lived highly esteemed not only by the members of that body but by others who knew him. Soon after he began practice he was appointed one of the surgeons to the Eye Institution, with Mr. Wilson and Mr. Barton, and was consulting surgeon to it at the time of his death. One of his sons is a member of the City Council, and another follows his father's profession. Our respected fellow-townsman, Mr. J. C. Needham, married one of his daughters.

Another octogenarian who was practising fifty years ago is Dr. Radford, then living in King Street. He is now in his eighty-sixth year, and is to-day taking as active a part in the duties connected with St. Mary's Hospital, in which he has always taken the liveliest interest, as if he were a young man. He attended my brother in his last illness. Nor are these the only instances of such remarkable longevity in the medical men of half a century ago. Some time during the first decade of the present century Mr. John Johnson Boutflower began practice in Greengate, Salford. About

the year 1823 he took his son into partnership, and both
were practising fifty years ago.   Mr. John Boutflower, the
son, is still living, and though in his turn he has a son
who assists him, yet I believe he still practises.   I am
not aware of his exact age, but a surgeon who has been
in practice at least fifty-six years must now be a very old
man.   Another instance is that of Dr. Harland, who fifty
years ago lived in Salford; and having many patients in
Manchester, as well as in Oldham, Rochdale, and other
towns, he used to meet them at 21, Market Street, where I
was an apprentice, and where he called every day.   He was
then a bachelor and an intimate friend of Mr. John
Dugdale, whose niece he eventually married.   He retired
from practice some years since, and is now, I think, a little
over eighty years old, and enjoying a peaceful old age at
his residence in Greenheys.   His son is curate of Stretford.
The late Mr. Roberton, who had a large practice, died a
few years since at an advanced age.   Fifty years ago he
lived in King Street, which it will be seen was then very
popular with medical men as a place of residence.   The
late Mr. R. T. Hunt, who also attained an advanced age
and died a few years ago, lived in Gartside Street, at the
time we speak of.   He was then assistant surgeon to the
Eye Institution, and at the time of his retirement from
Manchester to Disley, which took place a few years before
his decease, he held the position of surgeon to it.

The late Mr. Joseph Jordan, who attained such eminence
both as a surgeon and as a lecturer on anatomy, began
practice prior to 1814, and at one time was in partnership
with Mr. Blundstone, at No. 4 Bridge Street, where he was

in 1829. Mr. Jordan lived to a great age. The late
Mr. Heath, who had a large practice, and who also lived
to be an old man, was living in Cooper Street at the time.
Mr. James Braid, who made a great stir at one time by
his lectures on and practice of animal magnetism, was living
in Piccadilly, but afterwards removed to St. Peter's Square.

Amongst the leading surgeons were Messrs. John and
Robert Thorpe, James Ainsworth, John A. Ransome, and
W. J. Wilson. John Thorpe, the father of Robert, was then
the oldest surgeon in Manchester, and was practising several
years before the close of the last century. His house was
then in Cock Gates, Withy Grove, a place we should now
think very unfit for the residence of a surgeon. In 1829 he
was living in King Street; whilst his son, who began
practice somewhere about the year 1814, lived in Oldham
Street. Robert (or, as he was familiarly called, Bob)
Thorpe I remember very well; as well as James Ainsworth,
to whom my master once sent me with some slight accidental
injury. The latter began practice about the year 1808, at
the upper end of King Street. After residing there more
than forty years he died at Cliff Point, Broughton. Mr.
J. A. Ransome was practising in Princess Street in 1810,
and after some years removed to St. Peter's Square, where
he was eventually succeeded by either his **son** or nephew
Joseph. There were at this time two members of the
medical profession as well as two druggists members of the
Society of Friends—Mr. Ransome and Mr. Windsor.

Another surgeon practising at this time in Manchester
was Mr. Charles Greswell, living in Great Ducie Street, son
of the Rev. W. P. Greswell, incumbent of Denton. The

latter was a quaint-looking little old gentleman, well known, I believe, as a very learned man, who had another son in the Church, the author of some important works. Mr. Samuel Barton, who afterwards rose to eminence, was then living in Mosley Street. He retired from the profession many years ago, and after an absence from Manchester for a time returned, residing at Bankfield, near the entrance to Manley Park, where he died a few years since. A little higher up Mosley Street, on the opposite side, was the residence of Mr. Thomas Ashton, who, though he never had a large practice, was well known amongst the literary and scientific circles of Manchester. He eventually took the degree of M.D., and retired some time ago from Manchester. A few years since I had the pleasure of meeting him, and of finding him well. His father, who was the bread baker of the day, at No. 3, Piccadilly, was a wealthy old gentleman, having made a considerable fortune in his business. Owing to the very superior quality of his bread, for which he got a higher price than any other baker, he had almost a monopoly. He will be remembered by many, no doubt, as a big and very old man, moving about very slowly, with the weight of years bowing him down, and his feet encased in a huge pair of shoes. At the close of the last century he had a shop in High Street.

I have mentioned the late Mr. Thomas Turner else-where, and the age to which he lived. His career was a remarkably successful one from the first. Fifty years ago, his prescriptions, coming to be dispensed, were neither few nor far between. I well remember his neat hand-writing at that time, the style of which altered so little with

advancing years. Independently of his ability, the secret
of his success was not far to seek. He was remarkably
genial and kindly in his manner, and always brought sun-
shine into a sick room. If a poor fellow was down, he
would try to lift him up. If a patient thought it was all
over with him, he would try to cause "hope eternal" to
spring up in his breast. He preached the doctrine that it
is not work which kills men, but worry. He acted on it,
and proved the truth of it, for he was never worried,
worked to the last, and died at a very advanced age.

A well-known surgeon half a century ago was Mr. Benjamin Roberts, who began practice in Brazenose Street about
the year 1812. He removed to Stevenson Square, and
then to a house at the corner of Lever Street, and Back
Piccadilly. He was the brother of Mr. John Roberts, the
well-known stationer of Market Street. Their father was
one of the early Methodist preachers sent out by John
Wesley, beginning his labours in 1759, and was appointed
one of the ministers of Oldham Street Chapel in the years
1774-5 and 1799. Exactly opposite, in the same street,
lived another surgeon, who had a fair share of public
confidence, Mr. Thomas Fawdington. He was one of the
surgeons of what was then called "The Lying-in Hospital."
In Salford, besides Mr. John Boutflower, Mr. Gardom and
Mr. Thomas Brownbill enjoyed for many years extensive
practices, and held the offices of surgeons to the Salford
Dispensary. The father of the latter was a large brick-
maker, first in Manchester and afterwards in Salford. He
helped to level the mount on which the present Quaker's
Chapel was built, by making the clay portion into bricks.

Anyone acquainted with the medical men of Manchester fifty years ago will not think a notice of them complete without some mention of Mr. Heurtley, who practised as a surgeon for nearly half a century, residing during that time, first at the Infirmary, then in Spring Gardens, and afterwards in Oldham Street, where he died at an advanced age. At the beginning of the present century he was House Apothecary at the Infirmary, and afterwards went into practice. He lived and died a bachelor, and was rather remarkable both in appearance and dress, wearing pantaloons made after the fashion adopted by the dandies of a former period—fitting tight round the calf, and finishing off above the ankle. He set himself up as a great wit, and was very fond of punning. If he said a good thing which took, he never rested till he had related it to all his friends to whom he could gain access, and to some of them more than once. Not only so, but he took a great delight in proclaiming to everybody that he was an unbeliever in the inspiration of the Bible and the truth of Christianity. The consequence was that his practice was very limited, though, no doubt, his ability was great.

Besides the foregoing I well remember the following :—Mr. Jesse, of Downing Street, Ardwick, who had a large practice; Mr. Robert Crowther, of Longworth Street, who removed into Quay Street ; Mr. Gavin Hamilton, of Portland Street, who went to reside in Burlington Street, Chorlton Row, then a new neighbourhood, and who married Miss Ward, the actress, a daughter or other relative of Mr. Ward, the teacher of music, of Ward and Andrews ; Mr. George Ferneley, of St. Peter's Square ; Mr. Grindrod, of Oxford Road, now practising as a hydropathic physician, I believe, at Malvern; and Dr. J. P. Kay, in King Street. This gentleman attained considerable eminence both in his profession and as an author. He wrote the "History of the Cholera" in 1832, and, besides other works, one on Asphyxia. He retired from practice to become president of the Poor Law Board, assuming the name of J. Kay-Shuttleworth, and was made a baronet. The present Sir U. Kay-Shuttleworth is his son.

I must not omit to notice two or three men who, though they had not received a professional training, enjoyed a large share of public confidence—the first in the practice of physic, and the second in that of surgery. I refer to the Rev. James Schofield, and Mr. Edmund Taylor, "the Oldfield Lane Doctor." The former was formerly the minister of the chapel known as Christ's Church, near the barracks, in Hulme, and at the time we speak of was the minister of a similar chapel in Every Street, Ancoats. Patients from all the country round used to apply to him, and he had the reputation of curing the ailments of many who had been given up by the regular practitioner. He was very popular amongst the working classes, and took an active part in politics, being one of the leaders of the Radicals of that day, and a coadjutor of Henry Hunt, to whom a monument is erected in the burial-ground attached to his chapel.

The Oldfield Lane Doctor came from Whitworth, near Rochdale, to Manchester sometime during the first decade of this century, leaving either two or three brothers behind him known as the Whitworth doctors, who were as popular as Edmund Taylor afterwards became in Salford. He appears to have made a name for himself shortly after his settlement in Salford; for in the "Directory" for 1811 his name is entered thus: "Taylor, Edmund, Oldfield Lane Doctor, Oldfield Road, Salford." It is said that the Whitworth doctors had been celebrated for two or three generations. The whole family seem to have had a gift in that line, the female as well as the male members of it. A sister of Edmund Taylor married Mr. Maden, a wealthy gentleman and a magistrate, residing at Bacup, and she gratuitously practised the healing art amongst the poor to a late period of her life. I remember, when a youth, spending an evening at her house with my father and mother, when she gave them an account of her labours, stating that she devoted her mornings to this charitable work, having a dispensary fitted up for the purpose, and that the average cost of her drugs and medical appliances was £70 a year.

I used to be very fond of watching old Edmund Taylor's operations, and have spent many an hour in his surgery, frequently on a Sunday afternoon, for he was then always to be found at work. It was most interesting to watch the various cases of accident and forms of injury which presented themselves. The surgery, which had been a large kitchen, having a stone floor, a fireplace, and some benches round it, was at the back of the house, and opened into a large yard. Anyone could go in or out as he pleased, without any notice being taken, as the old gentleman attended to one thing at a time, and seldom noticed anybody or anything but the patient he had in hand, or the one thing he was doing. He went through his work at one uniform pace, and was never hurried or excited by anything. A great many patients were generally waiting their turns, and occasionally there were spectators like myself, but I was always struck with the decorum and stillness which prevailed. Though the old doctor would sometimes crack a joke with a patient, he seldom spoke in a loud voice, and there seemed to be a tacit understanding amongst those present to preserve quiet. Hanging up were several skins of leather, ready spread with a brown kind of plaister, from which occasionally he cut long strips with which to bind up some broken arm, dislocated shoulder, or other injured part. On his shelf were a number of stone bottles, about the size of ordinary medicine bottles, which were filled with a peculiar liniment, for which he and his brothers were celebrated. It was known as the " Whitworth Red Bottle," and seemed designed for universal application. Of this they used to dispense large quantities. Spirit of turpentine was one of the ingredients, and I remember, during my apprenticeship, once sending Taylor a large puncheon of that drug. He was assisted, at one time, by a son who died of consumption. His place was taken by a sister, afterwards Mrs. Ridehalgh.

A third, who was more of a quack, was the so-called Dr. Lignum, of Bridge Street, who was afterwards joined by his son. His real name, I believe, was Wood, and he chose to assume the Latin word for wood. He was the proprietor of a celebrated quack medicine, which is still sold, known as " Lignum's Antiscorbutic Drops."

The Pharmacopœia of fifty years ago contained the names of 444 drugs and their preparations, whilst that of to-day contains the names of no fewer than 802. The former did not contain the names of quinine, morphia, or iodine, three of the most commonly used drugs of the present day. In fact, so frequently are they prescribed in one form or another, that one wonders how the doctors managed without the two latter. Quinine was in use to a certain extent, though it was not officially sanctioned; but where one grain was then used I believe a hundred are now. The system of treating many diseases has indeed been completely revolutionized. Speaking generally, the practice used to be to pull down the system; now it is to build it up by a freer use of quinine and other tonics. But in nothing is the change more striking than in regard to the then common habit of blood-letting, as it was called. I suppose that in the last century it was even more common than it was at the time we speak of, so that if a person fell down in the street from exhaustion he was sure to be bled. Though the practice was becoming more restricted, yet it was very prevalent fifty years ago. I well remember my brother suffering from rheumatic fever, and seeing Mr. Gardom, one of the best surgeons in Salford, draw a basin full of blood from his arm—a thing which no sane medical man would do in the present day. Not only was the lancet used in this way, but cupping and the application of leeches were continually resorted to in cases of inflammation, which it was supposed impossible otherwise to subdue. It is no wonder if the doctors prescribed such treatment that the public believed in its utility. It was no uncommon thing to be told by persons that they found it conducive to their health to be bled periodically, and that such treatment was necessary for them. I remember a neighbour in Market Street, a thin, delicate-looking man, who used to believe in the necessity of periodical blood-letting, and who, if I asked him how he was, would sometimes reply that he had not been bled lately and did not feel very well. He would accordingly be bled. No wonder that he died in the prime of life.*

Fifty years ago the profession of dentistry was in its infancy. Then Manchester only contained six or seven dentists ; to-day there are over one hundred and twenty. The three principal ones were Messrs. Richard Helsby, in George Street ; John Faulkner, near the Wesleyan Chapel, in Oldham Street ; and Faulkner and Son, at the corner of Back Piccadilly, on the left-hand side of Lever Street.

---

* The case of Malibran, who died after first being bled, will be referred to in a succeeding chapter.

CHAPTER VI.

DRUGGISTS.

FIFTY years ago there were only sixty druggists in Manchester and Salford ; to-day, their number exceeds 260. So that whilst the doctors have increased in that time a little more than 100 per cent, the druggists have increased about 330 per cent. Not one of the sixty who were then in business as druggists is so now ; whilst, so far as I can ascertain, only two out of the whole number are living. These are Mr. Eli Atkin, of Newton Heath, and Mr. William Hyde Lamb. Mr. Atkin was an apprentice in the same shop as myself, but had completed his apprenticeship before I began mine, and was then in business, in partnership with Mr. Dale, as Dale and Atkin, in Swan Street. He afterwards relinquished the retail business, and became a drysalter and manufacturing chemist. Mr. Lamb was then a druggist in Shudehill, but shortly after removed to the corner of Lower Mosley Street and Windmill Street, and for some years was a member of the Town Council. He is now an estate and property agent, having an office near his old shop, but on the opposite side of the street.

The oldest member of the trade, at that time, was Mr. Daniel Lynch, who about the year 1790 began business in Market Street, near what is now the end of Corporation Street, but which, of course, did not then exist. He afterwards removed to the opposite side, higher up, next door to the Commercial Hotel, where he was in 1829. I have before stated that he held the chief office in the fraternity of Freemasons. There was another druggist who was in business in the last century, and whose name was retained in the firm of Atkinson and Barker, though he had retired from it before 1829. Mr. John Atkinson was in business in 1790 in St. Mary's Gate, and afterwards went into partnership with Mr. Robert Barker, occupying the shop at the corner of Market Place and St. Mary's Gate, which was pulled down a few years ago to make way for the splendid pile now occupying that and the adjacent ground, and which was at the time of its demolition in the possession of Messrs. Mottershead and Co. Mr. Atkinson was the inventor of that well-known mother's friend, "Infants' Preservative," which, we are informed, has received the patronage of royalty. When I first knew the shop, the firm had two assistants, who eventually went into partnership and opened a shop in Market Street, the firm being Ingham and Westmacott. They afterwards dissolved partnership, and both have since passed away. Mr. Westmacott was a relative (nephew, I believe) of the sculptor of that name, and had a taste for the art himself. At the time of his death his shop was at the corner of Market Street and Corporation Street, where he left a son as his successor, who also has artistic tastes.

Next door to Atkinson and Barker's, in the Market Place, was the shop of Mottershead and Brown. About the year

1790, Thomas Staines was carrying on business, as a druggist, in the Market Place, his house being at White Cross Bank, Salford. In 1815 he was in partnership with Mr. Mottershead, the firm being Staines and Mottershead, which was succeeded in a few years by that of Mottershead and Brown, and which existed fifty years ago. At that time Mr. Brown was dead, and shortly after the business was carried on in the name of John Mottershead. He was a descendant of the Rev. Joseph Mottershead, who was minister of Cross Street Chapel 54 years, commencing his ministry in 1717, and who died at the age of 83 years. I often had occasion to go to the shop, and remember Mr. Mottershead very well. He was a plain and homely man, both in his dress and manner, and, being a bachelor and living on the premises, he had an ancient-looking house-keeper, who used occasionally to come limping into the shop to see how its occupants were getting on. I heard it stated that she was the first person in Manchester who made fermented ginger beer in bottles. Mr. Mottershead had at that time two apprentices, one of whom, Thomas H. Taylor, afterwards began business in St. Ann's Square, where he continued many years. A few years since he relinquished it for another branch of business. The other apprentice was a nephew of Mr. Mottershead's, Thomas Roberts, who was afterwards taken into partnership, the firm being Mottershead and Roberts, and the business was continued by Mr. Roberts after Mr. Mottershead's death. More than thirty years ago, Barker, the successor of Atkinson and Barker, relinquished the retail business, when the corner shop, which was a larger and more convenient one than Mottershead's, was taken by him. The business was carried on by Mr. Roberts till the premises were pulled down, when it was disposed of to the two gentlemen who had so ably managed it for him, and who removed it to premises under the Exchange, Mr. Roberts having become the senior partner in the firm of Roberts, Dale, and Co., manufacturing chemists, Cornbrook. I well remember both Mr. Taylor and Mr. Roberts when they were youths behind Mottershead's counter.

The names of several of the druggists of that day are still perpetuated, namely, Lynch, Mottershead, Jewsbury, Bullock, and Goadsby, though the men themselves have been dead some time, and have no descendants now in the business. Mr. Francis Goadsby, father of the late Alderman Goadsby, was then a druggist in Chapel Street, his shop being on the Manchester side, between New Bailey Street and Blackfriars Bridge. Another venerable Salford druggist of that day was Mr. William Brearey, whose shop was then at Pendleton. He had a shop previously in Market Street, and afterwards removed from Pendleton to Upper Brook Street. Contemporary with the elder Goadsby and Brearey was Mr. James Brereton, who evidently believed, as well as his successors, that "a rolling stone gathers no moss," for, about the year 1810, we find him keeping a shop at the corner of Cateaton Street and Smithy Door, where I knew him in 1829, and which he continued to keep for many years. He was succeeded by his son, who in his turn was succeeded by Mr. Hughes, the present occupant. So that the old shop has only changed owners twice in about seventy years. Another druggist who

began business about the same time was Mr. John Cook ;
his shop was in King Street, a little lower down than the
Old Exchange entry, on the same side. I remember it in
1829, as it presented a rather old-fashioned appearance,
having bow windows with small panes of glass. There was
also another druggist's shop then in King Street on the same
side three doors from Deansgate, and next to Townsend's,
the music seller, occupied by Mr. Daniel Bullock. So that
King Street then contained two druggists, though there is
not one there now.

Oxford Road had only one, Mr. Thomas Sigley ; whilst
there was only one in the whole of Hulme. That happy
individual was Mr. Robert Middleton, of Chester Road.
Of course the Stretford Road was not then constructed.
There were four in the Market Place. Besides Atkinson
and Barker and Mottershead, there was George Vaughan,
who was also a seedsman and began business at the beginning of the century, his shop being in the corner next to the
Blue Boar court. Nearer to Market Street was Mr. Gilbert
Blackberd, also a druggist and seedsman, in the shop
now occupied by Mr. Henry Watkinson, the seedsman.
Mr. Thomas Watkinson, an elder brother, succeeded
Mr. Blackberd, and after some time gave up selling drugs,
confining his trade to the other branch. He died several
years since, and was succeeded by his younger brother.

Market Street at that time possessed four druggist's shops,
their owners being Stocks and Dentith, Daniel Lynch,
Robert Halstead Hargreaves, and Jewsbury and Whitlow.
The most popular street with druggists was Piccadilly,
which then contained six, two of the number being sons of

Wesleyan ministers. The first shop which was. so long
occupied by Mr. Standring, and which has only just been
pulled down to widen the entrance to Tib Street, was then
occupied by Mr. John Williams Gaulter. His father was
the Rev. John Gaulter, who in the early part of his career
was a contemporary of Wesley, at which time his name used
to be spelt Gaultier. In my early days he resided for a
time in Manchester, and I remember his tall and handsome
figure and venerable appearance, dressed in the costume of
the day with knee breeches, black stockings, and silver
knee-buckles. His son was a very gentlemanly man, and
began business about the year 1812. When I first knew
him his assistant was Mr. L. Simpson, who afterwards began
business in Princess Street, his shop being the first opened
in that street. It was thought at the time to be rather a
rash undertaking, but it succeeded. He retired many years
ago, when he disposed of his business to Messrs. Ransome
and Co.

Previous to this, Gaulter had two apprentices named
Jewsbury and Whitlow, who ultimately went into partnership, beginning business about the year 1825, in the shop
over the door of which the name of one of the partners
is still retained. It was one of three or four which
had just been rebuilt, and were then called " Egyptian
Buildings." Mr. Jewsbury's father was a yarn agent, and
also agent for the West of England Insurance Company,
and was the father of the two authoresses, Miss Jewsbury
(afterwards Mrs. Fletcher), who died in India, and
Miss Geraldine Jewsbury, the novelist. Jewsbury married
his partner's sister, whose mother kept the George and

Dragon Inn, at the corner of York Street and Fountain Street. The house was sold some time after her death, and the premises taken for the South Lancashire Bank, long since defunct.

About the year 1824 there was a hosier's shop at the corner of Swan Court, in Market Street, occupied by Mr. James Townsend. During some extensive alterations which were being executed at the next shop, some injury was done to the foundation of Townsend's shop. One Saturday afternoon a man going past was startled by the falling of bricks, and he shouted to Townsend warning him of danger. The latter had just time to escape, with his bag of money in his hand, when the building fell. Fortunately just at this time the shop (now No. 27) which had been occupied by Mr. Bentham, a bookseller, who had removed to the Market Place, was at liberty, and to this Townsend removed. After carrying on business some years longer he retired, and disposed of it to a Scotchman named Brown, who had resided in Manchester for some years. Mr. Brown had several children, and amongst them a bright, bonny-faced boy, called William Scott, who he was ambitious should become a druggist. Accordingly, when William was old enough, he was sent to Mr. John Lessey's, in Piccadilly, but did not remain long there, and was bound an apprentice to Messrs. Jewsbury and Whitlow. After some time they dissolved partnership, Whitlow going to Liverpool and Jewsbury retaining the business. For many years before Jewsbury's death, owing to some spinal injury, he lost the use of the lower extremities, and could not attend to business. He wisely took into partnership his former apprentice, then an assistant, who still survives to render services to his fellow-townsmen in various public capacities, as William Scott Brown.

I mentioned in a notice of Market Street, that in 1829 the alterations connected with the widening of the street were not complete, and that there was still standing on the left-hand going up, an old pile of buildings, the footpath in front of which was much higher than the carriage way. One of the shops in this old pile was that of Mr. Hargreaves, already mentioned, who began business there in 1796. He was also a drysalter, and had been a chemical manufacturer, in which he made a large fortune. I was often sent to him to inquire what he would charge us for some article which we had not in stock. As sure as I did so the old gentleman would seize a duster and commence a polishing operation on his counter-top. Whilst doing this he would mutter a complaint that my master was spoiling the trade (referring to the drysaltery) by cutting down the profits and underselling him. Then, after another rub or two, he would gruffly give me the information I sought. In due time the old buildings came down, and were replaced by the present ones, which stand on the site. Mr. Hargreaves retired from the business about 1844, and was succeeded by the late Mr. James Woolley. Three doors from Gaulter's, in Picca-dilly, was the shop of Mr. Samuel Dean, a druggist; and when I came to Manchester Mr. James Woolley was just completing his apprenticeship with Dean. I remember him calling to see the assistant in the shop where I was one Sunday afternoon about that time. He eventually opened a shop in King Street, near to the one now occupied by

Messrs. Wilson and Co., the ironmongers. When Mr. Hargreaves retired, Mr. James Woolley purchased his business. He was for some years a member of the Town Council, and greatly respected by all who knew him. He did not live to be an old man, and his business is carried on by three of his sons, who have greatly extended the wholesale branch of it, as well as the premises occupied by their father.

There were two druggists then in Manchester who were quakers. One of them was Mr. W. Ansell, whose shop was in St. Mary's Gate. He was a clean, pleasant-looking little man, very precise and methodical in his manner, and just the sort of man to inspire you with confidence in his accuracy. His was the only place then in the town where chemical apparatus could be purchased. He was succeeded by Mr. Dale, now of the firm of Roberts, Dale, and Co.

The other quaker druggist was Mr. George Danson, in Piccadilly, his shop being between the houses of Mr. Bloor, the pawnbroker, and Mr. John Windsor, the surgeon. A little lower down, and three doors from the Albion, was the shop then occupied by the late Mr. Thomas Standring, who afterwards removed to that which had been Gaulter's, and which has so recently been pulled down. It may be interesting here to state that fifty years ago the late owner of the site gave £3,500 for it, and it was recently sold to the Corporation for £22,500.

I have mentioned the name of Mr. John Lessey, in Piccadilly, to whom young William Scott Brown was first sent to learn the mysteries of a druggist's shop. He was the son of the Rev. Theophilus Lessey, one of the early Wesleyan ministers, and had a brother Theophilus, also a

Wesleyan minister, known as one of the most eloquent preachers of the day. Next door to John lived another brother, a surgeon. The sixth druggist in this street was Mr. R. Woodall.

Not only was there a noted surgeon, named Robert Thorpe, in Oldham Street fifty years ago, but there was also in the same street a noted druggist, named Ellen Thorp, who was quite as popular in doctoring women and children. In 1794 there were two lady druggists in Manchester, one being "Ann Cooke, druggist and seedsman, 27, Market Place;" and the other Ann Thorp, apothecary, 45, Oldham Street. She had a son, Issachar, who acquired a knowledge of the business when a young man, and who afterwards became a calico printer, having a warehouse in Fountain Street, and who, on the death of his mother, took her business. For a few years he had both businesses on his hands, and I doubt not that his wife Ellen assisted him at this time in the shop, and so became sufficiently acquainted with its duties to be enabled to follow them up after his death. The shop of Ann Thorp, in 1794, was a black and white half-timbered old house. Ellen Thorp, on the death of her husband, continued the business, which is still carried on by her successor.

About the year 1822 Mr. John Stocks, who had a shop previously at the corner of Thomas Street and Oldham Street, removed to Market Street. The shop to which he removed is now No. 41, but owing to a different method of numbering the streets, was then 21, and is the shop in which I served my apprenticeship. At the time Mr. Stocks removed to it, Mr. Eli Atkin was his apprentice, and Mr. Atkin informs me that there was at that time a tradition in the place that it was the oldest druggist's shop in Manchester. I have no means of tracing its history further back than 1794, at which time its occupant was George Buxton Brown. Soon after the beginning of the present century the business was transferred to William Wilson, who retained it till John Stocks became its possessor. Stocks took into partnership William Dentith, who had been a traveller for David Taylor and Sons, and the firm became Stocks and Dentith, but had not existed long before Stocks died. When I was an apprentice the premises belonged to a Mr. G. B. Brown, of Halifax, I presume a son of George Buxton Brown, who was there in 1794. After the death of Mr. Stocks, his widow retired from the business and I was bound an apprentice to the new firm of William Dentith and Co., my father paying down £100 as my premium. Mrs. Stocks, who was the sister of our almost octogenarian friend, Mr. Benjamin Rawson, of Ardwick Green, afterwards married Mr. Heap, a large stonemason, who built the steeple of St. Peter's Church, which at first was without one for some years. He also built St. Matthew's and Stand Churches, but unfortunately got involved in a law suit for extras with the Church Commissioners, which he lost. I understand Mrs. Pochin, the wife of the M.P., is his grand-daughter. Dentith had two other apprentices when I entered his service. The elder of the two was the son of the late Rev. Dr. Warren, and brother of Mr. Samuel Warren, Q.C., the author of "Ten Thousand a Year." He afterwards entered the service of Pole and Co., merchants, of London, who had a house at the Isthmus of Darien, to which he was sent, and where he died shortly after. The second was Henry Blaine, the son of a retired draper at Hull. After I had been rather more than two years with Dentith, he sold his retail business and went altogether into the wholesale, taking Blaine with him and leaving me with his successor. Shortly after my apprenticeship terminated, Blaine made overtures to me to go out with him to the Cape of Good Hope. I went to consult my father, who was at the time attending the Wesleyan Conference at Birmingham, travelling all night by the Red Rover coach. He in his turn (unwisely, as I thought) consulted a missionary named Kay, who had just returned from the Cape. The result of a five minutes' conversation with him was, that Blaine went out without me, founded the house of Blaine Brothers, and became the Hon. Henry Blaine, member of the Upper House of Legislature at the Cape.

A druggist's apprentice in those days had to work both harder and longer than at the present day. My master being a large soda water maker, I had the advantage of learning that branch, at which for the two first years of my apprenticeship I worked pretty hard. At that time there were only three makers of soda water in Manchester— Gaulter, in Piccadilly; Thompstone, in Cupid's Alley; and my master. In the shop was a soda water fountain, from which soda water was drawn by means of a strong glass globe, the mouth of which fitted tightly on to a nipple, and out of which it was poured into a tumbler ready for drinking. On one occasion Blaine was drawing a glass for a customer when the globe burst and laid open his cheek, thereby slightly disfiguring him for life.

After I had been with Dentith between two and three years he sold his retail business to Mr. Horatio Miller, of London, to whom I was bound over. Miller had been for some years an assistant with Godfrey and Cooke, of London, who were at that time the principal West End chemists, and had most of the aristocracy as customers. He afterwards went one or two voyages on board of a whaleship as medical attendant, which would be illegal in the present day. He had seen much of life, having mixed a good deal with London society, and was not long in Manchester before he made the acquaintance of a number of the professional and literary men of that day, with others of congenial tastes, whom he gathered around him. He was a believer in the fact that your grand stately "spreads" do not always yield the most pleasure, and preferred snug and less ostentatious social gatherings. Moreover, being a bachelor, he had no fear of the consequences if sometimes he brought in a friend to partake of a little "plain family dinner" without notice. After a while he seemed to become rather partial to me, used to read Shakspere and other authors to me after business hours, and often permitted me to be present when entertaining one or two of his friends, whose society I used greatly to enjoy.

Chief among these was Mr. Henry B. Peacock, the elder, better known as Harry Peacock, who was, I believe, one of the founders of the Prince's Theatre. Fifty years ago he had a tailor's shop in King Street, but had removed at the time I knew him into St. Ann's Square. I used to delight in his company, as his conversation abounded in wit, humour, and anecdote. In a diary I then kept for a short time I find his name frequently mentioned. Another frequent visitor was Charles Swain, the poet, whose dark lustrous eyes and intellectual conversation I well remember. Charles Wilkins, the barrister, occasionally dined with us. Though he afterwards became Serjeant Wilkins he did not attain to great eminence at the bar, and died after a somewhat brief career. He was known to his friends as anything but an affluent man. His forte was in addressing juries. To hear him was a rich treat, as he told them that it was now his "turn, under the direction and correction of the learned judge, to place the facts of the case before them," rolling his words out with delightful smoothness and distinctness.

Mr. Miller was also on intimate terms with Charles Calvert and William Bradley, the artists. I mentioned some time since in the *City News* that on one occasion Miller had promised to take a young lady to the flower show at the Town Hall, and that being prevented doing so he requested me to supply his place. She was Calvert's daughter, and became Bradley's wife, but at the time of my writing I had forgotten in what relation she stood to Bradley. After my reference to her in the *City News* she wrote me a kind letter, from which I may be allowed to give the following extract :—" I was the young girl you so kindly escorted to the flower show, and Mr. Miller, of Market Street, was a very kind friend of my father's, and visited at our house in Princess Street. The time of going to the flower show was prior to my marriage. I afterwards visited, along with my father, Mr. Miller's house, taking tea and spending the evening there, admiring the flowers he so prided himself

in arranging in vases ; and the circumstance is impressed on
my memory in consequence of Mr. Miller so much admiring
a gold chain I wore for the first time, being the first present
from Mr. Bradley, and which he put round my neck just
before I set out for Mr. Miller's house." Those who have
felt any interest in the notices of William Bradley which
have appeared in the *City News* will not be sorry to read
another extract from the same letter. The writer says :—
"Long years have passed since I saw you. I have been
eleven years in Sydney, N.S.W., with my present husband,
my two daughters, and my eldest son ; and having acquired
a comfortable competency after all the tossing of fortune,
or rather misfortune, I am now settled down in this place"
(naming a small town on the banks of the Thames).

Other visitors at Miller's house were Mr. Lot Gardner,
of High Street ; Mr. Joe Marsland, cotton merchant, of
Cockpit Hill ; Mr. Edward Saul, of the firm of Gardner,
Harter, and Co., drysalters ; Mr. William Hatton, iron
merchant, Blackfriars Street ; and Mr. George Condy, the
barrister. The latter was the son of an Irish Wesleyan
minister. He had very little practice at the bar, but was
one of the commissioners in bankruptcy, and for some years
was editor of the *Manchester and Salford Advertiser*, at the
time Mrs. Leresche was its proprietor, and its office was at
the corner of Spring Gardens and Market Street.

Mr. Miller having resided so long in London, and having
as I have said mixed a good deal in London society, had
become acquainted with many of the leading actors of the
day. Accordingly when any of them came to Manchester
he found them out and invited them to visit him. I have

a distinct remembrance of once dining with Charles Kemble, and of the pleasure I felt in assisting him to vegetables.

Macready was also a visitor at Miller's house when he came to Manchester. I have a vivid recollection of his coming in one morning having, in passing a newly-painted lamp-post, daubed the sleeve of his coat. It was a single-breasted brown overcoat, and I had the pleasure of helping him out of his difficulty. The manner of his thanking me was most polite and courteous, and the tone of his voice so striking that I used to think that if I heard the same words again uttered by the same voice, blindfolded, I should recognise it.

Dowton was another visitor. I suppose he was the finest representative of Falstaff of all who ever attempted the character. He was, in the early part of his career, a contemporary and a colleague of Mrs. Jordan, the intimate friend at one time of William IV. I have preserved a note, written by Mr. Clarke, the manager of the Theatre Royal, to Condy, the barrister, which I presume had been handed to Miller in explanation of Clarke's absence. There is no date to the note, but it will be seen the dinner party was on a Sunday. The following is a copy of the note :—

MY DEAR SIR,—I am on the doctor's list, and cannot leave house to-day. Will you have the kindness to make my apology to Mr. Miller, with whom I was to dine, and say that I very much regret not being able to meet him? Dowton relies upon your good offices to show him the way to the dinner table; he is domiciled at No. 70, Falkner Street; Andrews on door.—Yours very truly,

   Sunday morning.   RT. CLARKE.

 — Condy, Esq.

Andrews was a performer at the Theatre Royal, and took the characters of old men. He was the father of Mr. Andrews, of the firm of Ward and Andrews, professors of music.

Horatio Miller afterwards relinquished the drug business, and went into partnership with Mr. Robert Hindley, the brewer, Miller's Lane, Salford, sometimes known as Bob Hindley, and sometimes as Captain Hindley, from his having held the rank of captain in the Volunteers of a former period.* Afterwards Miller went to Fleetwood and then to Southampton, as agent for one or two steam-packet companies. The last I heard of him was that he was connected with the exhibition of the great Globe in Leicester Square, during the Great Exhibition of 1851, and that he had a trial with Mr. Wylde concerning it, and had lost his case. He occasionally indulged in writing poetry, of which I retain several specimens, and was somewhat of an adept at sketching and modelling. I have in my possession a caricature pen and ink sketch which he made of Dentith's head, which is a capital likeness. After finishing my apprenticeship I remained with him, at his request, as an assistant for two or three years, when we went into partnership together as soda water makers, the business being carried on in my name.

Altogether, my old master was not an ordinary man, and, in looking back, I think of him with the liveliest interest.

---

* In 1833 Mr. Hindley was elected president of the club known as "John Shaw's," and held the office till 1852, when he resigned, being 82 years of age.

CHAPTER VII.

BOOKSELLERS.

IN 1829, the first bookseller's shop you met with coming up Market Street on the left-hand side was that of James Everett. He was originally a Wesleyan minister, and, owing to a throat affection, he became after a time what is technically called by the Wesleyans a supernumerary, and entered into business for some years. He then re-entered the Wesleyan ministry, and in the year 1849 finally left the body. His shop fifty years ago was near the present end of Corporation-street, but he afterwards removed higher up to a shop near the end of New Cannon Street. As I used to make for him ten gallons of ink at once, and take it to him, I remember him well, being generally met by some quaint remark as to the quality of the ink. He resided in a kind of square, called Sedgwick's Court, which turned out of Deansgate, on the river side, between St. Mary's Gate and the Old Bridge. I recollect having been sent to his house one Sunday morning early with a request that he would preach at Oldham Street Chapel that morning. He was a popular preacher, and author of several works, the most noted of which were "The Life of Sammy Hick, the Village Blacksmith," and the *Wesleyan Takings*, which last was published anonymously. There was one which he published about sixty years ago, which made no small stir at the time, and of which the publication was suppressed, I believe. Hence I find the recollection of it has nearly passed away. One of the earliest things of the kind which I can remember is the handling of a copy of this work, which my father possessed, and looking at one of the illustrations. It was called *The Parson and the Cat*, and was intended to take off the parson-hunting tendency of the age. It was cast in the "John Gilpin" mould, and narrated in verse how a certain parson, returning home disappointed of his day's sport, espied a lad with a cat and induced him to set poor puss down and let the dogs be after her. The instinct of the cat induced her to get as far out of the way of the dogs as she could by clambering up the hind quarters of the horse, then up the back of the rider, then on to his head. There was a picture of the scene of the hat and wig of the rider flying away, and the cat setting her claws on to the bald head of the poor affrighted and tortured parson.

The next bookseller's shop on the same side was that of Ebenezer Thomson and Sons, who occupied the shop No. 20, at the corner of Cromford Court, next to the one in which I was apprenticed, which was then No. 21, the numbers running consecutively at the time. In 1790 the same shop was occupied by James Thomson, bookseller. In 1810 it was divided into two shops, one being occupied by James Thomson and Son, the son being Ebenezer, who lived at the back of New Windsor, Salford. In 1815 the shop was restored to its original dimensions, and Ebenezer had the business to himself, the father having retired, and residing at "Cheetham Cottage Town," Red Bank. In 1824 the firm was still Ebenezer, but in 1829 it was, as I have stated, E. Thomson and Sons, and a year or two after was changed to James and Joseph Thomson. They were known as dealers in books on mechanics and the various branches of civil engineering as well as general literature, their stock of new and second-hand books being one of the largest in the provinces. Their printed catalogue in 1829 extended to something like 600 octavo pages, and contained the names of 20,000 volumes. They dealt also in stationery and stamps and did a good business in book-binding. The younger brother, Joseph, died some years since, but I had the pleasure of meeting with James three or four years ago, when he was staying at the same hotel in Southport as myself, his residence being near Bowness.

The next bookseller to the Thomsons was W. Dean, near to the end of New Cannon Street. In 1810 the shop was next door to that of Mr. Hargreaves, the druggist, and kept by R. and W. Dean. In 1815 they had removed to the corner of Brown Street, where they remained some years, but in 1824 there was only William in the concern ; and in 1829 the business had crossed over to the other side of the street again. When the Deans were at the corner of Brown Street they printed the Manchester Directory for Pigot, and published it conjointly with him, Pigot being at that time merely an engraver and not a letterpress printer. James Pigot was an engraver in Back Faulkner Street in 1794, and afterwards removed to Fountain Street where he was at the time I came to Manchester. At that time his son was in partnership with him, the father living in Polygon Avenue, Ardwick, and James, the son, behind the premises in Fountain Street.

The next bookseller's shop or stall, between the shops of Watson, the trunk-maker, and Hargreaves, the druggist, in the old part of Market Street not yet pulled down, was that of old Weatherley, about whom so much has been said in the columns of the *City News*.

In proceeding up Market Street, we next come to quite a nest of booksellers, all close together, the first of whose shops was that of Thomas Forrest. His history, in one respect, is interesting, inasmuch as he came to Manchester to seek his fortune, with a fellow-journeyman printer, named Jeremiah Garnett, of whom I shall have more to say shortly. They worked together for a while on *Wheeler's Chronicle*, and when the *Manchester Guardian* was established Mr. Garnett joined it, ultimately becoming a partner. Forrest, sometime about 1822 or 1823, took a shop in the Old Exchange Passage, where he printed a history of Wales for Mr. Cathrall, the then editor of the *Chronicle*, and, about 1828, removed to the shop adjoining the then Brooks's Bank, in Market Street. He was the only bookseller who would allow the publications of the Unitarian body to lie on his counter. He had a good business in printing and stationery, which, after some changes, passed, in 1853, into the hands of his former apprentices, Messrs. Johnson and Rawson, who have somewhat extended it, and carry it on in the same premises.

After passing the shop of Mary Lowe and Co., tailors, and the Old Palace Inn, the next shop at the corner of

Palace Street, was that of Mr. John Roberts, a large
stationer. He was the son of one of Wesley's early coadjutors, and brother of Mr. Benjamin Roberts, the surgeon, of
Lever Street. Being an intimate friend of my father's I
knew him well, and have spent many days at his house in
Piccadilly, next door to Mr. Bloor's, and opposite the end
of Portland Street, when a boy, on a visit with my mother.
He began business about the first year in the present
century, and I have heard it stated that his father, being
stationed at the time at the Oldham Street Chapel, after the
service there one week evening, announced to the congregation that his son had begun business in Market Street,
as a bookseller and stationer. His business was noted as
the oldest stationery business, and also for the enormous
number of bill stamps which he sold, disposing, I believe,
of more than all the other dealers in them in Manchester
put together. He was a very upright tradesman, very
genial, lived to a good old age, and stuck to business nearly
to the last, leaving behind him a handsome fortune. He
had an only son, Thomas, who was remarkably corpulent
for so young a man. He died a few years after he was
married. Mr. Roberts did a large bookbinding trade, which
was practically managed by Mr. John Leigh, who married
Mr. Roberts' relative and assistant, Miss Andrews, and
who succeeded him in the business. After his retirement
Mr. James Cheetham took the business.

Three doors higher up the street was the shop of
Mr. Charles Ambery. He was, perhaps, more of a seller of
books than any hitherto named. He had not been in this
business long before 1829, having been a joiner previously,

but being connected with Bennett Street Sunday School—
with which Mr. Benjamin Braidley was also associated—
the latter provided him with the means of beginning business as a bookseller, for which he had already manifested a
taste.   He was well supported by Church people and did a
large trade.   I have occasionally seen what has been a very
handsome Bible and Prayer Book bound together, in the
hands of an elderly married lady, which was purchased at
his shop before she was married.

Next door to Mr. Ambery was the shop of Mr. John
Royle, the stationer.   I well remember him as a very old
man.   In 1810 he was in Deansgate, and in 1815 he was
lower down Market Street, near the shop which is now
Darbyshire's, the confectioner's, his house being in Hodson
Street, Salford.   After that he went still lower down, occu-
pying a site near the present omnibus company's office.
From there he went into the Market Place, where he was
in 1824, but at last reached the shop at the corner of
Marsden Square, where he was when I was an apprentice.

Crossing over the end of High Street, we next came to
the bookshop of T. S. Gregson, the first shop in Egyptian
Buildings, Jewsbury and Whitlow's being the second, and
Miles Craston's, the hatter, being third.   Gregson was the
author of a book which is now becoming rare, called
"Gimcrackiana," composed mainly of poetic and humorous
descriptions of Manchester men and things, a specimen of
which was given in a previous chapter on "Hookers-in."   Poor
Gregson gave way to a little failing, and his shop in a few
years gave him up.   It appears that he was in the habit of
frequenting the George and Dragon, at the corner of York

Street and Fountain Street, and that on one occasion he was turned out, and requested not to enter it again. At the time, he was assistant bookkeeper at the shop of a neighbouring firm, and shortly afterwards the following stanzas were found on the flyleaf of a rough day-book in his writing. The first is a quotation, I believe, and in the second he evidently tries to relieve his feelings :—

BLOWING-UP DAY.

Whoe'er has travelled life's dull round,
　Where'er his toilsome journey's been,
Must sigh to think how oft he's found
　His warmest welcome at an inn.

The contrary we here may trace ;
　For quaffing off an extra flagon
The writer, held in sad disgrace,
　Was banished from the George and Dragon.

After leaving the shop, it was taken by Mr. Benjamin Binyon, as a confectioner, who, whilst there, opened the Beehive Restaurant, under the Palace Inn, which was the first extensive restaurant established in Manchester.

The last shop on the left-hand side of Market Street was that of Joseph Gleave. He was an old Manchester bookseller, having been in business several years before the close of the last century, in Southern Street, a small street which turned out of Priestner Street, in Alport Town. He then removed to Alport Street, and thence to the corner of John Street and Deansgate. This was his principal place of business, where he published a Hebrew Grammar, by Dr. Bayley, "The House of Stanley," "Bennet's Oratory," and other works. A short time before his death, he opened

the Market Street shop as a branch. There was a John
Gleave, a dealer in second-hand books, in 1829, not far
from Marsden Square, who, I believe, was a son of Joseph,
but who was only there a few years.

In Piccadilly, nearly opposite the Infirmary clock, was
the shop of Mr. William Ellerby, who came here in
1826, as the agent of the Religious Tract Society, but
united with the agency a general bookselling business.
He wa s not originally well educated, but by rare
application and perseverance he became a very well
informed man on all general literary subjects, especially
those connected with theology and the rise and progress of
Puritanism and Nonconformity. Having been a commercial
traveller for fourteen years, he had gathered a great deal of
historical information, which enabled him to contribute a
series of articles to the *Congregational Magazine*, and greatly
to assist the late Mr. George Hadfield in the suit instituted
to recover Lady Hewley's property, whereby it was taken
from the Unitarians and handed over to the "Orthodox
Dissenters." He was also consulted on literary matters by
such men as the late Sir Oswald Mosley and Sir John
Bowring, when they had occasion to visit Manchester. He
revised and published an edition of Edwards " On the
Religious Affections," and also published several pamphlets,
from his own pen, on the Quaker Controversies, at the time
Isaac Crewdson and others seceded from that body. He
died in 1839.

Mr. Thomas Sowler was a letterpress printer at the close
of the last century, in partnership with Mr. Russell, at
Hunt's Bank, the firm being Sowler and Russell. After a

time they dissolved partnership, Mr. Russell joining a
Mr. Allen, and carrying on the printing business in Deansgate, and Mr. Sowler beginning business, as a bookseller, in
St. Ann's Square. At the time I came to Manchester,
Mr. Sowler had added the publication of the *Manchester
Courier* to his other business. Subsequently the book trade
was relinquished, the efforts and capital of the firm being
confined to the publication of the newspaper, and to a
general job printing business.

In 1829, not far from Sowler's shop, at the corner of Red
Lion Street and Exchange Street, the firm of Bancks and Co.
was in full swing, doing a very extensive business. They
ultimately collapsed, their failure being one of the elements
which assisted in eventually bringing down the Bank of
Manchester, to whom they were at the time indebted for
considerably more than £100,000. With them was Mr.
Benjamin Love, who, with Mr. John Barton, an assistant of
Mr. Gleave's, began business as Love and Barton, in a shop
in Newall's Buildings. They subsequently removed to the
former premises of the Bank of Manchester. Mr. Love is
dead, and Mr. John Barton has retired, the business being
now carried on by Mr. Henry Barton. Mr. Love possessed
some literary ability, and was the author of one or two works,
the most important of which was descriptive of Wesleyan
Methodism, he having at one time been a Wesleyan.
Among their assistants were Thomas Roworth and William
Hale, who, on completing their terms, formed the partnership which, as Hale and Roworth, began business in King
Street, subsequently removing to Cross Street. A few years
ago they separated, when Mr. Roworth removed to his

present shop in St. Ann's Square, where he has a considerable Church connection.

George, or "Old Bentham," as he was commonly called fifty years ago, had a small shop in the Market Place, doing an unpretending but not an unprofitable business among the market people and frequenters of the Exchange. In Newmarket Buildings, near to Market Street, at the same time, was the shop of Ann Hopps, the widow of John Hopps, who had his shop there at the beginning of the century, and whose name has been previously mentioned in these pages.

James Wroe, a well-known Radical fifty years ago, was a bookseller in Ancoats Lane. He began first with a stall in Port Street, and succeeded so well that in a few years he not only occupied the shop referred to, but about the year 1819 became the printer and publisher of the *Manchester Observer*, the office of which was in Market Street, near the Sun Entry. He was so violent in his politics that he printed several libels on the Prince of Wales in the *Observer*. He was prosecuted, convicted, and sentenced to pay a heavy fine, and to be incarcerated in Lancaster Castle for three years. Before the expiration of his term of imprisonment another indictment had been presented against him, and Joe Nadin was waiting in Lancaster to serve him with another warrant on his exit. He, however, somehow managed to escape him and got on to the Manchester coach, but before he got to Preston, I believe in consequence of the upsetting of the coach, he broke his arm and was again imprisoned. This led to his ruin, for he failed in 1826, and was confined as a debtor in the King's Bench.

He afterwards complained that he had been deserted in the hour of need by his Radical friends, some of the more wealthy of whom had promised to make good whatever he might lose in his advocacy of their views. He had some time previously sold the *Observer* to Mr. Thomas John Evans. He died in 1844.

Mr. Robert Robinson, who, in 1829, was a highly-respectable bookseller in St. Ann's Place, was related to the wife of Sir Benjamin Heywood, his son, the present Vicar of Swinton, being named Henry Robinson Heywood. In 1821 Robinson had a partner named Ellis; and in 1825 his partner was Mr. Thomas Bent, who afterwards went to London and established *Bent's Literary Advertiser,* as a journal for publishers and bookbuyers. Mr. Bent married a sister of the late Mr. John Richardson, of the Mosley Arms, and was not successful in business. His three daughters, the Misses Bent, were brought up by their uncle at the Mosley Arms, and took an active part in St. Ann's Sunday Schools during the incumbency of Mr. Richardson and subsequently.

The firm of Swain and Dewhurst were in business nearly fifty years ago as booksellers, their shop being between the *Manchester Times* office and the Dog and Partridge Tavern, in Ducie Place. The first-named gentleman was Charles Swain, the poet. I possess a copy of Henry Kirke White's poems, which my master purchased at their shop, and presented to me. They never did a large business, and after a while Mr. Swain became an engraver and lithographer in Fennel Street. His partner, Dewhurst, continued the book trade in Market Street. In a part of the back of the

Exchange, Webb and Simms had a bookseller's shop, the business being ultimately carried on by Geo. Simms, in which establishment Mr. David Kelly was brought up, who afterwards succeeded Charles Ambery It was Webb and Simms and Charles Ambery who first introduced the system of allowing a discount on books.

William Willis was at one time the largest bookseller in Manchester, and was employed when a boy by an old bookseller named Newton. He afterwards borrowed ten pounds from his father, and set up a bookstall on his own account. This so annoyed Newton that he bought the ground upon which his rival's stall was erected, and Willis had to remove to a piece of ground near High Street. He was afterwards joined by a partner, who brought one hundred pounds into the concern, when the new firm removed to a cellar in St. Ann's Square. In five years the partnership was dissolved, and he removed to another cellar in Market Street. He afterwards opened a shop in Hanging Ditch. Owing to his carrying on the publishing business, disaster overtook him, and he was much reduced in circumstances. He eventually became a Roman Catholic, abjuring many of the political opinions which he held at one time, and died suddenly.

In 1829 there was a bookseller named Samuel Johnson in Market Street, his shop standing on the site now occupied by Hyam's clothing establishment. He was originally a spinner, in the same factory, in Ancoats, in which the late Elijah Dixon also worked. Whilst he worked in the factory, he had a bookstall near Store Street, which he found to answer so well that he left the factory and took a shop near the Ancoats end of Lever Street. When the firm of W. and R. Dean failed, he bought the stereotype plates of several works published by them. His business largely increased, so that he was obliged to remove to other premises in Rochdale Road, and ultimately retired to the Isle of Man, where his son Joseph still resides, his son Thomas still continuing the bookselling business in Corporation Street.

Some of the booksellers, who have been named, were letterpress printers, and besides these and the printers of newspapers, who will be mentioned afterwards, the names of two or three others, who were in business fifty years ago, occur to my mind. Mr. Thomas Wilkinson had his office in Ridgefield, where it had been since 1817. He was succeeded by his son, the printer of this book, who now carries on the business at the "Guttenberg Works," at Pendleton. Mr. George Cave had his office in Pool Fold, afterwards taking into partnership Mr. Charles Sever. Mr. William Preston Aston was in St. Ann's Street; Mr. Joseph Pratt, in Bridge Street; Mr. John Swindells, in Hanging Bridge; and Mr. Mark Wardle, in Back King Street. But the two, of whom I have the best recollection, are James Patrick and Wilmot Henry Jones. The former had his office in Cockpit Hill, just below the shop in which I was apprenticed, and was the official printer of the racing lists during the season. How well I remember how ten or twenty men used to issue sometimes out of the entry leading to Cockpit Hill, about eight o'clock in a morning, crying "Patrick's krekt list of the running horses, with the names, weights, and colours of the riders." His place of business,

in 1820, was near to Newall's shop, in Market Street.   He
held the monopoly of the racing business for many years.

W. H. Jones's office was at the end of Barlow's Court, it
being only divided by Mr. Ronchetti's shop from my
master's, and I used to be very fond of running in and
having a chat with him when I had an opportunity.   He
was the printer of Bayley's " Festus," and was the first in
Manchester to print posters in colours.   I remember calling
in once, when he told me that he had a handbill to print for
a hatter, who had solicited his aid in its composition, and
asked me to give him an idea.   I told him that Lord
Chesterfield had said that if a man wore a good and well-
brushed hat and a well-polished pair of shoes, he looked a
gentleman.   The idea pleased him immensely, and he
worked it into his bill.

CHAPTER VIII.

SUNDRY TRADERS, ENGINEERS, AND PROFESSORS.

ONE or two references have been made to the fact that the names of many firms which existed fifty years ago exist at the present day, although their owners are no more. Not only so, but in several instances these old firms are carrying on business in the same premises as they were half a century and more since. Edward Goodall and Co., carpet dealers, were then occupying the same premises in King Street as now, though the shop was only half the size it is, the corner one, which was then occupied by Mr. Robert Gough, an ironmonger, having been added since. Mr. Edward Goodall died only recently, being upwards of 80 years of age. Satterfield and Co. were also in business in the same premises in St. Ann's Square as were occupied by them up to a recent date, and which are still occupied by their successors. At the time the firm ceased to exist I believe it was the oldest retail firm in Manchester. In what year Mr. John Satterfield began business I cannot ascertain, but it is certain he was in business as a linen draper on the same site in 1794, and as there is a brass plate on one of the pews of St. Mary's Church bearing the inscription, "John Satterfield, 1788," we may take it for granted that he was in business in the Square before that date. Another old firm of linen drapers which were in business in 1829, and are still occupying the same premises in Old Millgate, is that of Smith, Hill, and Co. I cannot learn that they were in business before the early part of this century, but in 1810 William Smith and Co. were carrying on business as drapers there, and continued to do so till about the year 1826, when William and John Hill were taken into partnership. I well remember them, having reason to remember John especially; for my master, Horatio Miller, having gone to London for a week, on his return informed me that Mr. John Hill, who was a customer, had noticed my conduct during his absence, and had told him how very attentive to business I had been, and he presented me with a copy of Shakspere as a token of his pleasure. Mr. William Hill was a leading man in Salford, of which he was boroughreeve on one or two occasions.

There was also at the time referred to a draper's shop in Chapel Street, Salford, between the Old Bridge and Blackfriars, which is deserving of notice, inasmuch as its owner some years afterwards became Mayor of Manchester, and received the honour of knighthood. The late Sir Elkanah Armitage first began business in the shop I allude to as a draper, about the year 1817, and some ten years afterwards began to manufacture bedticks and nankeens, having a warehouse in Bank Buildings, Cannon Street. In a few years the Salford business was given up, and his warehouse was removed to Cromford Court.

Fifty years ago Messrs. Hime and Hargreaves, music-sellers—now Hime and Addison—were in St. Ann's Square;

Mr. Henry Whaite was in Bridge Street; Mr. Charles Meredith, the law stationer, was in Ridgefield; Mr. William Broome, the accountant, was in Essex Street; Messrs. Sharp, Roberts, and Co., the machine makers, had their works in Falkner Street; Mr. Joseph Cockshoot, whose business has been merged in the Cockshoot Conveyance Company, was then a well-known hackney coach proprietor.

Mr. William Gibb, who will ever be remembered in Manchester in connection with the efforts he successfully made to obtain the privilege of having bonded warehouses here, was then a wine and spirit merchant in Spring Gardens. His name is still perpetuated in the firm of Smith and Gibb, his nephews in Oxford Road.

Another well-known firm in business here fifty years ago was that of Binyons and Co., who had then two shops, one in St. Ann's Square, the same as now occupied by them, and one on the right-hand side of Oldham Street. The firm then consisted of two brothers, Thomas and Edward, who began business in 1817. Tradition says their grandfather, having married Ruth Wakefield, whose father was a rich banker, at Kendal, provided the capital with which Richard Arkwright began the cotton trade. His eldest son, Thomas, was a cotton manufacturer, and the inventor of a cloth made from a mixture of silk and wool. He was the father of the Binyons, engaged in the tea trade, whilst his brother Benjamin was the father of Alfred Binyon, who in 1829 was a calenderer and a coal agent, but having married Lucy Hoyle, afterwards became a partner in the firm of Thomas Hoyle and Sons, calico printers. Thomas and Edward had a brother and two or three sisters, who were also engaged in business here at the time we speak of. The brother, Benjamin, was a partner in the firm of Binyon and Taylor, twine manufacturers, Peter Taylor looking after the manufacturing part of the business, at Hollinwood, and Benjamin Binyon being the salesman, and lodging with his sister Deborah, who kept a ready-made linen shop in Piccadilly. Two other sisters, Hannah and Ann, were tea dealers, nearly opposite the end of Portland Street. I should have said that Thomas Binyon served an apprentice-ship to a druggist, at Newcastle-on-Tyne, but not liking the business, went to Liverpool and learnt the tea trade. It is well known that the Binyons were all Quakers, and pos-sessed in an eminent degree the virtues for which the members of the Society of Friends are remarkable. The business is now carried on, in greatly extended premises, by George Henry Fryer, a nephew of the late Thomas Binyon, and our friend Thomas Harrison, whose scientific status is well known in Manchester. Several members of another well-known Quaker family, the Labreys, were carrying on the tea business in Manchester at that time, whilst one of the brothers was a guard on the Peveril of the Peak coach.

An old and respectable firm in business here fifty years ago was that of J. Fletcher and Co., corn millers and merchants, their business premises being then in Tib Street, shortly afterwards being removed to Hanging Ditch, where they at present remain. The founder of the firm was Joseph Fletcher, who at the beginning of this century was a baker, in Swan Street, near New Cross, to which business he added that of a grocer, taking the next shop for the purpose. In the course of time the shops were given up,

and the business of a corn miller was carried on, at the
Albion Corn Mills, in Tib Street, to which was added that
of a cheese factor, and the importation of Irish grain and
butter. Joseph Fletcher died about fifty years since,
leaving several daughters, three of whom are still alive, one
of them being eighty-three years of age. Another of them
was the first wife of Mr. Charles Bradbury, the well-known
collector of antiquities, and another is the mother of
Mr. Fletcher Moss, the present head of the firm. She is
still living, and remembers during one of the bread riots,
which occurred about sixty years ago, having to hide in the
cellar, when the shop and warehouse were broken into by
the mob. At that time flour and meal were selling at 120
shillings per load of 240 lbs., and the principal food of the
working classes was barley meal and oatmeal, the former
being an article of food which the poorest will scarcely
touch now. On one Saturday about this time forty loads
of it were "scaled" out in small lots as food to the
customers.

Another old firm of corn dealers in business fifty years
ago was that of James and Samuel Barratt, in Fennell
Street. They were brothers-in-law to Joseph Fletcher, Mrs.
Fletcher being a Miss Barratt. When the Fletchers gave
up the retail and went altogether into the wholesale, they
were much opposed by the Barratts, so much so that when
the former got new lurries painted blue, the Barratts, whose
lurries had been blue, immediately had them painted red.
Just at the corner of Swan Street and Shudehill was another
old corn dealer, named Hesketh, who more than seventy
years ago was in business in Chapel Street, Salford. He

was a friend of my father's, and a Wesleyan, and with his family attended Oldham Street Chapel.

Besides Samuel Prince and William Newall, already named, the principal grocers whom I remember were George Southam, father of the late Mr. Southam, the surgeon, of Salford; Richardson and Roebuck, both of the Market Place; and James and Thomas Fildes, in Shudehill, where they carried on a large wholesale business in addition to the retail. They had also a shop at the corner of Travis Street, London Road, which had been carried on by their father, Thomas Fildes, who took an active part in the establishment of the first Sunday school in Manchester. Near to his shop was a cellar, inhabited by a poor shoemaker named John Lancaster, who, in 1785, came to Manchester from Halifax, and almost immediately started a Sunday School in his cellar. Both he and his neighbour were Methodists, and Mr. Fildes, learning what he had done, joined him in the effort. The cellar was made warm and comfortable, and soon another cellar was added. Shortly afterwards, Thomas Fildes erected some cottages, over which was a large room, behind his residence in Worsley Street, to which the children were transferred. His grandson, Mr. James Fildes, of Spring Gardens, informs me that, so far as can be ascertained, this was the first Sunday School erected in Manchester, which would be about the year 1787. Mr. James Fildes, the elder, as a trustee of Oldham Street Chapel, was one of the principal defendants in the Chancery suit instituted by the Rev. Dr. Warren, and which, being decided by Lord Lyndhurst against the doctor, led to what is known among Wesleyans as the Warrenite division. During the hearing of the case, Sir Charles Wetherell, Dr. Warren's counsel, used to cause a smile by his persistently speaking of the defendant as " James Fil-dees."

Fifty years ago several respectable Italians were in business here, as carvers and gilders, looking-glass makers, and printsellers. In 1810 Vincent Zanetti carried on business, as a carver and gilder, at Wright's Court, Market Street, and his brother Vittore at a shop a little higher up Market Street. About the year 1817, Vittore Zanetti joined the late Mr. Agnew, the firm being Zanetti and Agnew. At the time I came to Manchester, Mr. Vittore Zanetti had retired in favour of his son, when the firm became Agnew and Zanetti, having removed to the premises still occupied by Messrs. Agnew in Exchange Street. Messrs. Grundy and Fox, printsellers, were at the time in business in St. Ann's Square, but shortly removed to the premises in Exchange Street, occupied so long by Messrs. Grundy. Mr. Joseph Merone commenced business, as a carver and gilder, at the beginning of this century, in Market Street, in the shop now occupied by the Milner Safe Company. I remember him there, in 1829, as an old man. Mr. Dominic Bolongaro began business, as a carver and gilder, about the year 1818, in Old Millgate, where he continued till he removed to the premises in Market Street, now occupied by his son, which was shortly after I took up my abode on the opposite side of the street. At this time there were two looking-glass makers, named Peduzzi, in separate shops in Oldham Street. Anthony commenced business, as a picture dealer, in Spear Street, during the first decade of the present century, and after settling in Tib Street for a few years, took a shop in Oldham Street. James Peduzzi, who, I believe, was Anthony's son, began business about 1822. I remember we had them both as customers for quicksilver. Joshua Ronchetti was a noted maker of barometers, thermometers, and specially of hydrometers, of the latter of which he had a large sale, on which at that time handsome profits were made. His first place of business was his house in Balloon Street, Withy Grove. He afterwards removed to Cateaton Street, and shortly after I came to Market Street, he became our neighbour. His son-in-law, Mr. Casartelli, succeeded him, and occupies the same premises. Baptist the father of Joshua Ronchetti, was a "weather glass maker," in High Street. Joshua had two sons, Baptist and Joshua, who followed the same business in London, with the latter of whom I was very intimate. Miss Ronchetti, his eldest daughter, died very recently. Another of these Italians, whom I knew well fifty years ago, was John Bianchi, in Tib Street. He was a maker of plaster of Paris, with which he used to supply those of his poorer countrymen, who were often seen carrying all the kings of Europe on their heads. Bianchi afterwards entered the police force, and proved himself to be a very intelligent and useful officer.

Besides the carvers and gilders already mentioned, the notorious Joseph Gale carried on that business in 1829, near the shop now occupied by the Milner Safe Company in Market Street. His sparkling wit, his humour, and his drollery were inimitable; and the tales which were told of the sly tricks which he played on his friends, and even on

casual acquaintances, were innumerable. He once met
with a man at the Wind Mill Tavern, in Bridge Street, who
had been getting married that day, when, pretending that
he had met him before and was an old acquaintance, he
led him off, and got him so drunk that the poor fellow only
found his way home to his newly-married wife the next day.
He served his apprenticeship to Mr. Dominic Bolongaro,
and whilst in Market Street failed in business, and then
commenced as a hatter in Ducie Place. When the
Exchange Arcade was built, he removed to King Street, near
the well-known shop of Miss Boardman, the confectioner.
He introduced a new feature into the hatting trade, and
kept a barrel of beer on tap, with bread and cheese for
his visitors. At length, during the mania for speculation
in shares, he became a share broker.

At present there are nearly 120 brewers in Manchester,
whilst in 1829 there were only 28, the largest of whom was
Mr. Benjamin Joule, of Salford, the father of Mr. Benjamin
St. John Baptist Joule, J.P., of Southport, the accomplished
organist and musician, and Mr. James Prescott Joule,
D.C.L., LL.D., F.R.S., so well known in scientific circles
for several important discoveries, but chiefly for that of the
mechanical equivalent of heat.

The late Alderman Bake was then a saddler in Port
Street, whence he removed to keep the Bull's Head Inn in
Barnes Street, which thenceforward was generally known as
"Jim Bake's." The late George Pilkington, the giver of
the statue of Humphrey Chetham now in the Cathedral,
was then a cashier and manager in the service of Mr. Ellis
Duckworth, the distiller, in New Cannon Street. As we

obtained the spirits of wine used in the business from thence, and being a neighbour, I knew him intimately. On Mr. Duckworth's retirement, George Pilkington succeeded him. A little lower down Market Street, not very far from the present site of the Omnibus Office, was the shop of Mr. James Varley, smallware dealer, and father of Mrs. Linnæus Banks. Mrs. Varley used to attend to the business as well as her husband. Being neighbours, I knew them very well, the impression left on my mind of Mrs. Varley being that she was a very agreeable, chatty, and intelligent lady.

Fifty years ago there was a confectioner's shop a few doors past the end of Bridge Street, in Deansgate, kept by Mary Harrison & Co. Though the shop was small, the business done in it was large. It would be interesting to know how many wedding breakfasts have been adorned by bridescakes which have been sent out from this establishment, for it used to bear a high character for the quality of these important elements of festivity. This old-fashioned shop, with its small panes of glass, has retained its original simplicity, resisting most resolutely to the present day the tendencies of the times towards glare and grandeur. At last, I understand, it is to follow the fate of so many other mementoes of a bygone age, and in another week or two will be demolished. The Miss Harrisons came from Buxton, and were known as the " Buxton Bakers." *

The name of Micah Furniss, silversmith and toy dealer, whose shop I well remember fifty years ago, at the corner of St. Ann's Square and St. Ann's Street, should not be

---

* The shop has lately been taken down, and the business removed.

omitted. It has been suggested to me that he was one of the very oldest traders in Manchester, but there is no evidence that he was in business in the last century. He was occupying the same shop, however, about the year 1810.

The most fashionable tailors fifty years ago were Scarr, Petty, and Swain, next door to Mr. Furniss, in the Square; Geary and Horne, their next door neighbours; John King, father of our respected City Alderman, whose shop was on the opposite side; Edward Varley, of Exchange Street; and John Skerrette Stubbs, whose shop was between those of J. Pickering, the music seller, and James Adshead, the hosier. Mr. Stubbs was originally a silk manufacturer in Market Street, and failed; he then commenced the business of a tailor, in the square, and succeeded so well that he paid off his former creditors in full, and died a wealthy man. He had a remarkably well made figure, which shewed off a good suit of clothes to perfection. On the opposite side of the Square was the shop of Jonathan Wimpory, the fashionable boot and shoe maker. The gentleman who reigned supreme as a hairdresser was William Stoby, of St. Ann's Place, whose charge for simply cutting the hair was a shilling. He began business at the beginning of this century in Queen Street, certainly not a street in which we should now expect to see carriages draw up at a hairdresser's door. If any gentleman wished to adorn himself in leather breeches, he would make his way to the shop of old George Perkins, which, fifty years ago, was in Old Millgate, and previously was in Shudehill. The principal auctioneer at that time was Mr. Capes, father of the late senior partner in the firm of Capes and Dunn, whose room, I have already stated, was in High Street. Another auctioneer who commanded a good share of patronage was William Morris, whose rooms were near Four Yards, in King Street, and who succeeded a well-known man named Howe, generally known as Lord Howe.

The most noted engineers of the day were Peel, Williams, and Peel,* of the Soho Foundry, Ancoats, and Galloway, Bowman, and Glasgow, of Great Bridgewater Street. These two firms began business soon after the commencement of the present century, the latter of the two consisting at first of Galloway and Bowman only, who then designated themselves millwrights. There were then three organ builders in Manchester: Robert Bradbury in Picca-dilly, Joseph Richardson in Bloom Street, and Renn and Boston in Dickenson Street—the latter being the most noted and most largely patronized.

Amongst the best known teachers of dancing at that time were Mr. Frederick Cooper, in Faulkner Street, who lived there for some years, and was succeeded by his son; Mr. Prosper Paris, in Brazennose Street; Mr. James W. Pitt, in Faulkner Street; and Mr. Thomas Palmer, in George Street. A very popular teacher of French was M. Alexander Mordacque, in George Street, whom I remember well as a little, sharp, elderly gentleman. His son, I remember, too, as a Grammar School lad. He subsequently entered the Church, and obtained his first curacy at Haslingden, or at some place near it. Other teachers of French were

---

* Mr. George Peel still survives, having been born in Halliwell Street, in 1803.

M. Eugene Vembergue, in Faulkner Street; and M. Louis
Amand Beauvoisin, in Clarence Street.

The principal teachers of music, whom I remember, were
Mr. Richard Cudmore, in George Street; Mr. Moses
Hughes, in the same street; Mr. James Hyde, in David
Street; Mr. William Sudlow, in Hanging Ditch; and
Messrs. Ward and Andrews, in Spring Gardens. The latter
taught what was called the " Logerian System of Music,"
their rooms being at the right-hand corner of Spring Gardens
and Marble Street, as you enter. Mr. Andrew Ward, at the
age of eighteen, was leader of the band of the Theatre
Royal, and died, in 1838, at the age of 49. Mr. Andrews
was the son of a popular comedian at the same theatre.
At the time we are speaking of, Mr. Ward's nephew,
Mr. David Ward Banks, was apprenticed to them. I became
acquainted with him during his and my apprenticeship, and
remember seeing him frequently riding down Market Street,
on horseback, early in the morning, on his way to the
country, once a week, travelling as far as Bury and Haslingden, to give lessons in music at various schools and private
families. He afterwards became very eminent in Manchester, as a teacher, an organist, and as a musical conductor.
On the occasion of the Queen's first visit to our city, 80,000
Sunday scholars were gathered in Peel Park; they were to
sing " God save the Queen" in her presence, as she drove
round the park, and Mr. Banks was selected as the conductor. Rehearsals had taken place in every Sunday
school to be represented on the occasion, for weeks beforehand, and every precaution was taken to prevent failure and
ensure success. When, however, the critical moment came,

through no fault of the conductor, the first verse was hardly got through when the whole thing collapsed. I was present amongst the children, as a teacher, and noticed that when the Queen's carriage drew up in front of the platform on which we stood, the children became so much excited, being seized with such a desire to have a good look at Her Majesty, with her gay surroundings of ladies and gentlemen, liveried servants, horses and carriages, that they forgot all about the object for which they were assembled, and ceased to sing. Poor Banks continued to beat the air with his baton, in his elevated stand, with all the violent energy of which he was capable, but it was of no use, and the affair ended with a loud shout of delight on the part of the singers, and a good laugh on the part of the Queen. The labour needed to organize such a gathering, and the arrangement of multitudinous details beforehand, formed an herculean task, which was voluntarily undertaken, principally by Mr. Robert Needham, the brother of our friend, Mr. J. C. Needham. His death occurred shortly after, producing the impression on the minds of many of his friends that it had been hastened, if not caused, by the anxieties and toils he had lately passed through.

CHAPTER IX.

NOTABLE PERSONS.

THE late Mr. John Brogden, the father of Mr. Alexander Brogden, M.P. for Wednesbury, at this time was a dealer in horses in Every Street, Ancoats. This led to a considerable intimacy with the late Mr. Samuel Brooks, who had always a great fancy for horses. Mr. Brogden relinquished his business, and became a contractor for cleansing the streets of the town, occupying the town's yard, which now forms part of the site of the new Town Hall. After this he became a contractor for the construction of railways, being best known for the construction of the Furness Railway, which crosses the sands at Ulverston. I well remember him and his good-looking wife, as I used to see them in the gallery of Oldham Street Chapel every Sunday morning.

I have a vivid recollection of the figure of an elderly gentleman whom I used to notice fifty years ago, as he tracked his way through the streets. It was impossible to see him without being struck by his appearance. He was a large-boned man, though not corpulent, was beginning to stoop a little, walked with rather a quick step, the expression of his face indicating that he was very much in earnest about something, and was most respectably dressed in black,

wearing the usual knee-breeches of the period, with silver
knee-buckles and black stockings, and having on a pair of
gold spectacles.   To those who knew him I think I need
not say that this was Mr. Thomas Fleming, who for many
years took such a lively interest in the improvement of the
town.   To him, in connection with Mr. George William
Wood, formerly M.P. for the southern division of the
county, is principally ascribed the merit of originating the
gas works of Manchester, and placing them on their original
basis, which has been so beneficial to the town.   At the
beginning of the century, where is now the Blackfriars
Bridge, Salford, was approached by means of a wooden
bridge four feet wide, the descent to which on the Manchester side was by means of forty steps, and which was
only intended of course for foot passengers.   Mr. Fleming
was the means of forming a company and raising the capital
in shares for the erection of the present structure, for
passing over which a toll was paid for many years.   The
speculation did not pay, and ultimately Mr. Fleming bought
up all the shares.   The foundation stone was laid by him
on the 4th of January, 1819, and the bridge was formally
opened by him on August 1st, 1820.   It has now been free
from toll several years.   It was owing to his energy, too,
that the widening of Market Street was originated and
brought to a successful completion.   He was a large
manufacturer of archil in Water Street, having begun that
business about the year 1790, in the same premises which
he occupied in 1829.

John Dalton, had not then received his degree of
Doctor of Civil Law from Oxford, and fifty years

ago was professor of chemistry, mathematics, and natural philosophy, residing with the Rev. William Johns, at his Academy in George Street. He was a Fellow of the Royal Society and President of the Manchester Literary and Philosophical Society. Most persons know that he was the discoverer of the Atomic Theory, and also that he was a Quaker. I occasionally saw him, the last time being about a year before his death, when I met him arm-in-arm with his attached friend Peter Clare, in York Street, as though they were proceeding from the Literary and Philosophical Rooms, in George Street, to Clare's house, in Quay Street. They were walking at a slow pace, owing to the doctor's feebleness, his arm resting on that of his friend. He had a beautifully calm and placid countenance, expressive of gentleness, thoughtfulness, and intelligence, and was generally dressed in black. There is a clock in the room in which he sat as president of the Literary and Philosophical Society, in George Street, which was made at his request, I presume by his friend Peter Clare, and which only gives one stroke on the bell in the course of the twenty-four hours. This is at nine o'clock p.m., and by its means notice was given at that hour to close a discussion— showing Dalton's methodical character.

Peter Clare was also a Quaker, and was Dalton's bosom friend. He was one of the secretaries of the Literary and Philosophical Society. His father, Peter Clare, was in business, at the close of the last century, in Deansgate, as a clock, watch, and smoke-jack maker, and about the beginning of the present one removed to Quay Street, where the son was residing in 1829, afterwards confining his attention

principally to the making of clocks, in which line both
father and son were celebrated in their day. I well remember the second Peter Clare. He was always remarkably neat and well dressed in a suit of black, wearing
knee-breeches with silver buckles, which showed his fine,
well-shaped legs, and a broad-brimmed hat. His linen was
of the purest white, and he presented a clean, happy, and
cheerful-looking face, which was not disfigured by a beard.
The sight of Dalton and Clare, as I saw them walking
arm-in-arm, was so striking that I could not resist stopping
to gaze after them, and their figures still seem to be photo-
graphed on my memory.

I well remember Mr. John Greenwood, the father of Mr.
John Greenwood of the Carriage Company, who was the
originator of omnibuses here a very short time before I
came to Manchester. He kept the tollbar at Pendleton
originally, and at the time I remember him he used to be
busy looking after his one or two very small omnibuses,
which ran to Pendleton at certain periods of the day from
the left-hand side of the lower end of Market Street. They
ran in the early part of the morning, at noon, and in the
evening, and for some years started from the place mentioned. Mr. Greenwood was a rather big man, wore knee-
breeches and coloured stockings, and had one of his hands
mutilated, I believe by a gun accident. At this time the
present Mr. John Greenwood, whom I well remember as a
young man, was a clerk in Trueman's cotton warehouse,
Ducie Place, near the old Post Office, behind the Exchange.
A little stout man named Penketh then drove his own small
solitary 'bus to Cheetham Hill. He afterwards sold it to

John Ramsbottom, and continued to drive for him. Afterwards the Cheetham Hill omnibuses, which had increased in number, were sold to Greenwood, Clough, and Turner. After a while the partnership was dissolved, and Turner retained the Cheetham Hill concern and Greenwood the Pendleton one.

George Wilson, the chairman of the Anti-Corn-Law League, and afterwards chairman of the Lancashire and Yorkshire Railway Company, I used to know about the time referred to very well. He was in the habit of frequenting the shop where I was an apprentice, before he became a public character, and occasionally had a chat with my master and the assistant, being very plain and unassuming in his manner. His father was a flour dealer, near to New Cross, and the son became a manufacturer of starch, at Newton Heath. He was a believer in phrenology, and afterwards became a member of the class formed by Mr. William Bally for the purpose of studying it. Bally was an Italian, and well known in Manchester as a great authority on that subject. I well remember how surprised I was when George Wilson was appointed to the office of chairman of the Anti-Corn-Law League, never suspecting his possession of those qualities which so eminently qualified him for it, and which the eyes of others had detected in him. Richard Cobden had a very high opinion of him, and used to say of him that he could always see the end of anything from the beginning. He had the weakness of indiscriminate generosity, being accustomed, at the latter period of his life, to keep plenty of loose silver and copper in his pocket, of which he would distribute to almost every suppliant he met. When remonstrated with on the subject, he would reply that if he relieved only one deserving person out of the lot he was glad. I once had the pleasure of spending a very pleasant evening with him in London, in the early days of the League, as we happened both to be staying at Thompson's boarding-house, in Bartlett's Buildings.

The late Alderman Charles James Stanley Walker lived to such a good old age, sitting on the bench to such a late period of life, that it is not many years since he passed from amongst us, and hence is well remembered by most Manchester people. I never saw him when he did not wear a swallow-tailed coat, which was always buttoned up to the chin. Fifty years ago his favourite colour was blue, the coat being adorned with smooth, bright, gilt buttons. His visage being free from hair, and his skin remarkably clear and smooth, he presented a very striking appearance, but always looked the gentleman. He descended from an old Manchester family, which had been Liberal in politics, on which account they had been much persecuted. His father, Thomas Walker, was the leader of the Liberal party here during the course of the first French Revolution, just after the breaking out of which he was appointed boroughreeve. His house and warehouse were attacked by one of the Church-and-King mobs of that period, and he was tried for treason in 1794, being defended by Erskine, who made one of his most celebrated speeches in his defence. I met the late C. J. S. Walker, on the occasion of laying the foundation stone of the present Withington Workhouse, when he told me that he remembered, when a little boy, his father lived in the last house in South Parade going from Deansgate, that the house was once attacked by a mob, and that he was taken out of danger's way at the back through the garden, which extended a long way behind. When Manchester was incorporated, he was elected an alderman, and was made a magistrate, to the duties of which he assiduously devoted himself to the last. He was the brother of Thomas Walker, M.A., a barrister, one of the police magistrates of the metropolis, and author of a book full of common sense, known as "The Original," containing several chapters on aristology or the art of dining, the art of attaining high health, the art of listening, and the art of travelling.

"Dictum Factum" was a gentleman tolerably well known here at the time I am speaking of. He was rather eccentric, and was afflicted with St. Vitus's Dance, which added very much to his apparent eccentricity. Notwithstanding, he was very genial, good-natured, and much respected. His name being Seddon, he took it as if written "Said done," which being translated into Latin is Dictum Factum. As he kept his carriage, he took this as his motto, had it painted on his carriage door, and it became the name by which he was familiarly known amongst his friends. It is said he was the author of the song known as "The Spider and the Fly."

Joe Richardson was another well-known character fifty years ago. He was the son of Mr. Joseph Richardson, who kept the King's Head, in Chapel Street, Salford, and was known for his splendid horsemanship, it being said he was the best steeplechase rider in the country. He was lightly

built, wore a pair of drab cloth knee-breeches and top-boots,
and always seemed to be riding through the streets. He
had such a command over his horse that it might have
been a part of himself. At the time of the late Alderman
Bake's death, it was stated in a Manchester newspaper that
after he went to the Bull's Head, which became such a
famous betting house, Mr. Bake himself used to bring home
the news of the winner of the St. Leger from Doncaster on
horseback. I must not dispute this, but I well remember
that after a time Joe Richardson was employed to do this,
using relays of horses. I can recollect what crowds used to
be collected about Barnes Street, waiting for the news. It
would be interesting to know how long the journey took
him.

I well remember that very corpulent, jolly-looking lady,
known as Dolly Rexford, whose father was the senior
partner in the firm of Rexford, Holland, and Taylor, wine
merchants, in Cross Street, his house being in Brazenose
Street. She was born in 1798, the year in which her
father died. Her mother, after her father's death, kept
the Grapes, in Deansgate, and, in 1829, was living a
widow, in Brazenose Street. Dolly became the wife of
Job Haigh (who at that time kept the Rising Sun, in
Swan Street), and died at the age of fifty-five. A notice
of her appeared in the *City News* of September 7, 1878, in
which it was stated that she was so stout, that when she
travelled on the Altrincham line, it took two or three railway porters to get her in and out of the train. It may be
that it is more difficult to get into a railway carriage than a
hackney coach of the old time, even for a lighter person, as

we all know; but I thought the statement a figure of speech. I once saw her get into a hackney coach—not a cab—opposite Ducie Place, in Market Street. The coachman had to give a good push behind, certainly, but she managed to get in.

A little later I recollect John Easby, a well-known character of his day, who was the then editor of *Bob Logic's Budget*, a despicable and scurrilous publication, the sale of which was encouraged, I regret to say, by the scandal which it retailed concerning various public characters, in this respect resembling some later publications. When a boy he was the recipient of Anne Hinde's Charity, and wore the livery of such, which consisted of green coat and vest, green stockings, and leather knee-breeches.

It seems to be convenient at this point to endeavour to present a negative picture of Manchester, which will give a good idea of the great changes which have taken place in its condition during the last fifty years. I have not tried to classify the objects named, but name them as they arise in the mind. Fifty years ago, then, there were in Manchester no Athenæum, no Bonded Warehouse, no Assize Courts, no Free Library, no Botanical Gardens, no police court, no public parks, no statues, no Concert Hall, no railway stations, no beerhouses, no members of Parliament; no bishop, dean, or canons; no mayor, aldermen, or councillors; no town clerk, no city or borough coroner, no Cathedral, no stipendiary for the city, no police, no County Court, no poor-law guardians, no Saturday half-holiday, no early closing, no manorial rights, no penny postage, no telegraphs, no local daily paper, no penny newspaper, no cabs, no omnibuses as now, no teetotal societies, no volunteers, no steel pens in constant use, no lucifer matches, no Stretford Road, no free trade. There were no ocean steamships, slavery was not abolished, neither were the corn laws. Everything was taxed—almanacs, windows, paper, soap, leather; bottles, and other glass; newspapers, advertisements, and hundreds of other things in common use, which are now as unburthened as the air.

———◆———

CHAPTER X.

PLACES OF WORSHIP.—CHURCH OF ENGLAND.

A T the beginning of the last century there were only two churches and two chapels in Manchester and Salford, viz. :—The Collegiate Church in Manchester, Trinity in Salford, the Presbyterian Chapel in Cross Street, and the Friends' Meeting House in Deansgate. Of these the only building now standing is the Collegiate Church, the others having been pulled down and rebuilt. The following facts will shew the earnestness of the religious revival of the eighteenth century.

Fifty years ago there were in Manchester and Salford sixty-seven places of worship and eighty-one ministers. To-day there are about 323 churches and chapels and 417 ministers, showing that they have increased about five-fold since 1829. The following table shows with tolerable accuracy the relative numbers of these pertaining to the various sects. The number as to 1829 I believe to be fairly accurate; there is some difficulty as to those of 1879, owing to the existence of a large number of mission-rooms, which I have endeavoured to exclude. There is also the consideration that the area is much larger than it was; that many places which were outside Manchester fifty years ago are now part of it. So that I cannot say that the numbers for the present year are more than an approximation to the truth, though I think a near one. The number of Wesleyan ministers does not include what are technically known as supernumeraries—that is, ministers who have given up the active duties of the ministry and yet do a good deal of preaching on a Sunday.

The difficulty has been to draw a line fixing the limit :—

	1829.		1879.	
	Places of Worship.	Ministers.	Places of Worship.	Ministers.
Church of England.........	20	33	110	175
Independent	8	5	34	30
Wesleyan	9	13	35	39
Roman Catholic	3	7	33	88
Various Methodist	6	5	49	34
Baptist	4	4	17	12
Presbyterian	1	2	13	13
Unitarian	4	5	12	13
Welsh	5	2	6	4
Swedenborgian...............	2	2	2	2
Jews	1	1	4	4
Quakers.......................	1	0	1	0
Various.......................	3	2	7	3
	67	81	323	417

The following twenty churches existed fifty years ago :—

1. THE OLD CHURCH.—In 1419 Thomas de la Warre, the then rector of Manchester, having succeeded to large patrimonial estates and to the advowson of the rectory, proposed to the parishioners to build, at his own expense,

and endow, a Collegiate Church, in lieu of the Parish Church. This was accomplished, and the present beautiful. church was built, at vast expense. The ancient parish comprised 32 townships, having an area of 35,000 acres. The church has accommodation for 3,000 worshippers, and the number of baptisms and marriages here, it is supposed, is greater than in any other church in the kingdom. The soft red stone of the exterior, fifty years ago, was in a very decaying state, since which time very extensive repairs have been effected, both inside and out, and a new tower has been built. Manchester was then in the diocese of Chester, the bishop of which was the Rev. John Bird Sumner, D.D., who afterwards was appointed Archbishop of Canterbury. There was consequently neither cathedral nor bishop, neither dean nor canons. We had instead connected with the Collegiate Church a warden, four fellows, two chaplains, and one clerk in orders. The warden was the Very Rev. Thomas Jackson Calvert, D.D., rector of Wilmslow, who succeeded the Rev. Dr. Blackburne. The latter was the youngest brother of Mr. John Blackburne, M.P., and of Mr. Isaac Blackburne, the distributor of stamps for Manchester. Dr. Calvert was appointed in 1823, two months after Dr. Blackburne's death. He was a fine, venerable-looking man, having a very clerical appearance, whose house was in Mosley Street. The four fellows were the Rev. John Gatliffe, who was also rector of St. Mary's; the Rev. C. W. Ethelstone, incumbent of St. Mark's, Cheetham, whose son succeeded him there; the Rev. John Clowes, of Broughton Hall; and the Rev. J. H. Mallory, who at that time either lived or had rooms in Pall Mall. The two

Chaplains were the Rev. C. D. Wray, also incumbent of St. Thomas's, Ardwick, and the Rev. Richard Rimmington, who was a customer of my master's. I remember him as a very genial, friendly, and gentlemanly man, dressed more like an ordinary gentleman than a cleric. Mr. Wray, it will be remembered, lived to be a very old man. The Clerk in Orders was the Rev. Moses Randall, who had been previously curate at St. Ann's. Mr. Humphrey Nichols, who only lately passed away from us, after benefitting the public charities by his accumulated wealth, was then Parish Clerk. He lived at Stony Knolls, and had Mr. Thomas Parry, whose house was close by in Fennel Street, as his deputy. I remember Mr. Clowes very well, from the fact that I heard him preach in the Collegiate Church one Sunday afternoon in lavender gloves. He was a tall man, and seemed to have unusually long arms.

2. ST. ANN'S CHURCH, a handsome Corinthian edifice, was founded by Lady Ann Bland, of Hulme Hall, in 1709, and was consecrated in 1712. The rector, fifty years ago, was the Rev. Dr. Jeremiah Smith, who was also high master at the Grammar School, and lived in Long Millgate. He had held the office of head master since the beginning of the century, at which time he was the curate of Trinity Church, Salford. He then became incumbent of St. Peter's Church, and afterwards rector of St. Ann's. The first rector was the Rev. Nathaniel Bann.

3. ST. THOMAS'S, Ardwick, was, I believe, the next in the order of consecration. When it was founded in 1741, and enlarged in 1777, Ardwick was a little village separated from Manchester by at least a mile of cultivated fields. In

1815, the Rev. J. Cooke was the incumbent, and after him the Rev. C. D. Wray, having as curate the Rev. W. Wordsworth. In 1829 the Rev. Nicholas William Gibson was Mr. Wray's curate, and he afterwards became incumbent.

4. TRINITY CHURCH, Salford, built in the Gothic order of architecture, had been founded by Humphrey Booth, a prosperous merchant of Salford, in 1635. It was, however, taken down and rebuilt in 1752, so that the present edifice is not 130 years old. The incumbent, fifty years ago, was the Rev. Samuel Booth, the father of the present rector of Chorlton-cum-Hardy.

5. ST. MARY'S CHURCH, a Doric edifice, was founded in 1753, by the Warden and Fellows of the Collegiate Church, the foundation stones being laid by the Revs. Messrs. Assheton, Foxley, and Moss. In 1829, the Rev. John Gatliffe was rector, and the Rev. R. Basnett, curate. The church was originally built with a very high spire, which was generally admired, but which, being considered unsafe, was taken down some years since. For seventy years after it was built, the church had on the summit of its spire a gilt ball and cross. In 1822, the rod which supported them was so much bent by a violent gale, as to become dangerous, and remained so for some months, to the terror of the congregation. At length, an enterprising and ingenious artisan, named Philip Wotton, in view of thousands of spectators, ascended to the top of the spire, and succeeded in safely landing both ball and cross. The ornamental pulpit, which the church contained fifty years ago, was the gift of the congregation to the rector, the organ having been the gift of Mr. Holland Ackers.

6. St. Paul's, Turner Street, was consecrated in 1765, but in thirteen years the congregation had so much increased that the church had to be enlarged. The Rev. J. Piccope was the incumbent in 1829. Though respectably dressed, he was not as clerical in his appearance as clergymen now are, and might have been easily mistaken for a dissenting minister of that day. I was present one Sunday morning at the service, and remember that there was a good congregation. The church is now converted into business premises, and in its place a much finer edifice has been erected in Oldham Road, near New Cross.

7. St. John's Church was founded by Edward Byrom, in 1768, and consecrated the following year, when the Rev. John Clowes was presented by the founder as the first rector. He was rector in 1829, and resided in Warwickshire, having two curates to attend to the spiritual wants of the parishioners. The Rev. Robert Dallas was the first of these; he resided in Quay Street, and at the same time held the office of Master of the Lower Grammar School. The Rev. Wm. Huntingdon was the other; he resided in St. John Street. Mr. Dawson, who lived at the cottage which, with its garden, once occupied the ground on which the Concert Hall and the adjoining warehouse now stand, was associated with Edward Byrom in building St. John's Church. Some dispute, however, arising, Mr. Dawson withdrew after he had paid for a portion of the building materials. He purchased the picture, by Annibal Caracci, of "The Descent from the Cross" in Italy, which is now over the communion table of St. Peter's Church, intending it for St. John's in the first instance, but, on the occurrence

of the dispute, he presented it to St. Peter's. A remarkable history of longevity stands connected with the history of this church, inasmuch as the two first rectors held the office for 107 years. Mr. Clowes died in 1831, at the age of eighty-seven, having been rector for sixty-two years, and Mr. Huntingdon, who was appointed to succeed him, died four or five years ago, having been connected with the church as rector and curate for more than fifty years. Mr. Clowes, the rector of St. John's, must not be confounded with the clergyman of the same name previously mentioned, who was one of the Fellows of the Collegiate Church. The Mr. Clowes of St. John's was the fourth son of Mr. Joseph Clowes, barrister, and was educated at the school of the Rev. John Clayton, in Salford, who was a friend of John Byrom and of John Wesley, and at Trinity College, Cambridge. Soon after he was made rector of St. John's he became acquainted with the writings of Emanuel Swedenborg, whose theological teachings he imbibed; and, strange to say, he was allowed to retain his position and yet to devote all his energies to spread those doctrines both by the press and in the pulpit.

8. St. Thomas's Chapel, Pendleton, was originally built at the expense of Mr. Samuel Brierley, and was consecrated 1776, when the Rev. James Pedley, assistant master of the Grammar School, was appointed incumbent, residing in Gravel Lane. The present St. Thomas's Church was built in 1830, and consecrated in 1831. The Rev. William Keeling was the incumbent fifty years ago.

9. St. James's Church was built by the Rev. Cornelius Bayley, D.D., in 1788, his house being in Charlotte-street.

For some time after the church was built, it was the practice
of the Wesleyans to assemble at Oldham-street Chapel on a
Sunday morning at nine o'clock, and hold a service which
lasted an hour and a quarter, after which they adjourned to
Dr. Bayley's church and formed a considerable portion of
his congregation.

10. St. Peter's, built by Wyatt, was also founded in
1788 by the Rev. Samuel Hall, who had been curate at
St. Ann's, when he lived in Greengate.   He was the first
rector, and afterwards resided in Oxford Road.   After him
the Rev. Jeremiah Smith, D.D., became incumbent, who
had previously been curate of Trinity Church, Salford, and
head master of the Grammar School.   In 1829 Dr. Smith
was rector of St. Ann's, retaining the office of head master
of the Grammar School, which he held for some years.
In 1824 the Rev. Nicholas Germon was the curate at
St. Peter's, and second master at the Grammar School, and
in 1829 was rector of St. Peter's, retaining his office in the
school.   I have stated already that St. Peter's was first
built without a steeple, which was added some years after,
and was built by Mr. Heap.   As just intimated, the painting
over the communion table, by Caracci, was purchased in
Italy and presented to the church by Mr. Dawson.

11. St. Michael's, Angel Street, was the third church
built during the year 1788, and is stated to have been
founded by the Rev. Humphrey Owen, one of the chaplains
of the Collegiate Church.   Fifty years ago the Rev. William
Marsden, B.D., was the incumbent; he succeeded the
Rev. M. Wrigley, and resided many years in Quay Street.
Mr. Marsden subsequently became vicar of Eccles, and was

one of three brothers—George, John, and William. John was a corn dealer, in York Street, in 1829, and a Wesleyan, whilst George was a very popular Wesleyan minister, who began his ministry in 1793, and died in 1858. Mr. W. Marsden had the living of Eccles presented to him, it was said, because he voted at the first Manchester election after the Reform Bill for Mark Philips and C. Poulett Thompson.

12. St. Clement's, Stevenson Square, was built in 1793, by the Rev. Edward Smyth, and was licensed but not consecrated. Mr. Smyth resided in Back Lane, near the church, at first; but in 1810 was living at Chorlton Hall, near to Grosvenor Street. He was succeeded by the Rev. William Nunn, in 1818, who was incumbent for twenty-two years, and died in 1840. He was well known as a minister, from the fact of his preaching Calvinist doctrines very strongly, but was greatly respected by all classes. This was shown by the large number who attended his funeral. When a young man, I frequently heard him preach, and was amongst the throng who witnessed his burial. His son is the incumbent of St. Thomas's, Ardwick.

13. St. Mark's, Cheetham Hill, was built in 1794, by the Rev. C. W. Ethelstone, one of the fellows of the Collegiate Church. He was the incumbent in 1829. At that time he had for his curate the Rev. Peter Hordern, who was also librarian at the Chetham Library from 1821 to 1834, and succeeded the Rev. R. H. Whitelock in the curacy of Chorlton-cum-Hardy. Mr. Hordern was the father of Lady Ellen Frances Lubbock, the wife of Sir John Lubbock, Bart, M.P. for Maidstone; she

died a few months since, having been married in 1856. Mr. Hordern was the son of the Rev. Joseph Hordern, at one time curate of Prestwich and vicar of Holy Trinity Church, Shaw, near Oldham. Mr. Ethelstone was succeeded by his son in the incumbency of St. Mark's.

14. St. Stephen's, Salford, was built in the same year, by the Rev. Nicholas Mosely Cheek, of Dale Street. In 1811 the Rev. Ebenezer Booth was the incumbent, and in 1820 the Rev. Melville Horn was his curate. In 1824 he had a second curate, in the person of the Rev. E. B. Shaw. In 1829 Mr. Booth was still the incumbent, and no less a person than the Rev. Hugh Stowell, who then had lodgings in Bolton Street, was his curate. Shortly after this a church was built for Mr. Stowell, in the Crescent, Salford, to which he removed.

15. St. George's, St. George's Road, though built in 1797, was not consecrated till 1818. It was opened for divine service on the 1st of April, 1798, but was for a short time, it is said, occupied by ministers of Lady Huntington's connexion. In 1811 Samuel Bradley, who resided in Faulkner Street, was the incumbent; and in 1824 the Rev. William Johnson, residing in Oldham Street, held the appointment. Fifty years ago the Rev. James White was the incumbent—the brother of Henry Kirke White, the poet.

16. St. Luke's, Chorlton-on-Medlock, was built by the Rev. Edward Smyth, in 1804, who resided close by, at Chorlton Hall. The church was licensed but not con- secrated. Its first minister was the Rev. Abraham Hepworth, LL.B., who kept an academy at Barrowclough's Buildings, Ardwick, his residence being at first in Rosamond

Street, then in Rusholme Lane, and afterwards in Grosvenor Street. In 1829 he still retained the incumbency, but had given up the school.

17. ALL SAINTS', Oxford Road, was founded in 1820 by the Rev. Charles Burton, LL.D., father of the present incumbent. He was the son of Mr. Daniel Burton, of the firm of Daniel Burton and Sons, calico printers, of Rhodes, near Middleton, whose warehouse was in High Street. In 1829 Dr. Burton lived in York Street, Chorlton Row (as Chorlton-on-Medlock was then called), where he kept an academy. He was not only connected with an eminent Wesleyan family, but began his career as a Wesleyan minister, and had a brother, James Daniel Burton, who was one. The brother was stationed in Manchester, about sixty-five years ago, as a supernumerary. Charles, afterwards Dr. Burton, when a young man, was appointed to the Maccles-field, Leek, and Buxton Wesleyan Circuits, and while in the latter, an old friend of mine heard him preach at the Wes-leyan Chapel, Chapel-en-Frith. He married the daughter of a wealthy gentleman in the Potteries, whose fortune, with his own, supplied the means for his college course, and of building All Saints' Church. He was considered a young man of great promise, and no doubt he would have attained a high position amongst the Wesleyans had he remained one. He was a believer in the near approach of the millen-nium, and many years ago lectured on the subject. He was a good Hebrew scholar, hence the text in Hebrew over the south entrance to the church, " This is none other than the House of God." He lived to a good old age, had a very clerical appearance, wore knee-breeches and black cloth

gaiters to the end of his days, and walked with a firm step, which indicated the vigour and robustness of his constitution. Some years ago the church was on fire, when the roof was destroyed.

18. St. Matthew's, Campfield, erected in the Gothic style, is built upon the site of the ancient town of Mancunium, and was founded in 1822. A short time previously an Act of Parliament was passed, known as Peel's Act, by which a large sum of money was granted for the purpose of building churches in this neighbourhood, commissioners being appointed to manage the fund. Out of this money the commissioners granted £14,000 towards the erection of St. Matthew's Church, which was constituted a District Parish Church. It is a fine specimen of modern Gothic architecture, possessing an elegant lantern tower and spire, and was about the first public work designed by the late Sir Charles Barry (then Mr. Barry), who was the architect of the Houses of Parliament, and also of the Manchester Athenæum and the Unitarian Chapel in Upper Brook Street. In 1829, the Rev. Edward Butterworth Shaw was the incumbent, living in Byrom-street; and the Rev. E. Dudley Jackson, the curate, living in Irwell Street. The Rev. William Kidd* was the incumbent here before he obtained the living of Didsbury. Mr. Dudley Jackson† is now the rector of St. Thomas's Church, Heaton Chapel, and is the author of one or two volumes of verse.

---

* Mr. Kidd was killed at the Didsbury Railway Station on the 18th of December, 1880.

† Mr. Jackson has also passed away since these lines first appeared in print.

19. St. Philip's, Salford, was consecrated in 1825, and was built by the aid of a grant of £14,000 out of the same fund. The first incumbent was the Rev. Oswald Sérgeant, son of Mr. Sergeant, of the firm of Sergeant, Milne, and Sergeant, solicitors, and clerks to the magistrates. Subsequently Mr. Sergeant was appointed one of the Fellows of the Collegiate Church, and afterwards, on that church becoming a Cathedral, one of the Canons, being a colleague of the Rev. Dr. Parkinson.

20. St. George's, Hulme, was founded in 1826, and consecrated in 1828. The same parliamentary grant was made as in the last instance; but as the building cost £20,000, £6,000 was raised by private subscription. The first incumbent was the Rev. Joshua Lingard, who lived in Moss Lane, and was the brother of Mr. Thomas Lingard, agent to the old Quay Company.

21. Though St. Andrew's, Travis Street, was being built in 1829, and was not consecrated for a year or so after, it may be as well to name it. It was another of what have been called "Peel's Churches," a similar amount of £14,000 having been granted by the commissioners towards its erection. It was consecrated in 1831, and the Rev. George Dugard was the first incumbent. I once had the pleasure of hearing the Rev. Dr. Hook, before he was dean, preach a most eloquent sermon in this church, his text being "I perceive that in all things ye are too superstitious."

CHAPTER XI.

PLACES OF WORSHIP.—INDEPENDENT CHAPELS.

FIFTY years ago there were eight Independent Chapels in Manchester. These were severally situated in Cannon Street, Grosvenor Street (Piccadilly), Mosley Street, Rusholme Road, Jackson Street, Chapel Street, Salford, Windsor Bridge, and Lees Street, Ancoats.

CANNON STREET CHAPEL.—The history of Independency in Manchester dates from the seventeenth century, when the Rev. John Wigan, with others, formed an Independent Church in the buildings now known as the Chetham College in 1649. In the year 1672, a small and inconvenient room in Cold-house Lane (now called Thornley Brow) was licensed for the ministry of the Rev. Henry Newcome, who came to Manchester in 1656 to succeed Richard Hollingworth at the Collegiate Church, but who, on the passing of the Act of Uniformity in 1662, vacated his post. In 1761 an Independent Church was formed there under the ministry of the Rev. Caleb Warhurst, the congregation increasing so much that in a short time it became necessary to look out for a more commodious place of meeting. A suitable situation was found at the upper end of what was then known as Hunter's Croft, Hunter's Lane, now called Cannon

Street, running on the south side of it into Hanging Ditch, near the corner of which streets John Byrom's house then stood. A chapel was built there, a little back from the lane, two cottages standing between. It appears that the Rev. John Newton, the friend of Cowper, and one of the authors of the Olney Hymns, was present at the opening in 1762, not to take any active part in it, but "to see some ministers and friends with whom he was acquainted." Mr. Warhurst lived with a Mr. Clegg, in Turner Street, and was only pastor of the church three years, as he died in 1765. For three years the church was without any minister, at the end of which time the Rev. Timothy Priestley, brother of the late celebrated Dr. Priestley, succeeded to the pastorate. There were, however, continual feuds between the pastor and his deacons. Dr. Halley tells us he was charged with irreverently ascending the pulpit stairs with his hat on his head, and with making packing-cases on Sunday nights. As to wearing his hat on the pulpit stairs, he seems to have treated the charge as an impertinence unworthy of notice ; and as to the packing-cases, while the deacons kept him so miserably poor, he thought it was his duty "to provide things honest in the sight of all men," as well as to remember the Sabbath day. Notwithstanding these things the church prospered, and he remained its minister for nineteen years, during which time the chapel was enlarged by the removal of the two cottages and its being brought to the front of Hunter's Lane. Mr. Priestley on resigning his charge went to London, when he was succeeded by the Rev. David Bradbury, from Ramsgate, who had not a very happy time of it in consequence of disputes with some of his members, who were Scotch, and who wished to appoint ruling elders. The result was that a division took place, when several members left the church, and assembled for public worship in a building in St. Andrew's Lane, near Church Street. In 1788 these seceders built Mosley Street Chapel. Mr. Bradbury, after many unhappy disputes and a large secession of members, resigned his charge and left the neighbourhood in 1795. In that year the Rev. William Roby, from Wigan, succeeded to the pastorate of Cannon Street Chapel, which, owing to his efforts, soon became too small, and it became necessary to build a larger chapel. An eligible site was found in Grosvenor Street, Piccadilly, and a chapel was built, which was opened for divine worship in December, 1807, when the church, consisting of 226 members, with its pastor and deacons, removed to it. At first it was intended to utilize Cannon Street Chapel as a branch of the Grosvenor Street one, but ultimately, with Mr. Roby's consent, it remained a distinct place of worship, and was enlarged in 1828. Amongst those who remained as worshippers at Cannon Street may be named the ancestors of Messrs. S. and J. Watts, of Portland Street, who then carried on the retail drapery business, in Deansgate. Fifty years ago the Rev. Samuel Bradley was the minister of Cannon Street, having been previously that of Mosley Street Chapel. He began his ministry at Cannon Street in 1827, and resigned it in 1844, having married a member of the Bellhouse family, who attended his ministry whilst at Mosley Street. His nephew, the late Mr. S. M. Bradley, the surgeon, was well known. In 1860 the chapel was sold for £2,800, and is now converted into business property, being occupied by

Messrs. W. and R. Lee. The church and congregation have erected large and commodious premises in Chorlton Road, to which they have removed. Their increase under the care of the Rev. J. A. Macfadyen, who became the pastor in 1863, presents a history which, though very interesting, is beyond the scope of these reminiscences. The marvellously complete and unique organization of the church is clearly exhibited in the "Year Book" of the church, compiled by Mr. Charles Bailey, the brother of Mr. John Eglinton Bailey, F.S.A., the learned author of "The Life of Thomas Fuller," and many other works.

GROSVENOR STREET.—We have seen that Grosvenor Street Chapel, Piccadilly, was built in 1807, and that the Rev. William Roby, with the greater part of his flock, removed to it from Cannon Street. He was the minister of Grosvenor Street Chapel fifty years ago, but died in the following year. Dr. Halley says he was a man of pleasing simplicity, and affected none of the formalities of a clergyman, while the style of his preaching retained something of the clerical character. Churchmen and Dissenters who loved the Gospel, loved to hear William Roby preach it. He preached to an exceedingly sympathetic congregation, which earnestly co-operated in forwarding his designs, whether of a philanthropic or a strictly religious nature. His efforts to promote the erection of places of worship in less favoured districts were only equalled by his zeal in providing means of instruction for young men who proposed to enter the ministry. Through his instrumentality, an institute was founded for this purpose, in Leaf Square, Pendleton, and afterwards at Blackburn, but which was

eventually developed into the Lancashire Independent
College, at Withington.   From Grosvenor Street Chapel, in
the year 1817, there were sent out as missionaries Robert
Hampson, to Calcutta; John Ince, to Malacca; Samuel
Wilson, to Greece; and to South Africa, Robert Moffat,
the father-in-law of Dr. Livingstone.   In the year 1821
Thomas Hughes was sent by Mr. Roby to Hoxton College,
and afterwards became the pastor of the Independent
Chapel at Stoke Newington.   In the same year Elijah
Armitage, the brother of the late Sir Elkanah, was sent out
with his wife and family to the South Sea Islands, to
evangelize the heathen and teach them the cotton manufacturing and other industries; and others were sent out to
other places.   While Mr. Roby was preaching at Grosvenor
Street, the Rev. Joseph Smith, a very popular preacher,
had collected a large congregation in Mosley Street Chapel,
and from these two congregations were formed several
others, as at New Windsor; Jackson's Lane, Hulme, since
removed to Stretford Road; and Rusholme Road.   In
1818 nineteen members were transferred from Grosvenor
Street to Salford, and formed the nucleus of a church in
Chapel Street.   Mr. Roby was assisted by three laymen, or
what the Wesleyans would call local preachers, who conducted the services in certain country chapels, which were
under his care.   These were, Jonathan Lees, smallware
dealer and property agent, St. Mary's Gate; John Powers,
woollen draper, Market Street; and Robert Powell, cashier
to Leese, Kershaw and Callender.   Mr. Lees sometimes
occupied the pulpit of Grosvenor Street Chapel, in the
absence of Mr. Roby.   Amongst the principal persons who

attended Mr. Roby's ministry were the following : The three partners in the firm of Fletcher, Burd, and Wood, the first of whom became a magistrate; the firm afterwards becoming Samuel Fletcher, Son, and Co., of Parker Street. Mr. Fletcher's connection with Roby Chapel extended over a period of fifty years. Mr. Burd became an alderman, on the establishment of the Corporation. There were also amongst the worshippers Mr. Samuel Brooks, the banker; Mr. Lewis Williams, cotton spinner, London Road ; Messrs. Rymer and Norris, solicitors, Norfolk Street; the family of the Armitages, one of the brothers afterwards becoming Sir Elkanah; Benjamin Joule, brewer, father of the present Dr. Joule and of J. St. B. Joule, J.P., of Southport; James Kershaw, afterwards M.P. for Stockport, and his brother-in-law James Sidebotham, recently deceased ; Thomas and David Ainsworth; Stephen Sheldon, grocer, Shudehill; Mr. (now Alderman) George Booth, and his brother Hugh ; Isaac Shimwell, smallware dealer, St. Mary's Gate ; and S. T. Porter, tutor to Benjamin Joule's two sons, who became the minister first at Westhoughton, and after, co-pastor with the Rev. Dr. Wardlaw for a few years, at Glasgow. Other members of the congregation were the late Alderman Rumney ; Thomas Wright, the Prison Philanthropist; Mr. John Griffiths, a hatter in Deansgate ; Mr. Edward Lewis, solicitor, who became a deacon, and was a member of the congregation for nearly fifty years; Mr. Hugh Sheldon; Mr. S. Goodwin, silk manufacturer; Mr. John Holt, lead merchant; Mr. David Fletcher, Mr. John Griffiths, Mr. John Acton, and Mr. George Beaumont, a woollen draper. It was Mr. Roby's custom to preach to

the young on the evening of the first Sunday in the new
year. At the conclusion of this service, on the first
Sunday evening in January, 1830, he was carried home to
his house, in Aytoun Street, in an exhausted condition,
and died in a few days, in the sixty-fourth year of his age.
Miss Maria Jane Jewsbury, who then lived in Grosvenor
Street, Oxford Road, penned some verses on the occasion,
beginning, " I never knew him, but I knew his worth."

MOSLEY STREET CHAPEL.—We have seen that this chapel
was built in 1788, principally by some Scotch seceders from
Cannon Street. The chapel was enlarged in 1819. The
first minister was the Rev. Mr. Kennedy, whom the seceders
invited from Scotland, but his stay was a very brief one.
His successor was the Rev. Joseph Smith, from Rotherham
College, who became very popular, and married a lady of
considerable property. He shortly after relinquished his
charge and entered the cotton trade, residing till his death
at Strangeways Hall, but continuing to attend the chapel.
The next minister was the Rev. Samuel Bradley, who held
the pastorate for some years, and eventually became the
minister of Cannon Street Congregation. His successor
was the Rev. Robert Stevens M'All, who was the pastor of
the church fifty years ago, and whose house was in Arlington
Place, Oxford Road, next to that of Mr. Richard Potter,
afterwards M.P. Mr. M'All was a minister at Macclesfield
at the time he received the pressing and unanimous invitation of the Mosley Street church and congregation to become
their pastor. He had been a student in the Edinburgh
University, where he obtained his degree of M.A. with
such distinction that the Senate afterwards spontaneously

conferred on him the degree of LL. D. without his previous
knowledge. Mosley Street Chapel stood on the right-hand
side of Mosley Street going from Market Street, at the
second corner of Charlotte Street, the first one being
occupied by the Assembly Rooms, which, like the chapel,
was a plain brick building. The principal entrance to the
chapel was by means of a colonnade situated in Charlotte
Street, there being also a door in Mosley Street. The
chapel itself was what it is the fashion with our æsthetic
friends to call a barn. But, barn or no barn, it was a very
comfortable place of worship, far more so than many places
which make great pretensions, but in which you can neither
see nor hear the preacher from certain positions. There
are many places of worship of a similar type in various
parts of the country, which have sacred and pleasant
associations, and which are revered and loved by those who
worship in them. During the ministry of Dr. M'All at
Mosley Street Chapel it has been stated that there were to
be seen more carriages drawn up at the chapel at the close
of the service than at any other church or chapel in
Manchester. The congregation often contained Churchmen and Dissenters of all creeds, who could appreciate
the highest style of pulpit oratory. I remember once
passing just when the congregation was coming out, and
being amazed at the number of carriages and coaches,
and at the crowd of people. I can call to mind one
occasion of my forming a part of the congregation when
Dr. M'All preached on a Sunday morning. The subject
of the discourse was the training of children, and I
well recollect how strongly he pleaded against corporal

punishment, arguing that the rod spoken of by Solomon in another passage must not be taken literally. It was my privilege to hear Dr. M'All preach his very last sermon. This took place at Oldham Street Chapel, on the evening of Easter Monday, 1838, when he preached the annual sermon to the Wesleyan Missionary Society of the Manchester district and to a crowded congregation. His text was from Isaiah : " Mighty to save." He preached two hours, pausing when half way through, the Rev. William Bunting giving out a hymn, which was sung by the congregation. Of his preaching it has been truly said " that his reputation for eloquence was only surpassed by the reality. His accurate scholarship, his cultured mind, his striking person, his natural dignity, and his elegance of gesture, added many charms to his close reasoning and his fervid oratory." The following gentlemen with their families used to attend the ministry of Dr. M'All: James Holt Heron, cotton merchant, whose house was in the Crescent, Salford, with his son, the present Sir Joseph Heron, and the rest of his family ; Dr. J. Phillips Kay, afterwards Sir James Phillips Kay-Shuttleworth; Thomas Harbottle, who was almost a giant in size ; J. S. Grafton, father of the present Frederick William Grafton, M.P., and his brother; Mr. John Roberton, the eminent surgeon ; Dr. Jarrold ; Richard Roberts, chairman of the Bank of Manchester ; W. R. Callender, father of the late M.P. for Manchester ; J. B. Clarke, of the firm of George Clarke and Co., cotton spinners ; Thomas H. Bickham and three sons ; Wood and Wright, calico printers, Clayton Vale ; William Woodward, wholesale grocer ; William Newall, grocer (Newall's Buildings) ; John Latham, cotton spinner; Hugh Warburton, afterwards councillor; Rev. Joseph Whitworth, father of the present Sir Joseph; Robert Barge, calico printer; Daniel Procter; James Dilworth, cotton merchant; Joseph Midwood, manufacturer; John Fildes, afterwards M.P. for Grimsby; William, now Alderman Sharp; James Lamb, cabinet maker; Thomas and Henry Boddington; Thomas Roberts, of Roberts, Dale, and Co., Cornbrook; Thomas Hunter, of the firm of J. C. Harter and Co., drysalters, Chapel Walks; Rev. Barzillai Quaife, tutor to William Romaine Callender, jun., afterwards M.P., and Samuel Pope Callender, afterwards a deacon at Zion Independent Chapel, the two sons of W. R. Callender, sen. ; John and James Edwards, the former being a prominent member of the Anti-Corn-Law League; Thomas Shimwell, now a partner in the firm of E. Potter and Co., calico printers; Joseph Ramsey, of High Street, who was secretary of the Juvenile Society; Henry Forth, afterwards of the firm of Forth and Marshall, commission agents, and William his brother; John Bradshaw, agent for Newall's buildings and for other property belonging to Mr. Newall, and who was also the dispenser of the poor's fund in connection with the church. He had three daughters, the eldest of whom became the wife of Mr. W. P. Ellerby, and the youngest of whom was drowned when the "Emma" was capsized. There was also Henry Pope, whose three daughters were married to George Hadfield, W. R. Callender, sen., and Thomas Harbottle. The present Samuel Pope, Q.C., is the grandson of Henry Pope, and was the nephew therefore of the late Messrs. Hadfield, Callender, sen., and Harbottle. The Rev. R. M. Davies, now an Independent minister at Oldham, was then a young man connected with the church, and was sent to study for the ministry at the Blackburn Academy (as it was then called), and afterwards at the Withington College. There was another young man who was a member of the congregation about this time, whose name ought not to be omitted. That is John Cassell, of the firm of Cassell, Petter, and Galpin, the eminent publishers. He was about this period a carpenter, having some of the habits of other working men ; but one evening was induced to attend a temperance lecture in Oak Street. Deeply impressed by what he heard, he became from that night a total abstainer. Fired with zeal in a cause which he believed would prove a blessing to his fellow-workmen, he shortly afterwards left the joiner's bench and became a voluntary temperance missionary, and joined the church, and, I believe the Sunday-school, at Dr. M'All's. Furnished with a watchman's rattle, he used to go from village to village and invite the people to his meetings, often suffering great privations in his work. Ultimately he got to London, where he met two good men who discovered the nobleness of his character and his ability, clothed him in a respectable suit, and sent him forth as a lecturer. By his love of reading and his remarkable spirit of perseverance his mind and manners rapidly improved, and he gradually lost his rough provincialism. Having married, he became possessed of a sum sufficiently large to commence to print—first temperance tracts, then a monthly periodical, and then a weekly paper, and became widely known as the editor of the *Working Man's Friend.* His publications soon became too gigantic for one man to

manage, and he entered into partnership with the eminent
printers Messrs. Petter and Galpin. Some years afterwards,
when spending a Sunday in Manchester, he went to the
Sunday-school with which he had formerly been connected,
and in an address to the scholars he alluded to his former
connection with the school. He died in 1865, at the early
age of forty-eight. After the decease of Mr. Roby the
following persons left Grosvenor Street Chapel and became
seat-holders at Mosley Street: James Kershaw, afterwards
M.P.; James Sidebotham; Joseph Thompson, grandfather
of the present Alderman Thompson; Elkanah, afterwards
Sir Elkanah Armitage; William Ellerby, stationer. There
was a Young Men's Mutual Improvement Society in connection with Dr. M'All's chapel, which used to meet in one
of the vestries upstairs, the entrance to which was in Back
Mosley Street. When a young man, on the invitation of
one of the members, I joined it. Its president was the
Rev. Francis Beardsall, a Baptist minister, who afterwards
went to America, and amongst its members were Mr. James
Lamb, Mr. W. P. Ellerby, Mr. John Fildes, then cashier to
Messrs. Barge, calico printers, and afterwards M.P. for
Grimsby; and R. M. Davies, then quite a young man,
employed in a Manchester house. In due course he
became the Rev. R. M. Davies, and received a call from
the congregation of an Independent church at Oldham, the
minister of which he remains, I believe, to this day. At
this time the corn laws were not abolished, but the subject
was exciting a good deal of attention; and being, as I have
said, a young man, when it came to my turn to read a paper
before the society, I made an attempt to prove that the

abolition of those laws would prove the ruin of the country. Referring to the time of which I am writing, one cannot help saying "there were giants in those days," for Manchester was often visited by several eminent Independent ministers from other places, who were deservedly very popular preachers, and who often filled the pulpits, principally of Grosvenor Street and Mosley Street, on special occasions. Amongst these were William Jay, of Bath; John Angell James, of Birmingham; Dr. Winter Hamilton, of Leeds; Dr. Raffles, of Liverpool; Dr. Harris, of Cheshunt; James Parsons, of York; John Ely, of Leeds; Thomas Binney, of London; and Dr. Liefchild, of London. When Dr. M'All left home he frequently had his pulpit supplied by Dr. Hamilton, of Leeds, and would make an announcement to that effect, saying, "My noble friend, Dr. Winter Hamilton, will supply my place." It has been my privilege to hear the whole of these preachers in Manchester. I never willingly missed an opportunity of hearing James Parsons, whose sermons had a peculiar charm for me. From a defect in his vocal organs he had a very weak voice, and was only heard when there was perfect stillness in the chapel. There seemed to exist a tacit understanding between his congregation and himself, the former preserving the most complete stillness during the sermon, until Mr. Parsons, at some suitable point in his discourse, made a pause, and thus gave his audience liberty to cough and clear their throats, of which they invariably availed themselves. To anyone hearing him for the first time, the effect of the whole congregation simultaneously being seized with a coughing fit, which as suddenly subsided when the preacher was ready to begin afresh, was very singular. But his hearers got accustomed to it. William Jay, of Bath, I heard at the opening of Ducie Chapel, Cheetham Hill Road. Dr. Winter Hamilton I heard one Sunday evening at Dr. M'All's chapel preach from the words, "Was Paul crucified for you?" Dr. M'All died in the very zenith of his popularity on the 27th of July, 1838, at the age of forty-six, and was buried in Rusholme Road Cemetery. There was a large concourse of people at his funeral, amongst whom I was present. His body was first taken to the chapel, where there was a service, and an address given by the Rev. John Ely. At the grave an oration was delivered by the Rev. John Angell James. Dr. Raffles preached the funeral sermon on the 5th of August following. On the monument erected to Dr. M'All's memory he is described as "of commanding and attractive bodily presence, of mental powers acute, brilliant, and profound, and gifted with an eloquence seldom surpassed." Mr. Alderman Joseph Thompson has kindly furnished me with a few additional particulars concerning Dr. M'All and his chapel, and Roby chapel, which are worth recording. The doctor preached long sermons, and the deacons, remembering the Sunday-school, tried to limit them, but in vain. One expedient tried was a gilded ball, which was to be released at twelve o'clock by the deacon who sat below, and set oscillating. It was tried once, and failed. The ball was let go, and swung backwards and forwards, but the preacher stopped it with his hand, and went on as if nothing had happened. John Owens, the founder of Owens College, formerly attended Mosley Street Chapel, and had a large square pew. When

Dr. M'All became so popular, and attracted such crowds, the half-empty square pew was regarded with covetous eyes by the deacons, who greedily snapped up every spare square inch of sitting room.   Mr. Owens was asked to be so good as to allow part of his pew to be let to others, but he was so offended as to leave the place, and after for a time joining the Unitarians, found his way to St. John's Church.   Mr. Thompson's grandfather was superintendent of the Sunday school connected with Roby chapel, in 1825, or earlier.   He kept a diary, in which he recorded his experiences of the difficulties of his office, and doubted his fitness for the post because the young teachers would go out of town, leaving their classes unprovided with substitutes.   How many superintendents are there at the present day who could echo the same complaint!   The diary evidences how earnestly and prayerfully he watched over his teachers and elder scholars, and how steadily he visited the sick and soothed the dying.   He had a son, Joseph, who died about 1837, who seems to have been a notable man in his day.   He was a capital man of business, so much so that he was appointed liquidator of a firm of calico printers at the age of twenty-two, Mr. Kershaw saying he would withdraw his opposition if Joseph Thompson, jun., would act as liquidator.   He was a fair musician, and had an organ, which was presented by Mr. Alderman Thompson's father to the Chorlton Work-house.   He joined in violin and violoncello quartetts and quintetts, Moses Hughes taking part therein.   After Mr. Roby died, he was the only person allowed to sit in his chair, in which he read the scriptures to the widow.

The chair is that in which Mr. Roby sat when his portrait was taken, and was bought by the grandfather. It is now in Mr. Thompson's possession. I have heard from another source that the gilded ball Mr. Alderman Thompson speaks of was intended to strike a little bell; that the apparatus was made by Peter Clare; and though made at Dr. M'All's suggestion, it utterly failed in its design. The Doctor became so absorbed in the flow of his own eloquence that he seemed to treat it as a slight impertinence, and took no notice of it beyond stopping its motion with his hand, but would go on without let or hindrance till one, and sometimes till half-past. I am told also that John Owens had a solitary sitting in the gallery of the chapel, previous to his occupying the large square pew downstairs.

RUSHOLME ROAD CHAPEL was built principally through the efforts of .the late George Hadfield, afterwards M.P. for Sheffield, and was opened for worship in 1825. The first congregation was composed mainly of persons from the Grosvenor Street and Mosley Street chapels. The Rev. James Griffin, a thin but interesting young man, became the pastor, under whom the congregation and church flourished. Besides Mr. Hadfield, amongst the worshippers there were to be found James, the father of Mr. Alderman Thompson; the Hopkinson family, including the present alderman; Dr. Henry Brown; Henry Waterhouse, architect; Thomas Crighton, machinist; Mr. Melland, surgeon; John Parry, lately deceased; Thomas Coward; Edward Wood; Charles Cutting; and Stanway Jackson. It happened that a certain day in September, 1829, had been fixed both for the ordination of Mr. Griffin and for the wedding of Mr. James Thompson. When this became known, Mr. Thompson put the wedding off till the following day, so as to be able to attend the ordination. Mr. Griffin often referred to it, and regarded it as the greatest compliment ever paid to him. Mr. Griffin for some years resided at Richmond Terrace, Stretford Road, during which he was a guardian of the poor for Stretford, which at the time was a part of the Chorlton Union. Mr. James Thompson was also a guardian in the same union, and was its chairman for some years before his death, which occurred in 1860.

JACKSON STREET CHAPEL, HULME.—I am not able to say in what year this chapel was built. Fifty years ago there was no stated minister attached to it, but shortly afterwards the Rev. James Gwyther was chosen as its pastor. He laboured very assiduously, and with such success that shortly it became necessary to seek for more commodious premises. Amongst the congregation at this time were the late Edward Goodall, of King Street, and his sister. A larger and more handsome structure was erected on the Stretford Road, which was named Zion Chapel, to which the church and congregation removed. Mr. Gwyther remained their pastor till the infirmities of age compelled him to give place to a younger man, when the Rev. Edward Simon succeeded him.

CHAPEL STREET CHAPEL.—We have seen that in 1818, nineteen members were transferred from Grosvenor Street, to form the nucleus of a church in Chapel Street, Salford, which was built near the end of New Bailey Street. Its first minister was the Rev. John Addison Coombs, who retained the position fifty years ago. He was ordained in February, 1820, on which occasion there was no laying on of hands. Dr. Winter, the uncle of Dr. Winter Hamilton, after the ordination prayer, ascended the pulpit to give the charge, and began by lamenting and blaming the omission. A large and flourishing congregation was gathered in the course of time by Mr. Coombs' ministrations, which included the late Mr. James Carlton, who then lived in Strangeways, and shortly afterwards in Broughton Lane; John Dracup, draper, Chapel Street; James Hilton Hulme, solicitor, of King Street, whose house was at Broughton; Thomas Gasquoine, cotton merchant, Bank Parade; Mr. M'Clure, of Acton Square; Mr. Edge, the surgeon; and Joseph Ward, now of Southport, who afterwards attended the ministry of Dr. Halley.

WINDSOR BRIDGE CHAPEL.—The minister of this chapel in 1829 was the Rev. James Priddie. He was Mr. Roby's assistant in 1816, on the occasion of his undertaking a fortnight's preaching excursion to the populous towns and villages within a distance of ten miles of Manchester, thus preparing the way, as at Ashton and Oldham, for the establishment of new churches. In this he was greatly assisted by Mr. Priddie. He subsequently resigned his position at Windsor Bridge and accepted a call to Halifax. He was succeeded at Windsor Bridge by the Rev. George Tayler. Mr. (now Sir John) Hawkshaw, C.E., who, I am told, has the scheme in hand for connecting France and England by means of a submarine tunnel, when engineer of the Lancashire and Yorkshire Railway, was a member of this congregation. The Rev. John Clunie, LL.D., who had a good boys' school in Leaf Square, was also for many years a member of the congregation, and when necessity arose conducted the services.

The chapel in LEE STREET, Ancoats, had no stated minister fifty years ago.

At the time of which we are speaking there were several Independent ministers in other parts of Lancashire, one of the most eminent of whom was the Rev. William Alexander. He originally came from Scotland and became the pastor of the Independent congregation of Prescot, then of Leigh, and afterwards of Churchtown, near Southport. He was a friend of William Roby, and much resembled him in spirit and in laborious zeal, frequently walking thirty miles in one day, sometimes preaching four times on a Sunday, and sometimes twice out of doors. He died at the patriarchal age of ninety-two, in the enjoyment of all his faculties. He was the father of the Rev. John Alexander, of Norwich, and grandfather of Mr. John Fletcher Alexander, the agent of the Liberation Society here, who was himself educated for the ministry.

CHAPTER XII.

PLACES OF WORSHIP.—WESLEYAN METHODIST CHAPELS.

METHODISM (to use its original name) was probably introduced into Manchester between the years 1733 and 1738. In the first of these years, Wesley had visited Manchester and preached three times in three different churches on one Sunday, one of them being the Old Church. On the 16th of March, 1738, he and Charles Kinchin, another member of the Holy Club at Oxford (so called in derision), rode into Manchester late at night, having ridden from Stafford that day. The next day they spent with John Clayton, incumbent of Trinity Chapel, Salford, another of the little band, "by whom," says Wesley, "and the rest of our friends here, we were much refreshed and strengthened." The day after, Wesley and Kinchin officiated at Trinity Church in the morning, and St. Ann's in the afternoon, Mr. Hoole, the rector having been taken suddenly ill. The Rev. Benjamin Gregory observes on this: " It seems clear that before a class meeting was formed in London there existed in Manchester, if not a Methodist society, at least a Methodist circle. One of these 'friends' was doubtless the celebrated Dr. Byrom, the poet and man of science, a

Fellow of the Royal Society, author of 'Christians, awake!' and translator from the French of the noble hymn, 'O thou who camest from above.'" This was twenty years before Manchester began to export its manufactures, and twenty-one years before the townspeople ceased to be obliged to have all their corn ground at the Irk mill.

The first evidence of the existence of a "Methodist Society" in Manchester is given in a letter dated 1747, from John Bennett to Wesley, who says: "Some young men of Manchester (that spoke with Mr. Charles when he was with us last) have begun a society, and took a room, and have subscribed their names in a letter to Mr. Charles, desiring you will own them as brethren, and visit them on your return." Their number was very small, for when Richard Barlow, the first Methodist here whose name is known, joined them, they were but fourteen or fifteen. The room which these young men had taken was a small apartment built upon a rock on the bank of the Irwell, on the north side of Blackfriars Bridge, at the bottom of a large yard known as the Rose and Crown yard, and which was filled with wood-built thatched cottages. The house containing the preaching-room was three storeys high. The ground floor was a joiner's shop; the rooms in the middle storey were the residence of a newly-married couple; and the preaching-room was the home of a poor woman, who there plied her spinning-wheel, while her husband in the same apartment flung the shuttle. Christopher Hopper, one of the early Methodist preachers, speaking of a service he conducted there, says: "I preached in an old garret that overhung the river near the bridge;

the coals were in one corner of the room, the looms in
another, and I was in danger of breaking my neck in
getting up to it. When the congregation was collected
the first evening it did not consist of more than from
twenty to thirty persons." Such was the beginning of
Wesleyan Methodism in Manchester.

The next important step in its progress was the building
of a chapel in Birchin Lane, at the back of High Street, in
1750. The building was standing in 1829, and was then
occupied as a warehouse by Mary Bealey, the well-known
bleacher, and equally well-known as belonging to a family
of eminent Wesleyans, to which reference has been made in
a former chapter. Before the chapel was ready to receive
the congregation, however, it had increased so rapidly that
the old room near the river would not contain it, and fairly
trembled under the weight so as to produce considerable
consternation. In the emergency the same building which
had received Newcome and his congregation before Cross
Street Chapel was built, proved a refuge for these early
Methodists, who obtained the use of the Cold House
Chapel for a time.

Amongst the first members connected with Birchin
Lane Chapel were Thomas Fildes, grandfather of
Mr. James Fildes, of Spring Gardens, and originator of
Sunday Schools in Manchester, referred to previously ;
Mary Bromley, for seventy years a Methodist, who died in
1826, at the age of eighty-nine ; Adam Oldham, a felt
maker, one of the first trustees of Birchin Lane Chapel, who
lived in a house on the site now occupied by the Albion
Hotel ; Richard Barlow, who for sixty-five years rose at

half-past four in summer and five in winter; Mr. Brierley, who met in Peter Kenworthy's class, and was in its early days leading singer at Oldham Street Chapel, and afterwards a magistrate; John Mosley, a hatter in Millgate; and Mrs. Bennett, the first female class-leader in Manchester.

Manchester, which at the present day contains thirteen Wesleyan circuits, in 1752 was only part of what was called the Cheshire circuit, and which included Lancashire, Cheshire, Derbyshire, Staffordshire, and part of Yorkshire. The contributions of the members of the society in Manchester towards the support of the ministry in one quarter of that year only amounted to £2. 3s. 5d. In 1765 Manchester became the head of a circuit, the first ministers who were appointed to it being James Oddie, John Oliver, John Murray, and Isaac Waldron.

OLDHAM STREET CHAPEL was opened by John Wesley on Good Friday, the 30th of March, 1781. He writes in his journal: "Friday, March 30. I opened the new chapel at Manchester, about the size of that in London. The whole congregation behaved with the utmost seriousness. I trust much good will be done in this place. Sunday, April 1. I began reading prayers at ten o'clock. Our country friends flocked in from all sides. At the Communion was such a sight as I am persuaded was never seen in Manchester before, eleven or twelve hundred communicants at once; and all of them fearing God." This building has always been looked upon by Wesleyans as next in importance and interest to City Road Chapel in London, and by Manchester Methodists it has been regarded almost in the same light as the Old Church is by

Episcopalians. There is a tradition amongst Wesleyans that John Wesley regretted it was built so far out of town. Little did he dream that in less than a hundred years it would be seriously discussed by the Conference whether it should be sold, because it was too near the centre of the town ! To name the ministers who have been appointed by the Conference to labour in the Oldham Street circuit would be to name those who have been the most eminent in the Connexion. Amongst them are found the names of Adam Clarke, Jabez Bunting, Robert Newton, Samuel Bradburn, Thomas Jackson, James Everett, Joseph Benson ; John Gaulter, whose son was a druggist in Piccadilly ; Joseph Fowler, father of Mr. Henry H. Fowler, the Liberal member for Wolverhampton ; James Wood, grandfather, and Robert the father, of Mr. Bateson Wood, solicitor of this city ; John Pipe, whose uncle was a rich man, and who, having made a will in favour of his nephew John, threatened to disinherit him on his becoming a Methodist, and died before he could execute his threat, John's two sons, Isaac and William, being in partnership as silversmiths in Market Street in 1829 ; Edmund Grindrod, whose daughter became the wife of Mr. W. C. Rippon, of the Manchester and Liverpool District Bank ; Miles Martindale, for some years governor of Woodhouse Grove School, near Leeds, where the author was educated ; George Marsden, brother of a late vicar of Eccles, before referred to ; John Stephens, father of the late Rev. William Rayner Stephens, at one time a notorious political agitator ; John Rigg, father of a former editor of the *Watchman* newspaper, and of

Dr. James H. Rigg, the well-known principal of Westminster Training Institution, and ex-president of the Conference ; and William Edward Miller, who became one of the most enthusiastic, energetic, and devoted of ministers. He was the son of Dr. Edward Miller, a man of literary taste, refined manners, and great eminence as a professor of music, and who was the popular organist of Doncaster Church for fifty years. He was the instrument of developing that profound astronomical talent which distinguished the late Sir William Herschell. The son, when a young man, followed his father's profession, and became an accomplished player on the violin. He went to India, and having heard that in the court of Tippoo Saib an exquisite instrument was in use by one of the Sultan's band, and having pushed his way to Seringapatam, he so enchanted the sovereign by his performance as to obtain possession of the prize. On his return to England it became the idol of his soul. When he became a Methodist, he was afraid it might be a source of temptation, and with unexampled firmness he laid it aside—though at the time he was esteemed the second, if not the first, performer in England—with the purpose never to touch it more, a resolution he kept to the day of his death. The violin is now in the possession of Mr. James Fildes, of Chorlton-cum-Hardy. Mr. Miller became one of the most earnest and popular preachers in England. His son was one of my schoolfellows at Wood-house Grove School. In 1829 the ministers of Oldham Street Chapel were John Burdsall, Abraham Stead, Samuel Dunn, and John Lomas. Burdsall lived at the corner of

Dale Street and Spear Street, and Dunn in Spear Street. From the hands of Samuel Dunn I received my note of admittance on trial into the Methodist Society, which is signed by him, and which I still retain. He was a disciple of Dr. Adam Clarke, inasmuch as he professed to hold his views on the "Sonship of Christ." In consequence he was not ordained for many years, until he abandoned them, which was after Dr. Clarke's death. He was a Cornish man, and had an impediment in his speech which prevented him sounding the R. Although he stood by Everett in his dispute with the Conference at a later period in reference to what were called the "Fly-sheets," and was expelled with him and Griffiths as members of the Conference, he took the Conservative side in politics. During his appointment to Oldham Street Chapel political feeling ran very high in Manchester, and he had noticed the name of Mr. Eli Atkin, who was then a member at Oldham Street, on the committee of some association formed to promote parliamentary reform. Mr. Dunn made it his business to see Mr. Atkin, in order to persuade him to have nothing to do with politics, and especially with the Liberal party. Mr. Dunn is still living in the enjoyment of tranquillity and peace after a somewhat stormy life, and is now reconciled to the Conference. During one of the open sessions of the Bradford Conference of 1878, when the public were admitted, I had the pleasure of seeing him on the platform, shaking hands with many of the preachers around him. The Oldham Street Circuit fifty years ago embraced Cheetham Hill and Oldham Road and the district between; Grosvenor Street and Oxford Road Chapels having been built a few years previously, the more wealthy portion of Oldham Street congregation had deserted it for the two former places. The congregation of Oldham Street Chapel at that time included Mr. John Roberts, the stationer, of Market Street, whose pew was in front of the gallery opposite the preacher, and which was kept locked, so that, as the chapel was often crowded in those days, he and his family could always gain access to it; Mr. John Brogden, father of Mr. Alexander Brogden, M.P., and his good-looking wife, who sat a few pews behind Mr. Roberts; James Morris, afterwards a partner in Satterfield's, and his mother, whose pew was near the last-mentioned; Joseph England, a well-known painter of Oxford Road; Alexander Braik, silk and shawl dyer, of Oldham Street, the predecessor of Mr. John Berrie, and who, with his wife, were good representatives of old Methodism; William Pollard, of Oldham Street, a tailor, and one of the earliest teetotalers, as well as a local preacher; Micah Rose, said to be one of the best and most obliging of tax collectors ever known, a native of Castleton in the Peak; Mr. John Hull, a tall, thin, venerable man, the representative of Mary Bealey, the bleacher, and whose eldest son married Mrs. Roberts' youngest daughter; Eli Atkin, now of Newton Heath, then of Dale and Atkin, druggists, Swan Street; Mark Abbey, baker, of Swan Street; William Dentith, druggist, of Market Street, who, with his apprentices, occupied a large square family pew downstairs near the pulpit, the next to it being that of Hugh Greaves, father of the late George Greaves, surgeon; James Fildes, wholesale grocer, father of Mr. James Fildes, of Chorlton-

cum-Hardy; James Redfern, of Market Street, with his
father and brother; Mr. Millward, father of Mr. Millward,
of Newton Heath; Mr. Samuel Stocks, father of
Mrs. Thomas Farmer, whose husband was a well-known
and wealthy Wesleyan and a liberal contributor to its
funds, who died a few years ago; and Mr. W. R. Johnson,
a friend of my master's, a partner in the firm of
Sedgwick, Son, and Johnson, drapers, St. Ann's Square,
and afterwards a partner in the house of Alexander Henry
and Co. He retired on a handsome fortune, and died a
few years since near Alderley Edge. Fifty years ago Oldham
Street Chapel contained no organ, but the orchestra
consisted of two violoncellos, a double bass (sometimes two),
and a bass horn. Mr. Thomas Swindells, of Heaton Moor,
who played the violoncello many years, still survives. The
leading singer was a fine old fellow, with a capital voice,
James Wilkinson. A few years later Robert Newton was
appointed to the circuit, and frequently preached at
Oldham Street on a Sunday evening, the service begining
then at six o'clock. He was always in the pulpit before
the time, seated and waiting for the clock to indicate that
moment, when he would rise and give out the first hymn.
He was very fond of that beautiful hymn of Scheffler's,
translated by Wesley, beginning, "O God of good, the un-
fathomed sea!" with which to begin the service. I do not
remember anything finer of the kind than Newton's giving
out of this hymn, followed by Wilkinson's setting to it the
grand old tune, known as Marienbourn, a crowded congregation joining in singing it. I need not say that Robert Newton,
with his large, bold, and handsome features, splendid

voice, and commanding presence, was one of the most popular orators of the day. It used to be seriously related of him that one evening he was preaching in Wakefield, and that a lady who was in the habit of attending the theatre, at the solicitation of a friend, went to hear him. After she had heard him give out his hymn, she became convinced that she was listening to no other than John Kemble. She went home and assured her husband that Jack Kemble was in the pulpit, and induced him to return with her. He did so, the result being that both husband and wife became members of the Methodist Society. Newton was gifted with a robust constitution, and for at least thirty years the whole of his time except Sundays was spent in travelling, mostly on the top of a coach, from place to place, making missionary and other speeches, and preaching for various objects. In this respect he was known from one end of the kingdom to the other. To return to James Wilkinson, he kept a music shop nearly opposite the chapel in Oldham Street, and next door to the smallware shop of Mr. James Varley, the father of Mrs. Linnæus Banks (who had another in Market Street). The family appear to have been musical, his son William being a teacher of music, and his grandson, whose name was Gregory, being an accomplished violinist, and one of the early members of Charles Hallé's orchestra. At that day the Wesleyan Schools on the Wednesday of Whit-week used to per-ambulate the streets, and assemble on Ardwick Green, where they sang several hymns, accompanied by a trumpet played by Peter Duckers, James Wilkinson standing in the centre and leading them.

IRWELL STREET CHAPEL.—The whole of Manchester and Salford was included in the Oldham Street Circuit till 1813, when Salford was separated from it and made a second circuit. The only Wesleyan Chapel then existing in Salford was Gravel Lane, which was built in 1790. Irwell Street Chapel, which subsequently became the head of the circuit, was not built till 1826. The first ministers appointed to the circuit in 1813 were Cleland Kirkpatrick, Thomas Dowty, and William Jones. Kirkpatrick, before he became a minister, was in the Royal Navy, and in an engagement with Paul Jones, the dashing American officer, during the War of Independence, lost one of his arms, which was substituted by a false one. Kirkpatrick's religion had not destroyed his sailor-like love of fun, for, on going to a village in a new circuit, arrangements were made for him to stay all night at the house of one of the members. He was shown to his room by the servant girl, who remained a moment or two to arrange the bed, during which he took off his coat, unfastened his false arm, and laid it on the table. Perceiving the girl's attention was arrested, and that she looked very bewildered at the operation, he went to the looking-glass and pretended to unscrew his head. This was too much for the girl, who flew downstairs almost head first, exclaiming, " Lors a' mercy, missis, the preacher's taken his arm off, and now he's a screwing his head off!" In 1829 the ministers of the Salford circuit were Jabez Bunting, Robert Wood (before referred to), and John Kirk. Bunting was born in Manchester, his father being a tailor. A short time previously his parents resided

at Monyash, in Derbyshire, where one of the early
Methodist ministers preached one night, when on his way
to set sail for New York, he being one of the two first
ministers who introduced Methodism there. Mrs. Bunting,
who was expecting to become a mother, heard him preach
from the prayer of Jabez, 1 Chronicles, c. 4 v. 10. She
resolved that if she should be the mother of a son, his
name should be Jabez, which came to pass. After being
an assistant to Dr. Percival, F.R.S., of King Street, he
entered the Wesleyan ministry in 1799, the same year
in which Robert Newton also entered it. The late
Mr. Robert Henson, of the firm of Broadhurst, Henson,
and Co., told me he heard Mr. Bunting preach one of
his first sermons, in a small room in Salford when quite
a young man. Since the death of Wesley no minister in
the Wesleyan body attained such an eminence as he did,
or was able to wield such an influence for the good of
the Connexion. It was often said that had his lot been
cast in Parliament nothing could have prevented him
being prime minister. He and Robert Newton were
the only two ministers who have been presidents of the
Conference four times. He was a friend of my father's
and I was frequently thrown into his society. I remember
meeting him at the house of Mr. John Roberts, the
stationer, when the conversation turned on the slender
attendance at the week-night services at the chapel.
Mr. Roberts said the reason no doubt was that the
congregation got such long sermons on the Sunday it
satisfied them for the week. "Nay, my friend," said
Bunting, "it is just the opposite; finding that people will

not come to the week-night services, when we do get them on a Sunday we therefore keep them a little longer." As an instance of this tact, I may be allowed to give the following anecdote. On one occasion, when he was President of the Conference, there was a vacancy in what is called "the Legal Hundred," that is, the hundred ministers who form the legal Conference in accordance with Wesley's poll-deed, such vacancy to be filled in this instance by seniority. There were two ministers equally eligible, Mr. Walker and my father, both having begun the ministry in 1804. Mr. Bunting put it to the vote which of the two should be elected. On counting the votes he announced them to be equal, and added, "which of you brethren will give way?" My father instantly rose and said : " I will, Mr. President." " Then, Brother Slugg," he said, " I give you my casting vote ; " and my father was elected amidst the applause of his brethren. Amongst other ministers appointed to the Irwell Street Circuit were William Atherton, father of the late Sir William Atherton, Attorney-General; Thomas Squance, one of the early missionaries to India; William Bramwell, Charles Attmore, and James Townley. Amongst the persons who formed the congregation of Irwell Street fifty years ago were Mr. Alderman Davies, of Salford, and his father; Mr. James Duke, silversmith, of the Market Place, his house being in St. Stephen's Street; Mr. John Morris, auctioneer (whose widow is still living, and whose pew contained several bonny girls, his daughters); Mr. George Peacock, draper, Deansgate, whose three sons are prosperous merchants at the Cape of Good Hope ;

Peter Drummond, draper, Deansgate, father of Dr. Drummond, and my brother's master; William Hill, of the firm of Smith, Hill, and Co., drapers, Millgate, who, as I have before stated, was boroughreeve of Salford afterwards; John Dale, of Dale and Hume, hat manufacturers, Water Street; Mr. and Mrs. Fynney Johnson, who had a large glass shop at the St. Mary's Gate end of Deansgate, where they kept open house for Wesleyan ministers; and Mrs. Crowther, the widow of the Rev. Jonathan Crowther, a coadjutor of John Wesley's, and President of the Conference in 1819. She received her ticket of membership from the hand of Wesley himself in 1790, and died in 1869, at the extreme age of ninety-five years. She had handsome features and a dignified though not a haughty bearing, and in her later years presented a pleasing picture of a fine old English lady. Her youngest son, Mr. Joshua Crowther, accountant, of this city, having been in the same form with me at Woodhouse Grove School, Mrs. Crowther became the first friend I had on becoming an apprentice. I frequently visited her family on a Sunday, and accompanied them to Irwell Street Chapel in the evening, and well remember all whose names I have mentioned. The chapel was a large and handsome structure, possessing a very fine mahogany pulpit and reading desk below. I remember Robert Newton one Sunday morning reading prayers, after which Jabez Bunting preached, during which Newton remained in the desk just beneath Bunting. I placed myself in the gallery, right opposite, that I might enjoy the sight of two such eminent men sustaining such relative positions, which to me was most interesting. Irwell Street Chapel had a burial ground attached, the chief rent of which, added to that of the ground on which the chapel was built, and the interest of a large debt left on the building, formed a heavy burden on the trustees for many years. A few years since a noble and successful effort was made to provide for the payment of the chief, and to pay off the mortgage.

GRAVEL LANE CHAPEL we have seen, after Oldham Street, is the oldest Wesleyan chapel in Manchester. It was built in 1790. Fifty years ago the principal seat-holder was Mr. John Downes, an extensive hat manufacturer, near St. Mary's Church. He married a sister of Mrs. Mary Bealey, the bleacher, and of Dr. Warren's wife, his house being in Strangeways. When I was an apprentice we used to do business with him. He was one of the most precise and exact men of business I ever knew. The father of the late Sir William Atherton used to preach in this chapel, and was what is called a memoriter preacher. Every sentence was carefully prepared beforehand and fitted into its place, like stones for a building. He was, in consequence, generally in a very nervous state whilst preaching, and used to lay hold of anything convenient and grip it fast. For this purpose, two good-sized knobs were screwed into the inside of the front of the pulpit of Gravel Lane Chapel, and are there to this day, so that he could lay hold of one or both. Some idea of his style may be formed from the following illustration I once heard him give. He was speaking at a missionary meeting, and said : " Some of you will say, you come to us and tell us that the gold and the silver and the cattle on a thousand hills are all the Lord's; and then you come to us at another time and begin to beg for the Lord; how is it?" Said he: " I'll tell you how it is; the gold and the silver are the Lord's, but he has lent it out, and many of you have some of it, and are paying so little interest for it that if you don't pay better interest the Lord may call it all in, both capital and interest.". I have his autograph, with scores of others of old Wesleyan ministers. Under his name he has written: " A man severe he was, and stern to view; I knew him well, and many others knew." A not very inapt description of himself.

BRIDGEWATER STREET CHAPEL was the third Wesleyan chapel built in Manchester. It was opened somewhere about 1800, but did not become the head of a circuit till the year 1827, having been previously a part of the Oldham Street one. Amongst those who worshipped there were Mr. Daniel Sandbach, a large tanner in Lloyd Street; Mrs. Mary Brewer, of Bridgewater Street, mother of Mr. John Brewer, of Wheelton, Brewer, and Buckland, Mr. Wheelton being the Sheriff of London imprisoned by order of the House of Commons, before referred to; Mr. James Sewell, cotton spinner, who is interred in the burial ground attached to the chapel, and one of whose family is the wife of Mr. Richard Haworth, J.P.; and Mr. Robert Barnes, father of the late Mr. Robert Barnes. Mr. Barnes the elder was an accountant, having his office for nearly twenty-five years at No. 2, Palace Street, his residence being at one time in Berwick Street, Chorlton Row, then in Faulkner Street, and finally at Newton Lodge, Oldham Road. He is buried in the ground attached to the chapel, against a wall which divides the ground from Bridgewater Street. In the vestry of the chapel is a well-executed portrait in oil of him in a good state of preservation, presented by the late Mr. Barnes. He died November 29, 1824, aged fifty-nine years. The late Mr. Robert Barnes bequeathed £3,000 to the trustees of the chapel in commemoration of his father, in order to provide for the ground rent and put the chapel and minister's house in good repair, making it a condition that the minister should always reside in the house. There is a very handsome mural tablet by Bennison and Son erected in the chapel to Mr. Barnes' memory, and recording the bequest. Fifty years ago the two sons of the elder Mr. Barnes, Thomas and Robert, were in partnership as cotton spinners in Jackson's Street, having removed from Oldham Road, where they first began. They were very successful and acquired a large fortune. At the death of Thomas, the elder brother, who was a bachelor, Robert inherited his property and carried on the business on his own account. He subsequently sold the business to W. R. Callender and Sons, and shortly after the sale told a friend of mine that for many years he had made a yearly profit of £8,000 or £9,000. He was an alderman of Manchester, and mayor in the years 1851 to 1853.

SWAN STREET CHAPEL.—At the beginning of the present century there were a number of pits of water, known as the Shudehill Pits, at the upper end of Shudehill, extending into what is now Swan Street. On a part of their site a Wesleyan chapel known as Swan Street Chapel was built in 1808, but which was converted into shops and dwelling-houses in 1823. I have heard my father refer to the fact of his having preached in the chapel. About this time Oldham Street Chapel was so full it was impossible to get a sitting.

CHANCERY LANE CHAPEL, ARDWICK.—In 1817 a building was erected in Chancery Lane, Ardwick, the upper part of which was used for a chapel and the lower for a Sunday school. When opened, the congregation included Mr. James Wood, of Wood and Westhead; Mr. Francis Marris, of Marris, Son, and Jacksons; the father and his family of Mr. John Napier, afterwards of the firm of Napier and Goodair, spinners and manufacturers, of Manchester and Preston, now of Plymouth Grove; and others of the more wealthy Wesleyans who began to reside on the southern side of the town. On the first Sunday of the school being opened a goodly number of scholars presented themselves, as well as teachers, amongst the latter of whom were a young man and his sister, the former being appointed teacher of the alphabet class. He lives to this day to witness the great development of Methodism during the last sixty-three years, and to be able to devote the leisure of a serene old age to the discharge of many active duties in connection with its operations. I allude, of course, to the venerable Mr. John Napier.

GROSVENOR STREET CHAPEL was built in 1819 and opened in 1820. The Revs. Jabez Bunting, Richard Watson, George Marsden, and John Stephens were the ministers who officiated on the occasion. Notwithstanding handsome subscriptions and collections, a debt of £5,000 was left on the premises, and remained nearly forty years, when successful efforts were made to remove it. At the same time funds were found for the erection of large and commodious day and Sunday schools on the site of what was the minister's house annexed to the chapel, the entire property being now free from all encumbrance. Amongst the first worshippers here were James Wood, with his interesting family; Edward Westhead, with his three sons— J. P. Westhead, some time M.P. for York; Edward, still living at Surbiton, in Surrey, who married the daughter of George Royle Chappell; and John, long since deceased, who married a daughter of James Wood; John Marsden, brother of the Rev. George Marsden, and of a late vicar of Eccles; Francis Marris and his son John; George Royle Chappell, with his fine family of daughters; Robert Barnes, with his excellent mother; Samuel Stocks, the father of the late Mrs. Farmer; William Allen, father of the member for Newcastle-under-Lyme; Robert Henson, a former partner of Mr. Broadhurst, the first City Treasurer; John Gom Baker, cotton merchant, Crow Alley; John Harrison; Mrs. Fogg; Thomas Townend; Luke Gray, manufacturer; Joshua Rea and his partner; John Lomas, of High Street; George Lomas; Joseph Hardy, drysalter, Ardwick; Charles Beswick; W. R. Johnson; William Burd, calico printer, and afterwards the first and indefatigable agent of the Star Life Insurance Society; and Mr. John Napier. There was another member of the Grosvenor Street congregation whom I remember, and who, though not a man of wealth or worldly position, deserves honourable mention, affording proof that there are other gifts than wealth which a man may contribute to any good cause which he espouses, and which are still more valuable. The Rev. Mr. Dale, the Congregationalist minister of Birmingham, in his admirable address to the Wesleyan Conference, which was held in Birmingham, spoke of the great importance of what is known as the class-meeting, and exhorted all Wesleyans to fidelity to their principles in this respect; pointing out how largely their success depended upon it. William Silkstone, the man I speak of, was one of the most devoted and successful class-leaders I ever knew. Although an overlooker in Wood and Westhead's mill, and, as such, occupied from early to late, yet for a number of years he had the charge of three large classes, numbering between one and two hundred members, and visited his absentees weekly, looking after their temporal and spiritual wants. After a long life of devoted labour he passed peacefully away, highly esteemed and greatly loved by the many that knew him. A mural tablet is erected to his memory in Grosvenor Street Chapel. I must not omit to mention the name of Mr. George Grundy, who has been a member of the Society and organist at Grosvenor Street for nearly fifty years, and is still found at his post every Sunday.

OXFORD ROAD CHAPEL was built in 1826, and at the same time Ancoats Lane Chapel, the trustees being the same. In addition to Messrs. James Wood, Edward Westhead, G. R. Chappell, Robert Barnes, and Robert Henson, who left Grosvenor Street and came to Oxford Road, the following worshipped there fifty years ago: John Fernley, T. P. Bunting, John Sandbach (father of the late John Sandbach), John Heyhurst, John Mason, and William Carter, of Ormond Street. The ministers of the

Grosvenor Street circuit at that time were Richard Watson, John Sumner, John Hannah, and William M. Bunting, son of Jabez Bunting. The repute of Richard Watson still exists as one of the greatest divines the Wesleyan body ever possessed, as well as a most eloquent preacher and speaker. I once was in his company, when a boy, my father having been invited to speak at a missionary meeting at Rochdale, at which Watson was to speak. I walked over from Bacup with my father, and met him at the house of Mr. Booth, the druggist. I remember him sitting on one side of the fire, and smoking from a long pipe. He was spare and tall, but had the head of a Socrates. Fifty years ago the Grosvenor Street circuit extended from Droylsden on the east to Northenden and Chorlton-cum-Hardy on the south-west, and included also Openshaw, Bradford, Ancoats, Oxford Road, and George Street, Hulme. In 1846 it was divided, Oxford Road becoming the head of a circuit, which was itself divided in 1867, Radnor Street becoming the head of the new circuit.

CHORLTON-CUM-HARDY.—Methodism appears to have been introduced into this little village at a very early date. It is said to have been introduced by a Methodist soldier in 1770, who came to Manchester with a few friends, and who, dressed in his uniform, preached on the village green. In 1800, class meetings were established in Chorlton, before which time services were held at a thatched cottage inhabited by John Johnson, behind the present National Schools, and in a barn at present occupied by Mrs. Higginbotham. The first chapel was erected in 1805. It was a small square building, in which the women sat on one

side and the men on the other. This gave place to a
larger structure (now used as a Sunday school) in 1827,
built at a cost of £690. The present chapel was erected
eight years ago at a cost of £5,600. The Sunday school
was opened in 1805, there being no other in the village at
that time. It is worthy of mention that the early race of
Methodists in Chorlton, before they had a chapel of their
own, used to attend the early service at Oldham Street,
which began at seven a.m., on the Sunday. Amongst them
was Jeremiah Brundrett, the grandfather of the present race
of Brundretts, which includes the wife of our friend
Mr. John Rowbotham, lately the valued committee clerk
of the Corporation.

CHEETHAM HILL.—Methodism was introduced into
what was then the village of Cheetham Hill through
the instrumentality of Mr. Samuel Russell, the partner of
Mr. Sowler, the grandfather of the present proprietor of
the *Courier*. Mr. Russell was the father of the wife of
Mr. John Napier, and in the first instance opened his
kitchen as a Methodist preaching-room about the year
1808. Such accommodation was soon found to be
inconvenient and insufficient. He next built a room
over his coachhouse, where the services were held for
some years. This, too, in time became too small, and the
first chapel was built in the village, which, since the
erection of the present large and handsome one, has
become the mortuary chapel of the cemetery there, which
contains so many of the Wesleyan dead. This has been
the principal Wesleyan place for burial for one or two
generations, and on that account is, to an old Methodist,

an interesting spot. The old chapel was opened in 1817, by Dr. Adam Clarke. Mr. Russell, who may be considered the father of Methodism in the place, was just permitted to see the accomplishment of that which he so desired, for he died shortly after the opening of the chapel.

CHAPTER XIII.

PLACES OF WORSHIP.—UNITARIAN CHAPELS.

IN the tabular statement which I have given of the number of churches and chapels existing in Manchester fifty years ago, the number of Unitarian Chapels is stated to be four. One of these, however, was in the suburbs. Hence there were only three Unitarian Chapels in the town—namely, in Cross Street, Mosley Street, and Greengate.

CROSS STREET CHAPEL is the oldest Dissenting place of worship in Manchester. The present chapel is the second built on the site, the first having been erected in 1693 for a Presbyterian congregation collected by Henry Newcome. This gentleman was not a Fellow, the Rev. C. W. Bardsley tells us, but a stipendiary curate of the Collegiate Church, which he crowded to overflowing by his simple and earnest discourses. In 1662, the Act of Uniformity was passed, and Newcome vacated his post. He preached his last sermon as an Episcopalian in Bowdon Church, whilst staying with Lord Delamere at Dunham Park. After officiating for a time in the Cold House Chapel already referred to, which was licensed for him, he became the minister of the first Cross Street Chapel as already stated. Jane Meriel, the wife of Edward Mosley, of Hulme Hall, helped to build the chapel, and became Newcome's patroness to the time of his death, and many individuals of rank were amongst his constant hearers. It is said of him, "that great men courted his acquaintance, and to the meanest Christian he was a most cordial friend." In 1715, on the birthday of James the Third, a Jacobin mob which paraded the streets, led on by Thomas Syddall, the peruke maker, proceeded to the chapel in Cross Street, smashed its windows and doors, overturned its pews and pulpit, and almost destroyed the place. Parliament granted £1,500 for its restoration, and it was enlarged again under the popular ministry of Dr. Barnes, in 1788. During the latter part of Mr. Newcome's life he was assisted in his work as a pastor and teacher by Mr. Chorlton, a fit coadjutor of Newcome, who died in 1705. After his death Mr. James Coningham, who had been educated at Edinburgh, accepted an invitation to become co-pastor with Mr. Chorlton, in 1700. One of the most noted of the early ministers of this chapel was Mr. Joseph Mottershead, who was educated at Attercliffe, near Sheffield, under Timothy Jollie, and was ordained when only twenty. He died in 1771, at the age of eighty-three, having been the minister of Cross Street chapel fifty-four years. His assistant was Mr. Seddon, who married his daughter. The latter was succeeded by Mr. Gore, and Mr. Mottershead by Mr. Ralph Harrison, whose only daughter married Thomas Ainsworth, and became the mother of William Harrison Ainsworth. She died in 1842. In 1780, Mr. Gore was succeeded by Dr. Thomas Barnes, whose popular style attracted a large

congregation, and who died in 1810, having been pastor
of the church thirty years. He was succeeded by
Mr. John Grundy, the uncle of our worthy ex-mayor, who
excited considerable attention by a course of lectures on
Unitarianism, which were published in two volumes octavo.
He afterwards removed to Liverpool, and died near Brid-
port in 1843. The Rev. John Gooch Robberds, born at
Norwich, and educated at the York College, became
Mr. Grundy's coadjutor on the death of Mr. Harrison.
The Rev. John Hugo Worthington became the colleague
of Mr. Robberds, until cut off by death when very young.
He was succeeded by the Rev. William Gaskell.
Mr. Robberds and Mr. Gaskell were the ministers in 1829.
Mr. Robberds was held in high esteem by his congregation
on account of his many fine qualities. Amongst other
accomplishments, he had an extensive acquaintance with
various ancient Eastern languages. He died in 1854, his
wife surviving him twenty years. She was the daughter of
the Rev. William Turner, of Newcastle-on-Tyne, and was
perhaps held in even greater esteem than her husband.
A simple but beautiful tablet, with brass plate attached,
recording the virtues of husband and wife, is affixed to the
west wall of the chapel. Mr. Gaskell was born at
Warrington, and still lives in the enjoyment of the cordial
respect and affection of his people after a fifty-one years'
ministry. Mrs. Gaskell died some years since, and is
buried at Knutsford, where her childhood and youth had
been passed. An admirable tablet on the east wall of the
chapel records her well-known talents and refined character.
The Cross Street congregation has always been remarkable

for the high social and intellectual position of its members.
In the year 1829 there were no less than a dozen gentlemen who afterwards became members of Parliament, and
five who became mayors of Manchester, who attended
either Cross Street or Mosley Street Unitarian chapels.
The following were members of the Cross Street congrega-
tion : Benjamin, afterwards Sir Benjamin Heywood, and
M.P. for the county; James Heywood, afterwards
M.P. for the northern division of the county; John,
afterwards Sir John Potter, M.P. for the city, and
three times mayor; Richard Potter, afterwards M.P.
for Wigan ; Thomas Bayley Potter, the present M.P. for
Rochdale; James Aspinall Turner, afterwards M.P. for
Manchester ;. Alexander Henry, M.P. for the county;
J. B. Smith, M.P. for Stirling and for Stockport; and
Robert Needham Philips, the present M.P. for Bury. Also
Thomas Potter, Alexander Kay, Ivie Mackie, and Abel
Heywood, afterwards mayors of Manchester; Edward
Holme, M.D., F.R.S., vice-president, and after John
Dalton's death, president, of the Literary and Philosophical
Society, of whom there is a portrait in the lecture room of
the society ; John Edward Taylor, proprietor and editor of
the *Manchester Guardian*, whose house was in the Crescent,
Salford ; John Touchet, merchant, of Chancery Lane, whose
house was at No. 29, King Street, and afterwards of Broom
House ; James Darbyshire, John Hall, Scholes Birch
Henry Marsland, cotton spinner, Marriott's Court ; Samuel
Marsland, of Nelson Street, Chorlton Row ; Samuel Kay,
solicitor, of the Adelphi, Salford ; Thomas Robinson, whose
house was · in Bond Street ; Samuel Alcock, executor of

John Owens, founder of Owens College; William, afterwards Sir William Fairbairn; and John Shuttleworth, who
was at that time a cotton and twist dealer, and agent to
W. G. and J. Strutt, of Derby, his warehouse being in
Newmarket Buildings, and his house in Oxford Road. He
afterwards was appointed stamp distributor for this district,
and on the incorporation of Manchester became an alderman.   Fifty or sixty years ago John Shuttleworth and
Absolom Watkin were perhaps the most effective speakers
in Manchester, Watkin being the more refined and
Shuttleworth being possessed of more power and energy.
It used to be said that as he was wont to give utterance to
very radical sentiments, the Government appointed him to
the office of distributor of stamps for this district to induce
him to keep his mouth shut.   He had a brother who at a
later date was a dissenting minister, and who was also a
very effective speaker during the Anti-Corn-Law agitation.
Few strangers who look at the plain uninviting edifice at
the corner of Chapel Walks, would imagine what a handsome interior it possesses.   There is still a very distinguished congregation to be found worshipping there.
The organ is a very fine instrument, presented as a memo-
rial of two highly respected gentlemen—Mr. John Carver
and Mr. James Darbishire. The accomplished amateur
organist who now presides at it is the son-in-law of one of
these gentlemen, and son of the other.   In addition to
several other tablets is one attached to a pillar in memory
of Sir William Fairbairn, D.C.L. and F.R.S., and another
on the east wall in memory of Samuel Jones, the banker,
and his wife, the uncle and aunt of Lord Overstone.

Mosley Street Unitarian Chapel stood at the corner of Marble Street, on the site now occupied by the establishment of Mr. H. J. Nicoll, and was built in 1789. The first minister was the Rev. William Hawkes, who died in 1820, after a ministry of thirty-one years, and was succeeded by the Rev. John James Tayler, B.A., who was the minister in 1829. A liturgy accommodated to the doctrines of Unitarianism was at that time used on the Sunday forenoon. This congregation was also wealthy and influential, and devotedly attached to their accomplished young minister. The following gentlemen were members of it about 50 years ago : George William Wood, M.P. for the county, and then for Kendal ; Edmund Potter, afterwards M.P. for Carlisle ; Robert Hyde Greg, afterwards M.P. for Manchester ; William Duckworth ; Dr. Henry, F.R.S. ; Peter Ewart, cotton spinner, whose house was in Cavendish Street, Chorlton Row, both he and Dr. Henry being vice-presidents of the Literary and Philosophical Society ; George Humphreys, solicitor, whose house was in Oxford Road ; Leo Schuster, who lived in Mosley Street ; John Kennedy, of Ardwick House ; Henry M'Connell, Leopold Reiss, Dr. Ashton, of Mosley Street ; Henry Houldsworth, cotton spinner, his house being at Ardwick Green ; and Edward Baxter, manufacturer, who lived in Mosley Street. The chapel was very plain, but, like other square places of worship of the last century, well adapted for seeing and hearing. The chapel and schoolhouse were sold for £10,000 to Mr. John M'Connell about 1834, and the handsome chapel by Barry, in Upper Brook Street, built for the congregation. Mr. Tayler remained the minister for a long period, in spite of many inducements to remove, but eventually went to London in 1854 to undertake the duties of Principal of the Manchester New College.

DAWSON'S CROFT CHAPEL, Greengate. This plain and unpretending place of worship, situated on the right soon after entering Greengate, was opened on Christmas Day, 1824. In 1829 the Rev. John Relly Beard was its pastor, and remained so for upwards of thirty years. He was born at Portsmouth, and came from the Manchester New College at York. He was a man of great industry and considerable learning, and received the degree of D.D. from a German University on account of his theological acquirements. The new chapel in New Bridge Street, Strangeways, was built in 1838, whither the congregation removed. Mr. Charles Sydney Grundy, the ex-mayor, has been a member of it for many years, both in the old and new chapels. Dr. Beard's successor was an intelligent, kind, and fine-spirited gentleman, Mr. Brooke Herford, whose removal from Manchester those who knew him best will mourn the most. I have a very pleasant remembrance of a friendly chat I once had with him in reference to a sermon on Inspiration which I heard him preach. It is remarkable that each of the four Unitarian ministers named undertook his charge here immediately on the completion of his course of study at the Manchester New College, and retained it at least twenty-five years. Mr. Robberds' connection with Cross Street Chapel ended only with his life in 1854; Mr. Tayler's pastorate of Mosley Street lasted more than thirty years; Dr. Beard ministered to the same people more than thirty years; and Mr. Gaskell still lives the highly-valued minister of the same congregation after fifty years of active service. This absence of change in the Unitarian pulpits speaks well for both ministers and people, and is certainly in remarkable contrast with general usage.

THE SUBURBAN UNITARIAN CHAPELS which existed fifty years ago are those of Platt, Gorton, Dob Lane, Blackley, Monton, and Stand. They may be called extra-parochial, being outside the boundaries of the borough, but are old enough and near enough to claim our notice. The particulars are mainly furnished by Mr. F. W. Holland, of Hyde Road.

PLATT CHAPEL, RUSHOLME.—In 1829 the Rev. William Whitelegg was the minister of this chapel, his house being in Chatham Street, Greenheys. He commenced his ministry there in 1810, and remained till his death in 1865, so that he was the minister of this chapel for fifty-five years, affording another proof how little given to change in their ministers the Unitarians are. Mr. Whitelegg at the same time held the office of secretary and librarian to the Portico Library and Newsroom in Mosley Street. This little chapel had an aristocratic appearance, looking like an appendage to Platt Hall, the residence of the Worsley family. In the rear used to be a sort of transept, fitted up with fireplace and dignified looking chairs, forming a grand pew for the great people at the hall at the time they attended this place of worship. The chapel had been built by a Mr. Worsley on the site of an older one erected at a cost of £95, in the year 1690, for Mr. Finch, who had been turned out of Birch, a domestic chapel near the place. Finch died in 1704 and was succeeded by Robert Hesketh. After him the Revs. Messrs. Whittaker, Haughton, Meanley, and Checkley occupied the pulpit previous to Mr. Whitelegg. There was a private walk from the hall to the chapel, where it was said the Mrs. Worsley of the day could gather a hundred varieties of roses on her way. Platt Chapel fifty years ago was but a dreary place, but has been greatly altered and improved. It is now well attended by a respectable congregation.

GORTON CHAPEL.—In 1829 the Rev. C. D. Hort was the minister of this place, many of his principal hearers being members of the Grimshaw family. The building was one of the many old-fashioned dissenting chapels which then existed, being about 150 years old, and stood in a large graveyard. It is now replaced by the magnificent Brookfield Chapel, which was built at the sole expense of Mr. Richard Peacock, of Gorton Hall.

DOB LANE CHAPEL, FAILSWORTH.—This old place of worship, like the one at Gorton, has recently disappeared, and in its place a spacious modern chapel has been recently erected. It forms a little exception to the remark made on a previous page, and at the time of which we are speaking changed its ministers pretty often. About fifty-two years ago Mr. George Buckland was the minister, and in about two years he was succeeded by Mr. Joseph Ashton, whose successor in two years more was Mr. James Taylor. The latter gentleman was a member of an old Manchester family, related to the Heywoods, the Percivals, and others of high respectability. One of the earlier ministers of this chapel was the Rev. Lewis Loyd, the father of Lord Overstone and brother-in-law of Samuel Jones, the banker, referred to in the account of Cross Street Chapel. Mr. Grindon, in his interesting book on " Manchester Banks and Bankers," tells us that one of the sixty-seven Lancashire ministers ejected from their livings under the Act of Uniformity was the vicar of Newton, and he it was who established the original Dob Lane congregation, though the old chapel itself was not erected till about 1698. The ancestors of several Manchester families now in high position were once members of the congregation—the Bayleys, for instance, one of whom became the wife of Mr. (afterwards Sir Thomas) Potter.

BLACKLEY CHAPEL.—The minister of this place was also one of the ejected, for whom the seceders built this chapel in 1662, described as long since draped with ivy, in a neighbourhood once famed for its thrushes. The pulpit of this quiet little chapel, now occupied by the Rev. J. Freeston, was occupied fifty years ago by the Rev. William Harrison. He was the son of Ralph Harrison, referred to already as the colleague of Dr. Barnes at Cross Street. Mr. Harrison's family were eminent for their musical talents, Ralph being the composer of " Warrington," and many other admirable hymn-tunes. William Harrison was the minister of this chapel for a very long period. Like that at Platt, it is now in excellent order, and is too small for its congregation.

MONTON CHAPEL, near Eccles, standing on an open green, with a spacious burial ground, and backed by beautiful trees, was a pleasing sight. The old chapel has been replaced by the splendid Gothic one which stands nearly on the same site. Mr. Silas Leigh, a young man in 1829, recently deceased, is said to have contributed more than £13,000 towards its erection ; and he and his sisters built, at their sole expense, the excellent school buildings adjoining. Monton Chapel had a very isolated position with respect to other places of worship, there being none nearer than Eccles or Swinton in one direction, and in a westerly one none nearer than perhaps eight or ten miles.

STAND CHAPEL in 1829 was under the charge of an estimable young minister, the Rev. Arthur Dean, who had also charge of the endowed school in the village. I believe he did not live long after this period, and has been succeeded by the Revs. John Cropper, P. P. Carpenter, and others. Mr. Robert Philips, father of Mark Philips, once M.P. for Manchester, formerly lived in King Street, and after his removal attended this chapel with his daughters. Both Mark Philips and his brother R. N. Philips, M.P. for Bury, when residing at the Park, Prestwich, were members of the congregation. Stand Chapel, like Monton, was for a century or more the only place of worship in the neighbourhood, All Saints' Church, Stand, having been built in 1826.

CHAPTER XIV.

PLACES OF WORSHIP.—VARIOUS.

GEORGE FOX, the founder of the Society of Friends, visited Manchester in the year 1647, when quite a young man. There was no meeting of Friends established in Manchester, however, for eight or ten years after, and where the meeting was first held is not certain. It was probably not far from Jackson's Row, for it is known that many members of the Society used to live in former days in Cupid's Alley and the neighbourhood. Certain it is that three of their number became the owners of a piece of land at the corner of Deansgate and Jackson's Row, in 1673, where twenty years later, the first meeting-house of which anything is known was erected. It appears that the land was originally purchased for a burial-ground, the first known interment in which took place in 1675, and the last in 1847. The land being required by the Corporation for the improvement of Deansgate, in 1877 the remains of the Friends who had been there buried were, in the most reverential way possible, removed from thence to the Friends' Cemetery at Ashton-upon-Mersey. The burial ground in Jackson's Row was the oldest in Manchester, excepting the one surrounding the Cathedral.

The chapel erected in 1693 in the course of time became too small, and in 1732 a larger one was built on the same site. This remained till 1795, when the meeting was removed to a new building erected on the site of the present meeting-house in Mount Street, but which fronted the street which now runs at the back of the chapel, and known as South Street. This again becoming too small, a fourth meeting-house was erected about 1829 or 1830, designed by Richard Lane, the architect. It fronted Mount Street, and still remains. Mr. Lane wisely built the meeting-house much too large for present requirements, and made arrangements for throwing a partition across when a smaller space is required, as in the case of ordinary religious meetings, leaving a second room at liberty for other purposes. During the building of it the Friends worshipped in a room in Dickinson Street, known as the Diorama.

My earliest recollections of the Friends' meeting-house are connected with the great Anti-Slavery agitation. The part which the members of the Society took in that agitation will always be one of their titles to honourable recognition and remembrance. It is true that John Wesley denounced slavery in the last century as well as many other philanthropists, but no religious body came to the front so early as the Quakers. They kept that position till the £20,000,000 was voted for the emancipation of every slave in the British dominions. When others slumbered they were up and doing; when the flame of zeal was dull they fanned it; and they were the most active members as well as the most liberal supporters of the

Anti-Slavery Society. That society was most fortunate in securing the services, as their advocate, of one of the most accomplished orators of the day, Mr. George Thompson. Whenever he visited Manchester the Friends' Meeting-house was always thrown open to receive the audience which his eloquence attracted. His denunciation of slavery was most withering, and his protest against the practice of buying and selling human beings was over-whelming. I never missed an opportunity of hearing him. This was before the Free Trade Hall was built; neither was there then any other room in Manchester, except the Corn Exchange, so convenient for the purpose. I well remember the pleasurable impression made on my first visit to the place, and how I enjoyed listening to Mr. Thompson's fervent but polished oratory. The scene of certain "potent, grave, and reverend seigniors," sitting in a long row behind the lecturer, and the crowded chapel, the audience being sometimes moved to tears and some-times to laughter, are present to the eyes of my mind now, whilst the tones of the lecturer's voice seem to be sounded in my ears. I believe Mr. Thompson came from Yorkshire, and was originally a Wesleyan local preacher. He was elected M.P. for the Tower Hamlets, and even-tually went to America, where he was once or twice mobbed by the slavery party. He died about two years ago. His daughter married Mr. Frederick Nosworthy, now of Liverpool.

I am indebted to the kindness of Mr. Alderman King for the following list of families who attended the Friends' Meeting-house about fifty years ago : Thomas Edmondson,

inventor of the railway ticket system; Dr. Dalton and his
friend Peter Clare; Isaac Crewdson, of Ardwick Green;
Joseph Crewdson, of Crewdson and Worthington; Thomas
Crewdson, the banker; and Wilson Crewdson, of Dacca
Mills—four brothers; Thomas Hoyle, of Mayfield, and his
three sons-in-law—William Neild (afterwards Alderman and
Mayor), Joseph Crompton and Alfred Binyon, all of the
firm of Thomas Hoyle and Sons; Thomas and Edward
Binyon, of St. Ann's Square, with George Robinson, after-
wards their partner; Samuel Eveleigh, hat manufacturer, of
Openshaw; Joseph Eveleigh, furrier and hat manufacturer,
of Oldham Street, afterwards a sharebroker, and a botanist
of some position in his day; Samuel Satterthwaite, furrier,
at one time in the Town Council; Thomas D. Crewdson,
Alderman, and nephew of the Crewdsons named previously;
James Hall and James Hall, jun., dyers, Salford;
Ishmael Nash, tea dealer and money changer, of Smithy
Door and Charles Street; Isaac Stephenson, sen. and jun.,
corn factors; John King, father of the present Alderman
King, St. Ann's Square; David Dockray, Rusholme Road,
formerly in the Manchester trade; George Danson,
chemist, Piccadilly; J. H. Cockbain, silk mercer, Picca-
dilly; William G. Ansell, chemist, St. Mary's Gate;
Joseph, John, and Joseph Rooke, jun., manufacturers of
iron liquor, Scotland Bridge; John Raleigh, Oldham Street,
and Joseph his son, fustian manufacturers; George
Bradshaw, originator of *Bradshaw's Railway Guide;*
John A. and Joseph A. Ransome, surgeons; John Fernely,
M.D.; William Boulton, merchant; Benjamin Pearson,
blanket manufacturer; John Windsor, F.R.S., surgeon;

John Rothwell, dyer, Water Street; William White, surgeon, St. John's Street; John B. Brockbank, builder; John Robinson, accountant; John Wadkin, sen. and jun., the latter a smallware manufacturer; Henry Wadkin, sewing cotton manufacturer, at one time in the Town Council; Nathaniel Card, one of the originators, if not the originator, of the United Kingdom Alliance; Matthew Corbett, builder, Pendleton; Peter Taylor, cotton merchant, Back Square; Michael Satterthwaite, bootmaker, Salford; John Robinson, draper, Oldham Street; David Holt, cotton manufacturer (referred to previously); Joseph Flintoff; John Goodier, calenderer, Poolfold; William and Jonathan Labrey, tea dealers; William Fowden, merchant; John Harrison, printer, Market Street, and his partner Joseph Crosfield, the latter being afterwards at the District Bank; Godfrey Woodhead, Smithy Door (who died at Huddersfield, at the age of seventy-two, a little while ago); Josiah Merrick, merchant, and his son Roger; Robert Barker, confectioner, Smithy Door; Charles Cumber, for many years master of the Friends' School, Mount Street; Alexander Morris, draper, Smithy Door; John Collinson and George Simpson, brewers, Newton Heath; Isaac Nield, fustian manufacturer; James Nodal, schoolmaster, Camp Street, and his sons Aaron and John Nodal, Aaron being subsequently one of the first three councillors elected for Ardwick Ward, and an active member of the Anti-Corn-Law League; John Thistlethwaite, confectioner, Oldham Street; Henry Nield, confectioner, Deansgate and Bridge Street; James Thompson, cotton spinner; Henry Waterhouse (still living), father of Mr. Crewdson Waterhouse;

Edward Corbett, surveyor, son of Matthew Corbett already mentioned; John Storey, grocer, Gartside Street; John Bradshaw, watch and clock maker, Deansgate; William Johnson, surveyor; John Worthington, of Crewdson and Worthington; Thomas Atkinson; Benjamin Binyon and his partner, Peter Taylor, of Hollinwood, twine manufacturers; and Deborah, Hannah, and Ann Binyon, sisters of the Messrs. Binyon.

A secession in the body took place in 1837, in the December of which year the so-called Evangelical Friends' Meeting-house was opened in Grosvenor Street, Chorlton-on-Medlock (now used as a Baptist chapel). The leader in the secession was Mr. Isaac Crewdson, who held views on some points at variance with the general body of the Friends. He was followed by several members of eminence in the town; and the controversy and secession eventually led to the families of the Neilds, the Windsors, the Ransomes, the Simpsons, and many others leaving the Society altogether.

After the building in Jackson's Row ceased to be a place of worship it was used by the Friends as a school, which was at the beginning of the present century presided over by Mr. John Taylor, the father of Mr. John Edward Taylor, the founder and former editor of the *Manchester Guardian.* Until recently the Friends' Meeting-house in Mount Street was the only one in the district, but owing to so many of the members now residing in the suburbs, two smaller meeting-houses have been built of recent years, one at Sale and one at Eccles.

BAPTIST CHAPELS.—Of these, in 1829 there were three in Manchester—one in St. George's Road, one in York Street, and one in George Street. There had been one in Fleet Street, but it had then ceased to exist. The first minister of York Street Chapel, which was built in 1807, was the Rev. W. Stephens; and he was succeeded by the Rev. John Birt, who was the minister in 1829. The chapel held its own for many years against the advancing tide of business requirements, but a few years ago it succumbed, and has now disappeared, a handsome structure having been built in Moss Side West with part of the purchase money. The George Street Chapel was built more recently, and has also ceased to exist many years ago. In 1829 its minister was the Rev. Thomas Upcraft, who was succeeded shortly after by the Rev. John Aldis. The chapel stood on the same side of the street as the Literary and Philosophical Society's rooms, nearer to Piccadilly.

GADSBY'S CHAPEL.—At the time we are speaking of the Rev. William Gadsby, or as he was familiarly called, Billy Gadsby, was at the height of his popularity. His chapel was at the left-hand side of St. George's Road, going from Shudehill. It was built in 1789, and Mr. Gadsby began his ministry at it 1806, when about thirty-three years of age. I find his name in Pigot's Directory for 1811, entered as "minister of Anabaptist Chapel, St. George's Road." In 1815 he was living at 175, Oldham Road; in 1820 at Lees Place, Ardwick; in 1824 at 20, Great Ducie Street; and in 1829 at Cheetham Crescent, Cheetham Hill. I remember something of his appearance, which was not clerical according to the notions of the present day.

He was rather over the average height, wore knee breeches—frequently both they and his stockings being coloured—and an unstiffened white neckerchief tied in a bow. His face had a somewhat quaint and humorous expression, and his countenance was rather florid. The valley of Rossendale fifty years ago contained several Baptist chapels, and when my father lived at Bacup, Mr. Gadsby frequently preached in one or other of these chapels. He was very popular in the district. On these occasions he used to let fly his envenomed arrows at the Arminian doctrines of Methodism, which are so much opposed to the Calvinism he preached. I do not care to repeat the sayings which it was currently reported he had uttered, some of them both coarse and bitter beyond belief. Every Tuesday evening he preached in his own chapel, when the congregation consisted generally of the members of his church. On these occasions he laid aside all controversy and the style which he adopted sometimes when in the presence of a mixed congregation, and talked to his flock as a father to his family. The only time of my hearing him was on such an occasion, when his discourse was a beautiful 'and experimental exposition of divine truth. He died in 1844, having been the minister of the chapel thirty-eight years.

LLOYD STREET PRESBYTERIAN CHAPEL.—Fifty years ago this was the only Presbyterian place of worship in Manchester. Its ministers were the Rev. Dr. Jack and his assistant, the Rev. William (afterwards Dr.) M'Kerrow, then a young man, Dr. Jack living in Lloyd Street and Mr. M'Kerrow in Oxford Road. I was in the chapel once, having been dining one Sunday with a Scotch friend in

Oxford Road, when I went with him in the afternoon and heard Mr. M'Kerrow preach. The chapel was of the usual type of the chapels built in the last century, and stood at the corner of Lloyd Street and Mount Street. The Scotch Kirk in St. Peter's Square was built shortly after this, and has been since removed to Bloomsbury. I remember Dr. Chalmers preaching at the old Mechanics' Institution in Cooper Street, and making a collection for the new chapel in St. Peter's Square. The old chapel in Lloyd Street has been pulled down some years, and in its place a handsome structure has been erected in Brunswick Street, Chorlton-on-Medlock, where Mr. M'Kerrow ministered many years. He has so lately passed away, and was so deservedly and universally respected, that it is needless to make further reference to him.

ROMAN CATHOLIC CHAPELS.—In 1829 there were three Roman Catholic chapels in Manchester—one in Granby Row, at which the Revs. James Crook and John Parsons officiated; one in Rook Street, behind Mosley Street, at which the Revs. Joseph Sherwood and Thomas Maddocks officiated; and one in Mulberry Street, Deansgate, at which the Revs. Henry Gillow, Daniel Hearne, and John Billington officiated. The eldest of these chapels was the Rook Street one, which was erected rather more than a hundred years ago, and was enlarged in 1832, but which is now numbered amongst the things which have passed away, the site being covered with warehouse property. Who the first minister was I do not know; but in 1780 the Rev. Rowland Broomhead was appointed to it, where he remained without a colleague forty years,

and died in 1820, aged seventy years, being buried at
St. Augustine's, Granby Row. The next Roman Catholic
chapel erected was the one in Mulberry Street, which was
opened in 1794. In 1811 the Rev. Edward Kenyon was
the minister of this chapel, and for some years after ; in
1820 the Revs. Thomas Lupton and Joseph Carr officiated;
and in 1824 the Revs. Henry Gillow and Michael Trapps.
This chapel is still in existence, and it has three ministers
attached to it. Granby Row Chapel was opened in 1820,
the building (of which John Palmer was architect) costing
£10,000. The first ministers were the Revs. John Ashurst,
Joseph Sherwood, and Thomas Rigby. Forty or fifty years
ago high-class sacred music was not as accessible as now,
and when an Italian opera company visited Manchester it
was customary for the members of it to sing at the Roman
Catholic chapels on Sunday, and for a charge to be made
for admittance. I remember going to Granby Row Chapel
one Sunday evening, when quite a young man, with a
friend, and paying half-a-crown for admittance to hear an
Italian named, I think, Donzetti, sing. At the time of what
is known as the "potato famine," which preceded the
abolition of the Corn Laws, there was great distress
amongst the poor, particularly in the St. George's and
Oldham Road Districts. The Rev. Daniel Hearne was
then located at the chapel in Livesey Street, Oldham Road;
and in the same street lived the Rev. John Smith, a
Wesleyan minister. These two men set a noble example
by uniting themselves together in the work of Christian
charity by house-to-house visitation and the distribution of
relief without distinction of sect or creed.

THE JEWISH SYNAGOGUE, fifty years ago, was situated in Halliwell Street, Long Millgate, nearly opposite the shabby footbridge at present leading to the Victoria Railway Station. At the end of the last century the number of Jews in Manchester was very small indeed, and their synagogue was a little upper room situated in Garden Street, Withy Grove, which remained till about the year 1810. At this time amongst the worshippers there was the great Rothschild, then an unknown young man, about twenty-five years of age. He had established himself in Manchester as a merchant in the last years of last century, his warehouse being first in Brown Street, and his house in Downing Street, Ardwick. In Pigot's Directory for 1811 his firm appears as " Rothschild Brothers, merchants, 5, Lloyd Street ; " but in that for 1815 the name is wanting, the presumption being that he had left Manchester previously. About the year 1810 the upper room used as a synagogue was abandoned for a small building in Ainsworth's Court, Long Millgate, opposite what was so long known as the " Poet's Corner," and approached by a flight of wooden steps. The reader at this synagogue was Israel Lewis. After the battle of Waterloo and the proclamation of peace, there was a great influx of Germans and others into Manchester from the Continent, amongst whom was Mr. Emanuel Mendel, the father of Mr. Sam Mendel. Many of these immigrants were Jews, who of course increased the size of the Jewish congregation very much, so that it became necessary to provide larger premises. Accordingly, in 1825 the Synagogue in Halliwell Street was opened, having for its rabbi the Rev. Abraham

Abrahams. Fifty years ago it was a respectable looking place, externally very much resembling many other places of worship at that time existing: I once ventured to peep inside during divine worship and remained for a short time, during which I received the most polite attention from a gentleman near me.

CHRIST CHURCH, KING STREET, SALFORD.—Fifty years ago the late Mr. Joseph Brotherton was the minister of this chapel, his house being at that time in Oldfield Road, eight doors from the Oldfield Road doctor. Amongst Swedenborg's earliest disciples were the Rev. John Clowes, rector of St. John's (before referred to), and his curate, the Rev. William Cowherd. The former, as is well known, never left the Church of England, but the latter decided to cast in his lot with the followers of Swedenborg in forming a new church. Cowherd laid the foundation of the New Jerusalem Church in Yates Street (now called Peter Street) in 1792. After preaching there some time differences arose amongst his congregation as to forms of church government and other matters, and in 1800 he built, at his own expense, the above-mentioned chapel, the roof of which fell in in less than five years. He was a man of considerable powers as a preacher, of scholarly habits, and extensive reading. He demanded, as a condition of membership, abstinence from flesh meat and intoxicating beverages, but many of his adherents did not accept this part of his creed. The nickname of " Beefsteak Chapel " was frequently applied to the chapel in former days. In connection with it Cowherd had a large and commodious school, capable of accommodating one hundred boarders. He died in 1816, aged fifty-seven, and on his tombstone was inscribed at his own request the words, "All feared, none loved, few understood." Joseph Brotherton, who was originally a cotton spinner and manufacturer, though the recognised minister of this chapel, never assumed the title of Rev., and in one of the two directories of the period of which we are speaking he is styled "gentleman." For twenty years he represented Salford in Parliament, and was ever an active and earnest worker in the accomplishment of the various social reforms which marked the first half of the present century. In 1868 the old chapel in King Street was relinquished, and in its place a new one was opened in Cross Lane, Salford, of which the present minister is the Rev. James Clarke.

There were two other places of worship in Manchester in 1829 also called Christ Church—one in Christ Church Square, Hulme, near the Cavalry Barracks; and the other in Every Street, Ancoats. The earliest of the two chapels was the one in Hulme, at which in 1815 the Rev. J. Clarke was minister. He was succeeded by the Rev J. Schofield, or, as his name was sometimes spelt, Scholefield, who was the minister in 1820. After him the Rev. T. B. Strettels was appointed; and after him the Rev. J. Gaskell, who became its minister about the time we are speaking of. Mr. Gaskell retained the post many years, and became one of the guardians of the Chorlton Union. On the building of Every Street Chapel, somewhere about 1823, Mr. Schofield was appointed its minister. He became a popular quack doctor and a notorious Chartist, being a great friend of Henry Hunt, to whom a monument is erected in the burial ground connected with the chapel. Reference has been made to him previously.

Although Cowherd, the founder of Christ Church, had embraced the doctrines of Swedenborg, the three chapels just named have not been regarded as strictly Swedenborgian. The members of that body designate their chapels "New Jerusalem Chapels," of which there were two in 1829—one in Peter Street, opened in 1793; and one in Bolton Street, Salford, opened in 1813—which remain without addition to the present day. If one may judge from this, no increase has taken place in the body during that time. In 1802 the Rev. R. Jones became the minister of Peter Street Chapel, and remained so till his death, in 1832. I was once in the chapel, and heard the Rev. J. H. Smithson preach on the resurrection of the body. I was also once in Bolton Street Chapel, having been attracted by the announcement of the subject of the discourse. Over the door was the inscription *Nunc licet*, words which Swedenborg said he saw written over a gate in the spiritual world, signifying that now it was allowable to enter into the mysteries of faith. As Mr. Hindmarsh, a former minister of this chapel, and Cowherd differed on the subject of vegetarian practice, the inscription was said to mean that it is allowable to eat flesh meat. Hence, the term "Beefsteak Chapel," which was sometimes jocularly applied to the old King Street Chapel, was a sarcastic nickname originally given to the Bolton Street one. The minister in 1829 was the Rev. D. Howarth, who succeeded the Rev. R. Hindmarsh.

CHAPTER XV.

LAWYERS AND MAGISTRATES.

THERE were in 1829 five barristers who had offices in Manchester, viz., Mr. Robert Brandt, whose house was at Pendleton; Mr. John Frederick Foster, the police magistrate, his house being in Mosley Street; Mr. Edward Jeremiah Lloyd, whose rooms were in King Street; Mr. James Norris, chairman of the Quarter Sessions, his rooms being in St. James's Square; and Mr. John Walker, who resided in the Crescent, Salford. Mr. George Condy, who it will be remembered, became a friend of Horatio Miller's, came to Manchester about a year afterwards. He became editor and joint proprietor of the *Manchester and Salford Advertiser,* and a Commissioner in Bankruptcy. It was said of him at the time of his death that he was an accomplished scholar; that there was hardly a branch of literature or art which he did not appear to have studied; and that, as a critic of music, painting, or drama, he had few equals.

One firm of solicitors in business in 1829 was Eccles, Cririe, and Slater, to whom the late Mr. Stephen Heelis was articled. In 1810 the firm was Sharpe, Eccles, and Cririe, in King Street. They then removed to Red Cross

Street, now known as Cross Street; and about 1822 Mr. Sharpe retired and Mr. Slater was received as a partner. Mr. Edward Bent was then in practice in King Street. Thomas and Joseph Nadin were also in practice in offices adjoining the Queen's Theatre. They were sons of Joe Nadin, the former deputy constable, and were the chief shareholders in the theatre.

The principal town's business was conducted by the firm of Sergeant, Milne, and Sergeant, in St. James's Square, Mr. Oswald Milne being clerk of the magistrates acting for the division of Manchester, and sitting at the New Bailey. John Frederick Foster was the stipendiary, but was designated the "police magistrate," and was assisted by six other magistrates, viz., Mr. James Brierley, of Ardwick; Mr. R. Fielden, of Didsbury; Mr. Ralph Wright, of Flixton; the Rev. C. W. Ethelstone, of Smedley; Mr. John Greaves, of Pendlebury; and Mr. Isaac Blackburne, the distributor of stamps in Brown Street. Mr. Wright was the same gentleman of whom it was said that having engaged a coachman, with whom he had agreed that he should be allowed to take vegetables out of the garden, he found him once taking home some potatoes, and had him apprehended, contending that they were not vegetables. The son of William Sergeant was named Oswald, and entered the Church, in 1829 possessing the curacy of St. Philip's, Salford. He was afterwards transferred to be one of the Fellows at the Old Church. Mr. Oswald Milne's brother John at that time was coroner for the hundred of Salford. William Smalley Rutter, who became coroner at the death of Mr. John Milne, was previously employed as clerk to

Oswald Milne, at the New Bailey. Mr. Alfred Milne, who was the late chairman of the Quarter Sessions, was the son of Oswald Milne.

Our venerable and respected fellow-townsman Mr. James Crossley, shortly before the time we are speaking of, became a member of the firm of Ainsworth, Crossley, and Sudlow, in Essex Street, his house being in Cheetwood. Mr. John P. Aston, of this city, served the latter part of his time to Mr. Crossley, whilst his brother Mr. Edward Aston served his time with Mr. James Barrett. The first time I saw Mr. James Crossley, was at a meeting called one forenoon at eleven o'clock in the large room behind the York Hotel, next to the Town Hall, in King Street. The object of the meeting was to organize an opposition to the incorporation of the town, and Mr. Crossley being called upon to speak, said that you might as well on meeting a strong, robust-looking individual in the street lay your hand on his shoulder, look him in the face, and say, " My good fellow, you look very ill ; let me advise you to send for your doctor," as talk of incorporating the town.

Mr. James Chapman, the first borough coroner, was then practising as a solicitor in Fountain Street, having been in practice for ten or twelve years. For some time we had two coroners and two inquests for the borough, Mr. Chapman holding one in virtue of his appointment under the Corporation, and Mr. Rutter holding a second under his appointment as coroner for the county, in the belief that Mr. Chapman's appointment was illegal. On one occasion Mr. Chapman summoned Mr. Rutter before the magistrates on a charge of assault in connection with an inquest, the latter being held to bail to answer the charge at the sessions. The year following the validity of the charter of incorporation was confirmed by the judges.

Mr. George Hadfield, the solicitor, afterwards M.P. for Sheffield, was in partnership with Mr. Grave, the firm being Hadfield and Grave, their office being next door but one to Mr. Chapman's, in Fountain Street. Mr. Hadfield began practice prior to 1815. Mr. Alexander Kay, afterwards Mayor of Manchester, was then in practice as a solicitor in Brown Street, having had his office previously in Exchange Street. He resided with his father, Alexander Kay, a cotton merchant in St. John Street, where he had resided since he began practice about the year 1813.

Mr. John Makinson, the father of the present Salford stipendiary, had his office then in Brown Street, but in 1830 removed to Market Street near to the end of Pall Mall, where he remained many years. He married the daughter of the Rev. Jonathan Crowther, one of Wesley's later coadjutors. Mr. Crowther's eldest son was connected with the press, and became reporting agent for the *Times* for Birmingham and the district. He was the brother of Mr. Joshua Crowther, the accountant, and died many years ago. During my apprenticeship I became acquainted with James Johnson, an articled pupil of Mr. Makinson's, our acquaintance ripening into close friendship. He was the son of Mr. John Johnson, of the firm of Johnson and Sharrocks, wire drawers, of Dale Street, and brother of Mr. Richard Johnson, of the firm of Johnson, Clapham, and Morris, who still carry on the same business in connection with the same premises.

My friend married a daughter of Mr. Angus of London, a large landed proprietor in Australia before the discovery of goldfields there. After he had married his health began to fail, and being advised to leave England and settle in Australia, he set sail with his wife and two children, died on the passage when off the Cape of Good Hope, and was buried in the great blue sea.

Mr. Thomas Potter then had his office in Princess Street, and had for an articled pupil a little before this time Percival Bunting, son of the celebrated Rev. Dr. Bunting. Afterwards he had for an articled pupil the son of one and grandson of another celebrated Wesleyan minister, Bateson Wood, whose grandfather, the Rev. James Wood, was another of Wesley's coadjutors, and filled the office of President of the Conference in the year 1800, and again in 1808. The Rev. Robert Wood, the son of the latter, and father of Mr. Bateson Wood, was a very popular minister amongst the Wesleyans, and was stationed in Manchester several times, the last occasion being in the Grosvenor Street circuit in the years 1835 to 1837. Professor Williamson married his daughter. Mr. Potter began practice in Clarence Street, Princess Street, about 1817, and afterwards removed to the same premises in Princess Street which he had in 1829, and which are still occupied by Mr. Wood, who before Mr. Potter's death became his partner. In the list which I gave of some of Horatio Miller's friends, I omitted the name of Charles Wood, the solicitor, Brazenose Street. He began practice at the commencement of the century in Hulme Street, but soon removed to the former street. During my apprenticeship his daughter Rose recovered £3,500 from a gentleman in London for breach of promise of marriage.

There was one gentleman in practice fifty years ago who was in practice in the last century, namely, Mr. John Owen, who was originally in King Street, but after a while removed to Gartside Street. The following, who were also in business fifty years ago, were so at the beginning of the century :—Higson, Bagshaw, and Higson, of King Street; Henry Cardwell; Cooke and Beever, Mr. Cooke's father being in Greengate as a solicitor in the last century; Robert Ellis Cunliffe, whose house was at first in Princess Street; and John Thomson. Other principal attorneys were Atkinson and Birch, of Norfolk Street; Kay and Darbyshire, Marsden Street; and Aldcroft Phillips, of King Street.

In addition to the names of those attorneys who were in business in 1829, and who had been so at the beginning of the century, I must mention that of Duckworth, Denison, and Humphreys. In 1794 Mr. George Duckworth was in practice at 38, Princess Street; and in 1810, at the same address, was the firm of Duckworth, Chippindall, and Denison; whilst in 1829, at 38, Princess Street, was the firm of Duckworth, Denison, and Humphreys. There was a Jeremiah Buckley in practice in Brown Street in 1829, who was so at the beginning of this century. Mr. William C. Chew was practising in Swan Street fifty years ago, whilst the firm of W. C. Chew and Son are still there.

I must not forget the celebrated Jack Law, who, fifty years ago, was in partnership with Richard Coates in Piccadilly. He had a large practice in the police courts,

and possessed those qualifications which best enabled him
to cross-examine a witness with effect. I once heard him
cross-examine a woman in an affiliation case, and well
remember its terrible severity. I omit repetitions and
flourishes. He produced a letter and inquired who had
written it. "My brother," said the woman. "And it is
just as true that your brother wrote that letter as that
which you have just sworn; the one's as true as the
other?" "Yes." "Now, then, did not a man called
H—— P—— write that letter?" "Yes." Of course the
case was dismissed. John Law was in practice in St. Ann's
Churchyard at the beginning of this century, and had a
brother David, who in 1794 kept the Crown and Thistle in
Half Street. Mr. John Law's opponent was generally
Mr. Edward Foulkes, of the Star Yard, who had been in
practice there since the year 1808. Solicitors do not seem
to have increased in number to the same extent as some
other trades and professions, for whilst fifty years ago there
were 127, I believe there are not more than 280 now.

CHAPTER XVI.

THE POST OFFICE.

THE earliest intimation which we have of the existence of a post office in Manchester is furnished by Mr. J. Owen, who tells us that the *London Gazette* in 1687 gives the name of Edward Holland as the postmaster. In the next century we hear of Thomas Illingworth as filling the office. It has been stated that in 1721 letters were forwarded three times a week to London, and that it then required eight days for an interchange of communication. In 1790 Manchester paid £11,000 in postages, being a larger amount than was paid in any other provincial town, the whole of the business being transacted by Mrs. Willat and two clerks. This lady succeeded her husband, John Willat, on his decease, in 1772, of whom it was said that he was second to none in this part of the kingdom in the knowledge of his profession. Mrs. Willat died in 1801, and is buried with her husband in St. Ann's Churchyard, where their gravestones may be seen. She was succeeded by Mr. James Harrop, printer, bookseller, stamp distributor, medicine vendor, and post-master, at 40, Market Place. In 1804 he resigned the office of postmaster, when the Rev. Richard Hutchins Whitelock was appointed. He resided at Chorlton-cum-Hardy, of which place he was incumbent, being vicar of Skillington, in Lincolnshire, at the same time. He resigned the office of postmaster rather more than fifty years ago, and died in 1833. His successor was Mr. Robert Peel Willcock, a relative of Sir Robert Peel, who on his death was replaced by Mr. John St. Lawrence Beaufort, the present post-master. So that there have been only two appointments made to the office in seventy-five years, viz., from 1805 to 1880.

Fifty years ago the Post Office was a low, shabby-looking building, at the back of the Exchange, on the opposite side of Ducie Place, to which locality it had been removed in 1808. In a short time after this the Exchange was enlarged at the back, when the Post Office was removed into the Exchange, occupying the hinder portion. In 1840 it was removed to Brown Street, where it now stands.

The history of the Post Office will show the progress which the town has made very accurately. We have seen that in 1790, just ninety years ago, the business of the Post Office was conducted by a lady and two clerks. In 1829 it required the aid of the postmaster and eight clerks to manage it. In 1879 no fewer than 244 clerks were employed by the office. In 1829 there were twelve letter-carriers and three country messengers; last year there were 244 letter-carriers and 187 messengers. So that, including 338 telegraphists, the number of persons employed in the Manchester Post Office at the close of 1879 was 1,013. The names of the eight clerks employed in 1829 were Thomas Knowles, chief assistant; Henry Andrews, first clerk and agent for newspapers, and clerk of the roads for the Chester District; Charles Jones, Samuel Brown, William Hayes, Charles Reynolds, Edward Wilson, and John Eldershaw. Of these I knew Andrews, Wilson, and Eldershaw, the latter being a very corpulent man. It was announced that "orders for all the London newspapers, Packet, London Shipping, and Army and Navy Lists are received at the Office and attended to by Mr. Andrews." This was then the principal Agency for supplying London newspapers. Eventually this business was conducted by Mr. Eldershaw, and after a time was given up by the Post Office, when it was continued by Eldershaw on his own account. Edward Wilson was originally the schoolmaster and parish clerk at Chorlton-cum-Hardy in the time of Mr. Whitelock, the incumbent, who, before he gave up the office of postmaster, appointed Wilson one of the clerks. The names of the letter-carriers were Thomas Sumner, James Ellison, Edward Lowe, Thomas Watts, William Hetterly, James Heywood, Matthew Sumner, William Owen, Samuel Davies, John Barnes, George Barnes, and John Buxton. Thomas Sumner was the inspector of the letter-carriers, and delivered letters in the Market Street district. He was a jovial little man, and had a deep and sonorous voice, which qualified him for the post he filled on Sundays as clerk to Mr. Piccope, the incumbent of St. Paul's. The twelve districts then were Market Street, Cannon Street, King Street, Mosley Street, Millgate, St. John's, Knott Mill, Ardwick, Ancoats, St. George's, Windsor, and Salford. The three messengers were despatched to Pendleton and Eccles, Cheetham Hill and

Radcliffe, Longsight and Gorton. There was not a single sub-office in the whole of Manchester and Salford, but there were four receiving-houses—one in Downing Street, one in Ancoats, one at New Windsor, and one at Knott Mill—at which letters were called for twice a day. The office was open every day from eight till ten, except on Sundays, when no letters were delivered from ten to twelve; it then was open till half-past one, and again at the delivery of the Birmingham and London letters about half-past four or five.

This was the day of high postages, when every London letter cost elevenpence at least, and every Liverpool one sevenpence. The rates of postage for single letters were as follows:—

				s.	d.
Not exceeding 15 miles				0	4
Above 15 miles and not exceeding 20				0	5
,,	20	,,	,,	30	0	6
,,	30	,,	,,	50	0	7
,,	50	,,	,,	80	0	8
,,	80	,,	,,	120	0	9
,,	120	,,	,,	170	0	10
,,	170	,,	,,	230	0	11
,,	230	,,	,,	300	1	0

And one penny for every excess of one hundred miles. Letters to and from Scotland were charged an additional halfpenny. These were the rates, as I have said, for single letters, which were to be written on a single sheet of paper, no matter how large, and which must be folded up without the aid of any kind of envelopes, such things being almost unknown at that day. If a letter should contain a loose piece of paper, however small, it was charged double postage, and if treble or quadruple the charge was in proportion. So that every letter as it passed through the office had to be carefully examined, and as many senders of enclosures were adepts at concealment, the letter had frequently to be held up before a lamp for examination. If suspected it was charged double or treble postage, which must be paid before delivery, the burden of proof that it was only single being with the recipient. A notice was put up at the office that overcharges on letters were allowed from ten to four. I was occasionally sent whilst an apprentice with a letter which had been wrongly charged double. The clerk was generally reasonable, who on making himself acquainted with the contents, and on a declaration being made to the effect that the letter was only single, would return the extra charge. It will be seen what an amount of labour was involved in the despatch of letters under the old system, for not only had each letter to be examined for the purpose just stated, but the clerk had to make up his mind what the postage would be, and then mark it with pen and ink in large characters on the direction. This was one of Rowland Hill's arguments in favour of a uniform postage to be paid by means of a stamp—that the cost would be proportionately diminished.

The privilege of franking letters, which belonged to members of the two Houses of Parliament, was very extensively used; in fact in many instances was greatly abused. The franking was done by the member writing his name in one corner of the directions, a practice which is still often adopted, although the privilege is abolished. Invoices in those days were always sent with the goods— in the case of a pack, sewn under the direction; of a hamper, laid on the top of the straw under the lid; and of a cask, nailed under the cardboard direction. Many great and needless delays in the transmission of the mail bags took place. Letters from Manchester or Liverpool passing through London to Dover, Brighton, and other places, were always kept waiting at St. Martin's-le-Grand for fourteen hours.

There were only two deliveries a day, at nine a.m. and five p.m. Only one mail was despatched daily to and from London, leaving Manchester at half-past nine a.m., and the one from London arriving here at four o'clock p.m. There were two mails to and from Birmingham, one to Carlisle, two to York, two to Liverpool, two to Sheffield, and one to Ashton, Blackburn, Bolton, Bury, Chester, Huddersfield, Oldham, and Knutsford. Fifty years ago foreign letters were despatched to France, Spain, Italy, Sardinia, and Turkey, every Sunday, Monday, Tuesday, and Thursday; to Portugal every Monday; to Holland, Guernsey, Switzerland, Prussia, Denmark, Sweden, and Russia every Monday and Thursday; to North America, only once a month viz., on the Tuesday before the first Wednesday in each month; to South America, Maderia, Gibraltar, and the Mediterranean, on the Monday before the first Tuesday in each month. Letters for places abroad to which there were no regular packets—as China, New South Wales, Sierra Leone, and many parts of South America—were forwarded in sealed ship letter-bags by vessels sailing from London and other ports, and were charged 1s. 9½d. for each single letter, which had to be prepaid. To France the postage of a single letter was 1s. 11d. ; to Germany, Russia, Prussia, and Denmark, 2s. 5d. ; to the Mediterranean by the Malta packet, 3s. 3d. ; and to the United States and all British North America, 2s. 3d.

The Penny Postage Act came into operation in 1840. The prejudice which had to be overcome on the part of the Post Office authorities and the legislature before it became law are almost incredible. When the Act came into operation, and before the invention of the penny stamp, a penny envelope was supplied by the Post Office to the public, having a very pretentious device engraved around the direction, designed by William Mulready, R.A. I have one of them now before me, on which Britannia is seated on an eminence with a tame old lion crouching at her feet, and her arms and fingers extended as far as possible, as if she were sending out letters to all the world from her finger ends. Right and left of her are assembled representatives of the various nations of the world—some of them writing letters, well clothed Europeans shaking hands with naked savages, surrounded by specimens out of Wombwell's menagerie of elephants, bears, and other wild animals. The pretentious character of the design caused it to be generally ridiculed, and after a time it became supplanted by the more sensible penny stamp which has continued to the present.

CHAPTER XVII.

THE STAGE-COACHING DAYS.

PERHAPS in nothing does the Manchester of to-day present such a contrast with that of 1829, showing the social advancement which has been made in the last fifty years, as in the means of locomotion, and the ease with which both passengers and goods are now moved from one part of the country to another. Fifty years ago the majority of the people rarely took a journey of a score or two miles simply for pleasure. The annual visit of husband, wife, and children to the seaside, which is now an institution, was then a rare exception. All this is due, of course, to the development of railways; so that as I came to Manchester at the beginning of 1829, and the Liverpool and Manchester Railway was not opened until September, 1830, I was enabled to witness the last days of the old stage coaches, which were then in their hey-day, and I saw them in their perfection. I had not been here long before I became greatly interested in them, and their proceedings presented a new world to me, in which I took the greatest delight. I made myself acquainted with their names, their times of departure and arrival, and to a great extent the names of the coachmen and guards. Living in Market

Street, through which all the principal coaches passed, in whatever part of the premises I was on hearing the sound of a coach going up and down the street I knew what coach it was, whether it was going out or coming in, and the exact time of the day without looking at a watch. To see a London coach start or arrive afforded me intense pleasure.

In 1754, we are told, "a flying coach left Manchester and arrived in London (barring accidents) in four days and a half." Six years later a considerable improvement had taken place through the instrumentality of John Handforth, Matthew Howe, Samuel Glanville, and William Richardson, and the journey was performed in three days, "if God permit," the inside fare being £2. 5s., and the outside half the price. In 1773 it is on record that a coach named the Diligence left Manchester for Liverpool at six a.m.; that the passengers breakfasted at Irlam, dined at Warrington, drank tea at Prescot, and dropped comfortably into Liverpool at nightfall. The journey to Liverpool was performed on Monday, Wednesday, and Friday, and the return journey on the alternate days. In 1779 there was only one stage coach to London.

Fifty years ago there were four coach offices from which the principal coaches started. The chief of these was the Royal Hotel office, which was lately occupied as a druggist's shop. All the principal mails started from this office, the proprietor of which was Henry Charles Lacy, who was also the landlord of the hotel. The other three were, the Swan office, occupied by Weatherald, Webster, and Co., near to the present site of Woolley, Sons, and Co.; the

Peacock, occupied by the late John Knowles and his father ; and the Star, at the corner of the Star Yard and Deansgate. Besides the Mail there were two London coaches which started daily from each office, the four-horsed coaches each carrying, besides coachman and guard, eleven outside and six inside passengers. Two or three of them were only pair-horsed coaches, and as the Mail carried very few passengers, and as the coaches were not invariably full, it is probable that not a hundred persons then travelled from Manchester to London daily.

The four principal mail coaches, viz., those from London, York, Birmingham, and Liverpool, were timed to arrive at the Royal Hotel each day at four p.m. To me their arrival was a matter of great interest, and I embraced every opportunity of witnessing it. To see them drive into the Royal Hotel yard one after the other, almost to a minute, was an unfailing delight. I have seen the London mail coming at full speed down Piccadilly, whilst I have heard the horn of the guard of the York mail as it came down Oldham Street ; then the Birmingham mail, which came down Oxford Road, turning out of Mosley Street ; whilst the Liverpool mail, which had deposited its bags at the Post Office, behind the Exchange, as it came up Market Street ; all arriving nearly at the same time. The front part of the old yard at the Royal Hotel, which went into the back street, is now built up, but the shape of the arch yet remains. The London mail started from the Royal Hotel at twenty-five minutes past nine a.m., and arrived at the Swan-with-Two-Necks, Lad Lane, at seven the next morning, thus occupying twenty-one hours and thirty-five minutes in the journey. Its route was through Macclesfield, Leek, Ashbourne, Derby, Leicester, Northampton, and Dunstable. The Defiance, which started from the same office, occupied twenty-two hours and a quarter in the journey, but some of the London coaches occupied twenty-four hours. Some time before the railway to London was completed, a coach was started which, by changing horses more frequently, completed the journey in seventeen hours.

The mail coaches were invariably painted dark red and black, and each had four horses and both coachman and guard, the latter being dressed in a red coat, and a hat having a broad gilt hatband, and he generally wore top-boots. There was only one seat behind, which the guard occupied; he was generally provided with a brace of pistols placed within reach. His horn was always a plain long tin one, which sounded but one note and its octave, but in the open country could be heard a great distance. It was blown to give the horsekeepers notice to be ready to change horses and to arouse in the night the keepers of the toll-bars, who were generally quick-eared and had the gate open when the mail arrived. The guards were often very respectable men; and I remember one on the Carlisle mail which passed through Garstang, where my father once resided, who had been to college, and was known on the road as "The Collegian."

The most popular London coaches were the Defiance from the Royal Hotel, the Telegraph from the Star, the Independent from the Swan, and the Peveril of the Peak from the Peacock. One of the guards of the Telegraph was a tall, well-built man named Pretty. He had been a musician in the Grenadier Guards, and always attracted much attention as the Telegraph proceeded up Market Street, by his splendid playing of the bugle. The Peveril of the Peak used also to attract a good deal of notice on account of four handsome piebald horses attached to it as it left the Peacock at noon. In the midsummer of 1828 I paid a visit with my mother to some relatives near Dunstable, and we returned to Lancashire by the Peveril of the Peak, which was then only a pair-horsed coach. We joined it at a place called Market Street, near Dunstable, at about ten o'clock p.m. I well remember the night was wet, and the inside of the coach being full, my mother was obliged to travel outside, and sat next to the driver. Being then only a two-horsed coach it had no guard, and I sat behind.

At some small town through which we passed, about three or four o'clock in the morning, we changed horses and had a horse put in which backed the coach against a garden wall. It was a beautiful morning, and I had a lady companion who was charmed with the beauties of the sky ; whilst I, a timid lad, was full of fears as to the safety of the coach. However, we got off all right, and came to Manchester through Derby, Matlock, and Buxton—a magnificent drive—and we arrived about four o'clock.

In 1829 the Red Rover had not begun running to London, but started a year or two afterwards. It became a very popular coach, known as a "Patent Safety," as it was supposed that it would not upset if the axle-tree should break, inasmuch as it did not reach from wheel to wheel in a straight line, but was bent downwards towards the ground. Its chief proprietors were Weatherald, Webster, and Co., and it started at 8 p.m. I travelled by it to Birmingham in August of 1836, and remember getting to Stone at two o'clock in the morning, and finding a cottage near to the place of changing horses, which was open, where coffee and toast were supplied, and a good fire kept up, for the accommodation of the passengers of the many coaches which passed through the place during the night. The ride through the Black Country in the dead of the night, when the darkness was here and there illuminated by the lurid flames which the various furnaces shot forth, accompanied by curious noises, was very impressive and suggestive. A vivid imagination would not have had much difficulty in picturing Dante's Inferno.

There were about thirty coaches a day to Liverpool by way of Warrington, one of the most popular being the Doctor, driven by Tom Coxson, a man who had one leg shorter than the other. It used to leave Liverpool at five a.m., arriving here at nine; returning at six p.m., and arriving at ten. The man who was reputed to be the best driver out of Manchester was Jerry Scott, the driver of a Leeds coach.

It was the practice in those days to secure a place on an important coach beforehand, generally the day before, and sometimes even two or three days. A " way bill " was sent with the guard, or, if none, by the coachman.

There were generally five coachmen and five guards to a London coach. The coachman used to drive one coach out about forty miles and another in on the same day, whilst the guard went through. He used, for instance, to leave Manchester on a Monday, arrive in London on Tuesday, leave there on Wednesday, arrive here again on Thursday, rest on Friday, and start again on Saturday. Both coachmen and guards, not only on the London coaches but on all others, expected a fee on finishing the journey. The usual fees on a journey to London were a shilling to each coachman and half a crown or five shillings to the guard. Many of them were most respectable men. One of the guards of the Peveril of the Peak was one of the Labreys, whose brothers were tea dealers. I remember Horatio Miller, my master, who had travelled with him from London, saying that he had been struck with the shape of his head and face, and that he would make one of the best Falstaffs he had seen. The resources for stowing away luggage were very limited, and necessarily the size and style of the trunks and boxes which passengers then took with them were in striking contrast with the contents of the luggage van of a railway train of the present day.

Accidents happened to stage coaches, and persons were sometimes killed owing to the upsetting of the coach. I well remember, when a boy at school, the sensation caused there by the intelligence of the death of the father of a schoolfellow from this cause, when three Wesleyan ministers, the Rev. John James, father of the Rev. Dr. James, late of this city, the Rev. E. B. Lloyd, and the Rev. George Sargent, left Halifax by coach to attend the Wesleyan Conference at Sheffield. On going down a hill known as Shelley Bank, near Huddersfield, the coach was upset, all the passengers being thrown to the ground, and Messrs. Lloyd and Sargent were killed. Sometimes there was opposition between two coaches, when there was generally a strife between the coachmen who should keep first on the road. A good deal of excitement was created all along the route amongst those who lived by the roadside, and amongst the inhabitants of the small towns and villages, as the coaches passed, as to which took the lead, every person having his favourite coach. The dexterity with which the horses were changed on these occasions was amazing. There was generally a man to each of the four horses, which stood ready harnessed, the coachman never leaving the box, and the word "right" was given in two or three minutes, and some-times less. When home for my holidays once at Garstang, I remember the North Star and Royal Bruce coaches passing through to Kendal and changing horses each afternoon, and on one occasion the coachmen got off their boxes and began fighting, but of course were stopped by the passengers.

Having heard that there was an old coachman of the Peveril of the Peak, named Watmough, living at Wilmslow, I lately went over to see him. Though eighty-two years of age I found him as lively and vigorous as most healthy men are at seventy, and for his age very erect. He was living in a good house in comfortable circumstances, and in reply to a remark from me as to his health said: "Other drivers when they felt cold used to drink brandy and water, and then shortly would want another glass, but I never drank anything but water." His father was an officer in the Blues, retiring on full pay after 37 years' service, and young Watmough also had a commission in the Scot's Greys, which he sold previous to his marriage. He became fond of horses and of driving, and took up the occupation of driving a stage-coach simply from the love of it. He at first drove the Lady Nelson in opposition to the Lord Nelson to Nottingham. Eventually a coalition was effected, and a coach was run by the two opposing parties called simply the Nelson. On this Mr. Watmough was transferred to the fast coach before referred to, which was timed to reach London in 17 hours, running at the rate of 11 miles an hour. He and a driver named Taylor had to drive to Derby, and they agreed each to take the coach to Derby and back on alternate days, so that each might avoid lodging in Derby, and sleep at home every night. Poor Taylor was afterwards pitched off the coach and killed, near Macclesfield, leaving a wife and seven young children. Watmough not liking the route of the coach, and preferring the one taken by the Peveril of the Peak, made an exchange with one of the coachmen of the Peveril, known as " Ned White," and continued to drive the latter for ten years. Instead of having five coachmen to London, the Peveril had only three; and Watmough drove it as far as Loughborough, horsing the coach and driving his own horses for two or three stages. The rate at which the Peveril travelled was 10 miles an hour.

In driving through Longsight he once met with a serious accident; he was pitched off the box and the coach fell upon the lower part of his body. His right thigh was dislocated and pushed into the region of the ribs. He had three medical men in attendance upon him—Dr. Bardsley and

Messrs. Jesse and Harrison—and it was with difficulty that the dislocation was reduced. His arm was also injured, but he was able to resume his duties in three months. I can remember Mr. Watmough's features very well, having so often when a lad watched him as he sat on the box, reins in hand, waiting for the guard's "All right."

One of the most famous coachmen who used to drive a coach out of Manchester to the Potteries, was a man known as Bob Hadley. He was the son of a large coach proprietor in Coventry, and was an eccentric and amusing fellow. Being full of fun, anecdote, and sometimes of practical joking, he was a general favourite. At one time he was guard on a Birmingham coach, when he wore a red hat with a brim about ten inches wide, and a bright scarlet coat. Afterwards he became the driver of the before-mentioned coach to the Potteries, when he wore sometimes a white and at others a black hat with an outrageously broad brim, and a suit of a most extraordinary pattern—a very large check of such dimensions as to attract the gaze of the multitude. As an illustration of the speed attained by stage coaches, I may say that I have before me a printed card, recounting the performance of a coach named L'Hirondelle, from Birkenhead to Cheltenham on the 1st of May, 1833, William Greeves being the guard. It appears to have left Birkenhead at 49 minutes past 5 a.m., and to have arrived at Cheltenham at 28 minutes past 3 p.m., performing the whole journey of 131 miles in nine hours and 39 minutes, averaging about 13 miles an hour. The card exhibits a list of the eighteen places through which the coach passed, with the times of arrival at each place.

CHAPTER XVIII.

TRAVEL AND GOODS CARRIAGE BY ROAD AND CANAL.

THE names of other coaches to London were the Herald, the Hawk, the Tally-Ho, the Bruce, the Express, the Bang-up, and the Traveller. To Carlisle there were the Invincible, the Sir Walter Scott, and the North Briton; to Leeds, the Cornwallis, the Pilot, the Duchess of Leeds, the Highflyer, the Umpire, and the Defiance; to Chester, the Victory and the Dart. I remember taking a journey by the Victory in 1829 or '30, starting from the Royal Hotel at a quarter before six a.m., through Altrincham, Bucklow Hill, and Northwich, to a village called Kelsall, a little this side of Chester, where my master had a small property, and where he sent me to serve some legal notice on one of his tenants. To Buxton, there were the Royal Buxton, the Duke of Devonshire, and the Lady Vernon; to Nottingham, the Champion and the Lord Nelson, the latter of which used to drive to the Palace Inn, and which had for its guard one of the tallest, handsomest, and best built men I ever saw, wearing a white neckerchief, black coat, and top boots. I recollect seeing him once lift a corpulent lady down from the top of the coach with the same ease with which I should lift a child from off a table.

To Southport there was only one coach to carry all the visitors to that place, except those that went by the passage boat as far as Scarisbrick, which left the Duke's Quay in the summer every morning at six. The coach was named the Pilot, and left the Buck and Hawthorn, St. Ann's Street every day (except Sunday) at twelve. What few passengers found their way to Blackpool from Manchester fifty years ago travelled by the Union, the Butterfly, or the Duke of Manchester to Preston, whence they were transferred to a pair-horsed coach which went every evening in the season to Blackpool. I remember making my first journey there by this coach, soon after the railway was opened to Preston.

On the first of May there was always a grand turn-out of stage coaches, which formed a procession through the principal streets, the coachmen and guards making themselves and their horses as fine as they could. Many of the horses had new harness on that day. On the King's birthday all the mail coaches that could be spared formed a procession in a similar way, the guards generally having their new red coats on. The procession on the King's birthday always included the military, and was a very grand affair. In the evening the gentlemen of Manchester in those days used to dine together at the Exchange room, the price of the dinner tickets being a guinea, which included wine.

In these old coaching days, before the railway system was developed, the mode of travelling adopted by the "nobility and gentry" was that of "posting," which was a recognized institution all over England. On the principal roads, at intervals of twelve or twenty miles, were inns known as posting-houses, where a number of suitable horses and postboys were kept. These latter were sometimes grown-up boys and sometimes men of small stature and light weight. When a gentleman was about to take a journey in this way he would employ his own travelling carriage, or else hire a postchaise, and, on starting, would apply to a posting-house for horses and a postboy to drive him to the next posting-house on his route. At the second posting-house he would engage fresh horses and a boy to the next, and so on to the end of his journey. Generally the postboy rode one of the horses as a postillion, and was dressed in a short jacket reaching to the waist, frequently red, and sometimes blue, or occasionally brown, plentifully adorned with small bright buttons on the breast. He wore buckskin knee-breeches and top-boots with spurs, and a velvet skull-cap with a peak. Where there was more than one posting-house in a small town, each proprietor had a distinctive colour for his postillions' jackets. Scores of these houses were ruined by the introduction of railways. In some instances their proprietors were able to retire, but others were not so fortunate. The usual number of horses to a vehicle was two, but very wealthy and very grand people used four, with two postillions. I well remember, when at Garstang in the summer, that the number of these equipages which used to pass through on their way to the lakes and to Scotland was very large.

When an apprentice, I recollect being in King Street one Sunday afternoon, and seeing a carriage and four of this kind proceeding up the street at a very rapid pace, and noticed a gentleman with dark piercing eyes leaning his head in one corner. Lad-like, I ran as hard as I could to see where the carriage stopped, and saw it stop at the Albion. Though too late to see its occupant step out, I learnt that he was Kean (the elder), who had posted from Liverpool, where he had been fulfilling an engagement, and was about to fulfil one in Manchester. I have a lively recollection also of seeing a carriage and four opposite the door of Mr. Lewis, the newsagent, at the lower end of Market Street, one afternoon about two or three o'clock. Out of it had stepped Mr. Charles Murdo Young, the publisher of the *Evening Sun*, who had posted all the way from London, bringing the joyful intelligence that the Reform Bill had passed the House of Lords.

The subject of posting brings to my mind another circumstance which it may be interesting to name. When Lord Brougham was at the zenith of his popularity he posted from London to his seat in the north, and when near the end of his journey some slight accident happened to his carriage. Somehow the news got to London the next day that his carriage was overturned and Lord Brougham was killed. The following morning the *Times* contained a long and masterly biographical notice of him, with free criticisms on his character and ability as a lawyer and a statesman, written by Thomas Barnes, the editor, in his best style. So that Lord Brougham enjoyed the unique luxury, which is so rarely granted to any man, of reading for himself what would have been said of him had he been dead.

Before leaving the subject of travelling I must not omit to mention the "passage boats" which sailed from

Manchester to Runcorn, Bolton, Warrington, Worsley, and Wigan. These were fitted up with large deck cabins, surrounded with windows, like the Iona on the Clyde, so that a person could be under cover and see the country. They were each drawn by two or three good horses (on one of which a postillion in livery was mounted) at the rate of six miles an hour. One of the Runcorn boats started from New Bailey Bridge on the river and went by way of Warrington, whilst the other went on the canal by way of Stretford, Altrincham, Lymm, London Bridge, and Preston Brook. Both left here at eight a.m. and arrived at Runcorn at four p.m., the fare being 3s. 6d. for the fore cabin and 2s. 3d. for the after. I once sailed in this way to Runcorn on a beautiful summer's day, after their speed was accelerated, when we arrived about one p.m. I never enjoyed anything of the kind better. I also once sailed from Bolton one fine summer's evening, leaving there at five and arriving here about seven. The passage the other side of Ringley was delightful.

The great highway for the transport of goods fifty years ago was the canal. Amongst the carriers Pickford and Co. took the lead both by land and water. Their canal warehouse was on the right-hand side of Dickinson Street going from St. Peter's to Portland Street. The other carriers by water to the south had their warehouses at Castlefield. Of these I remember Kenworthy and Co., Snell, Brice, and Co., Ames, Bach, Green, Heath, and Robins, Mills, and Co. There were about thirty such carriers at Castlefield. There was also a large canal warehouse at the lower end of Deansgate, near to Knott

Mill, known as the Severn Warehouse. To Liverpool by the Mersey and Irwell there were the Old and New Quay Companies, and the Grocers' Company. The water carriers to Hull, Leeds, and other parts of Yorkshire had their warehouses at the end of Dale Street, where was a large open space of ground through which the canal passed, surrounded by warehouses, known as the Rochdale Canal Yard. The principal carriers to Hull from this wharf were John Thompson and Co., the founders of the firm of Thompson, M'Kay, and Co., and Barnby, Faulkner, and Co. Besides Pickford and Co., one of the great carrying concerns of Manchester has been that of Carver and Co., which fifty years ago was carried on under the name of Carver, Scott, and Co. About the year 1800 Thomas Carver was a carrier at Halifax, having one cart. He soon after began to send a wagon to Manchester once a week, on Tuesday, his son William riding on a pony, and returning the same day. In 1815 his warehouse was in Dale Street, but shortly after he removed to a warehouse in Portland Place, at the Piccadilly end of Portland Street, and the firm became Carver, Hartley, and Co., but in a few years it became Carver, Scott, and Co. About 1824 business had so much increased that instead of sending a wagon once a week, one was despatched every day, and Mr. Carver came to reside here, when he built the warehouse at the David Street end of Portland Street, with a house for himself in David Street. Mr. William Carver continued to reside in David Street till about 1844, when he went to live at Mount Clifton, near Old Trafford.

I remember Mr. Faulkner very well as a very gentle-

manly man, and a friend of my master. He lost his wife
and two children in the ill-fated Rothsay Castle. This
steamer, which was very lightly built, and was only intended
for the navigation of the Clyde, sailed from Liverpool one
morning in August, 1831, for Beaumaris, with about 150
persons on board. When off Abergele a terrible storm
arose, increasing every moment in violence, so much so
that the affrighted passengers besought the captain to
return, and some of them offered him money to do so
without avail, for he determined to proceed. After being
subject to the buffeting of the waves many hours, at
midnight, near Puffin Island, the vessel became a wreck,
and out of the 150 persons on board only about twenty-
three were saved. One of these was Mr. John Nuttall, the
druggist, of Bury, a friend of my master, and from whose
lips I have heard a narration of the dreadful catastrophe
and of his rescue.

The carriage of goods by land was effected by means of
wagons and carts, of which above one hundred left Manchester, some of them daily and others two or three times a
week, to various places, as near as Eccles and as remote as
Bristol and Edinburgh. One of the principal carriers of
this description was Ann Johnson, a widow, whose husband
had previously carried on the business, her warehouse
being in Oak Street. These wagons were large, substantial
vehicles, having very broad strong wheels, and the goods
were covered by a hood. They were generally drawn by
four houses, and were accompanied by a substantial-look-
ing carter dressed in a "smock-frock." How rare it is to
see one of these overalls in Manchester now! It appears

these wagons were sometimes drawn by six horses, for I have one of Ann Johnson's advertisements now before me, at the head of which is a woodcut of one drawn by six horses. In the advertisement it is stated that the wagon for Liverpool leaves every evening at seven o'clock, and arrives there at nine the following morning. Her wagon for Birmingham left Manchester every Wednesday and Saturday evening at eight o'clock, arriving there in two days, whence goods for Bristol were forwarded by Gabb and Shurmer, arriving there on the fourth day after their departure from hence. Goods from London by Pickford's boat were in like manner delivered in Manchester in four days after leaving London.

Parcels, as already intimated, were often despatched by coach as the quickest means of conveyance; but another means was adopted of carrying them more speedily than by wagon but not quite so fast as by coach, and that was by Pickford's van. This was a large oblong vehicle, like an immense box, on springs, drawn by four horses, with a coachman in front and a guard behind. There were two which left Pickford's van warehouse in Marsden's Square daily, except Sundays, one to London and one to Liverpool. The one to London made the journey in thirty-six hours. Reminiscences of these vans used to be seen in the signs of several public-houses called the Van Tavern. The signboards bore faithfully-executed pictures of Pickford's van, with horses, coachman, and guard. One of the last of these signs which I can remember disappeared a few years ago from the corner of a street turning out of Chester Road.

CHAPTER XIX.

OPENING OF THE RAILWAY TO LIVERPOOL.

We miss the cantering team, the winding way,
The roadside halt, the posthorn's well-known air,
The inns, the gaping towns, and all the landscape fair.

WE can now afford to laugh at the dogmatism of those who once declared and "demonstrated" the impossibility of the success of railway locomotion. The opening of the railway between Manchester and Liverpool was effected in the face of the most determined opposition, into which as usual a large amount of sentiment was imported. Agriculturists shuddered at the thought of the invasion of their peaceful retreats, and the sullying of the purity of the fleeces of the sheep by clouds of smoke. Members of Parliament in their places declared that railways would prove dangerous and delusive speculations, and were unknown to the constitution. Medical men vividly depicted the horrors and dangers which would attend their use. The most strenuous opposition, however, came from the proprietors of the Mersey and Irwell Navigation, the Bridgewater Canal, and the Leeds and Liverpool Canal, and from the Earls of Derby and Sefton.

After a vigorous discussion in a Parliamentary Committee for thirty-seven days, the first clauses of the bill were negatived by a large majority, and the first bill was withdrawn. A second was introduced into Parliament, which, being largely backed by public opinion, was more successful. Amongst other false notions which were current, was a vague idea that the development of railways would diminish the demand for horses. I well remember how the stationers' windows contained caricatures representing, for instance, poor half-starved horses looking over the railings at a passing train, and holding conversations as to their own condition and prospects.

Despite all this ignorant opposition, the 15th of September, 1830, arrived, on which day the line was opened by the Duke of Wellington. I well remember the day. It seemed to me as if the towns by which Manchester is surrounded had emptied themselves, and poured their adult population into Manchester and the neighbourhood. It has been calculated that not less than 500,000 persons were congregated along the line, from Manchester to Liverpool, to witness the grand procession of engines and carriages which was to proceed from Liverpool to Manchester. The cortège consisted of eight engines and thirty-three carriages, which contained the directors, their friends, and a large number of nobility and gentry. Besides the Duke of Wellington, who was then prime minister, there were present Sir Robert Peel, home secretary; Lord Leveson-Gower, secretary for Ireland; Prince Esterhazy, the Marquis of Salisbury, the Earls of Wilton, Cassilis, Glengall, Gower, and Lauderdale; Viscounts Melbourne,

Combermere, Sandon, Belgrave, Grey, Ingestre, the Bishop
of Lichfield, Lords Stanley (afterwards Earl of Derby),
Skelmersdale, Wharncliffe, Fitzroy, Somerset, Delamere,
Colville, Dacre, Hill, Granville, and Monson ; the Right
Hon. William Huskisson, M.P. for Liverpool ; Sir George
Murray, afterwards a candidate for the representation of
Manchester ; General Gascoyne, Admiral White, the
Marchioness of Salisbury, the Countess of Wilton, and
Mrs. Huskisson. The engines were the Northumbrian,
North Star, Rocket, Dart, Comet, Arrow, Meteor, and
Phœnix. The procession occupied both lines of rails, the
Northumbrian, drawing the state car, moving on the
southern line of rails, whilst the remaining seven took
the other line.

The morning opened most propitiously as to the weather,
and about half-past ten I set off with my brother and a
friend to witness the wonderful sight of a train being moved
without horses. We proceeded along the banks of the
railway for a mile or two before we found a vacant spot,
which we occupied, but were soon surrounded by a crowd
of others. Whilst waiting for the expected procession a
thunderstorm passed over us. We waited as patiently as
we could till nearly one o'clock, but still no procession
came in sight. It seemed strange, for the procession was
to leave Liverpool at ten. The patience of everybody was
becoming exhausted, when the sound of an approaching
engine was heard, and there was a cry of "They are
coming." We were all excited, and every neck was
stretched to see the procession. Instead of this there
was a solitary engine—the Northumbrian—with the present

Earl of Wilton, then a comparatively young man, on board. In those days he was often in Manchester on horseback, so that I knew him by sight and was able to recognize him as he passed on the engine, which was dashing along at full speed.   In ten minutes it returned, also at full speed, carrying, besides the Earl, three or four other gentlemen. Everybody was sure that something strange had occurred, and by-and-by the news spread that an accident had happened to Mr. Huskisson.   There being no signs of any procession the crowd for the most part dispersed, and I retraced my steps homeward.

It appears that the procession started from Liverpool at half past ten o'clock, amidst the shouts of an immense throng and the sounds of joyous music, and reached Parkside, about seventeen miles from Liverpool, in safety. Here the engines stopped to take in fresh water, during which process the Duke of Wellington, Mr. Huskisson, and other of the passengers left their seats to stroll about.   The Duke had returned to his seat, when a recognition having passed between him and Mr. Huskisson, the latter hastened to the carriage of the Duke, and was shaking hands with him when a cry was raised that the other train was approaching on the opposite rails.   Many persons availed themselves of the warning, and moved off the line, but Mr. Huskisson, who seemed for the moment to lose his presence of mind, stepped back on to the other line, and was knocked down by the engine, the wheels of which passing over his thigh fractured it in a fearful manner.   He was raised from the ground by the Earl of Wilton and others, and being placed in the car appropriated to the musicians, was taken to Eccles, where he found an asylum in the residence of the Vicar. The Earl of Wilton and Mr. Stephenson proceeded to Manchester on the Northumbrian engine as quickly as possible, and on making inquiries for surgeons, Messrs. Whatton, Ransome, Garside, and White being on the ground, mounted the tender and returned with the Earl to Eccles to administer professional aid to the sufferer. He expired at nine o'clock the same evening, having retained his consciousness to the end.

The carriages arrived in Manchester about three o'clock p.m., and returned to Liverpool almost immediately. The various festivities which had been arranged in order to celebrate the occasion were abandoned, the Duke spending the evening in seclusion with the Marquis of Salisbury. The next day he quitted Lancashire, and could not be induced to take part in any of the public rejoicings to which his presence gave rise, and of which he should have been the object. When the accident happened, the Duke proposed that they should return to Liverpool without finishing the journey; and it was only on Mr. Bulkeley Price, the Boroughreeve, representing to him that the disappointment to such a vast crowd as was assembled at Manchester might lead to some disturbance, that he replied "There is something in that," and consented to go on.

In the adoption of a new system of travelling, as with many other changes, it seemed impossible to jump from old practices and habits into a new order of things without passing through a transition state. For instance, as there had been only two classes of passengers by coach—inside and outside—so there were at first only two classes of trains. There were seven trains a day each way, four first-class and three second-class. The first-class went at 7 and 10 a.m., and 2 and 5 p.m. ; and the second-class at 7-30 a.m., and 1 and 5-30 p.m. On Tuesday and Saturday, which were then the two principal market days, the last train left at 6 p.m. In a little while two additional trains were despatched. On Sunday, the first-class train left at 8 a.m. and 5 p.m., and the second-class at 7 a.m. and 6 p.m., the time occupied in the journey being one hour and three quarters. The fares were, by first-class trains in coaches holding four inside, 7s. ; and in those holding six, 5s. ; by second-class trains, in glass coaches, 5s. ; and in open carriages, 3s. 6d. This was the classification adopted by the railway company, but we see that virtually there were four classes of passengers, and three classes of fares. The railway then terminated at the corner of Water Street and Liverpool Road, where the booking-office was. The company, shortly after the opening, took an office at the corner of New Cannon Street and Market Street, where passengers could be booked, and whence passengers by first-class trains could be conveyed by omnibus, free, to the office in Liverpool Road. There were four of these omnibuses provided, each of which had the word "Auxilium" painted on it. The trains were started by the blowing of a horn.

What I have termed the transition state was marked by other peculiarities. As has been stated, when a passenger travelled by coach he had to be booked, his name being entered in a book and on the way bill. So you could not travel to Liverpool without being booked, and your name entered. The clerks (one of whom, named Mackenzie, I knew) were provided with books made of yellow paper, containing foil and counterfoil, on each of which your name was written, when one part was torn out and given to you. Edmondson's system of tickets had not then been invented. Again, there was nothing like the promptitude we now enjoy in starting the trains, owing to late arrivals. After a time a notice was issued to the effect that. "in order to insure punctuality in the time of starting, which has frequently been prevented by persons claiming to be booked after the appointed time, no passenger, unless previously booked, will be admitted within the outer door of the station after the clock has struck the hour of departure;" and, strange to say, it was added, "passengers too late to take their seats or otherwise prevented going, may receive back half the fare paid, if claimed not later than the day after that for which the places were booked." Hence there can be no doubt that persons were frequently booked some time before the journey was begun. Another striking circumstance was that at first there were no wayside stations except at Newton, and the train stayed anywhere on the line to suit the convenience of passengers. After a few months, sixteen places were appointed at which the train stopped, and an announcement was made that "with a view to obviate in some measure the inconvenience occasioned by the frequent stoppages to take up and set down passengers on the road, all short fares, excepting those to Newton, will in future be taken by the second-class trains only." The first-class trains were only

to stop at Newton.   The directors announced that they
were determined to prevent the practice of supplying liquor
on the road, and requested the passengers not to alight, and
added that "the second-class trains would stop at any of
the sixteen places named, but to avoid delay passengers
were requested to *have the money ready to pay the guard.*"
Before this regulation as to liquor was issued I took a
journey to Liverpool in the stand-up boxes, and well
recollect on the return stopping at Patricroft, opposite to
an inn on the left-hand side, and seeing a young woman,
carrying along a large tray of glasses containing liquors
and cigars, which she supplied to many of the passengers.

The first-class carriages contained three compartments,
the middle one resembling the body of a stage coach,
something like a capital U, whilst before and behind it
were smaller ones, resembling a post chaise.   The carriages
containing outside passengers were oblong open boxes,
painted blue, without seats and without roof.   In a little
while seats were provided, and after that a roof was
supplied, supported by iron rods.   Just as every stage-
coach was designated by some name, so during the
transition stage each first-class carriage was designated in
like manner.   Amongst the names which I remember
were King William, Queen Adelaide, Duke of Wellington,
Sir Robert Peel, Earl of Wilton, and William Huskisson.

It was some time after the opening of the line before
I could get to see a train in motion.   At length, one summer's evening when in Oldfield Road, I got on the railway
embankment, and to my inexpressible delight a train from
Liverpool passed.

CHAPTER XX.

GOVERNMENT OF THE TOWN : CURIOUS OFFICIALS.

The government of the town was far more democratic fifty years ago than it is to-day; for instead of the governing body consisting of forty-eight councillors, a mayor, and a few aldermen, the town was governed by 240 of its principal citizens, who were sworn in as commissioners. At their head were the boroughreeve and two constables. Instead of several hundred blue-coated gentlemen perambulating the streets to keep order, the town was divided into sixteen* districts, in each of which, according to its size, from ten to forty inhabitants were appointed as special constables, charged to preserve the peace within that district. One of their number was appointed the conductor. For instance, in the Oxford Street district, which was bounded by Bond Street, Brook Street, Mosley Street, and the river Medlock, Mr. Thomas Sowler, the proprietor of the *Courier*, was

---

* Fourteen of these districts are the same which now exist ; but there were two others which were designated thus :—" No 15 District —(Extra)" and " No. 16 District—(Extra)." To these two districts special constables were appointed, as to the others, No. 16 having as many as thirty-four.

the conductor, and amongst the specials under him were James Pigot, jun., the publisher of the Directory, whose house was in Marble Street, and Mark Whitehead, the calenderer, of Back Mosley Street. Mr. Emanuel Mendel, the father of Mr. Sam Mendel, was one of the constables of St. John's district; Mr James Bake (afterwards alderman) of St. Clement's; Mr. William Glasgow, millwright, and his brothers John and David, of the St. Peter's districts. Amongst the 240 commissioners were Messrs. Samuel Brooks and his brother John, Elkanah Armitage, Thomas Bazley, and Hugh Hornby Birley; John Edward Taylor, and Jeremiah Garnett, proprietors of the *Manchester Guardian;* Mark Philips, afterwards M.P. for Manchester; Thomas and Edward Binyon, Samuel Fletcher, Thomas Fleming, and William Labrey.

The commissioners divided themselves into the six following committees, with the names of the chairmen and deputy-chairmen :—(1) Improvement, Gilbert Winter and J. Bradshaw; (2) Finance, Benjamin Braidley and William Haynes; (3) Watch, Nuisance, and Hackney Coach, William Haynes and William Neild (afterwards Alderman Neild); (4) Lamp, Scavenging, Fire Engine, and Main Sewer, Henry Forth (afterwards of Forth and Marshall) and John Barlow; (5) Accounts, Benjamin Braidley and John Edward Taylor; (6) Paving and Soughing, Thomas Hopkins and George Hall. On this last committee were David Bellhouse and Jeremiah Garnett. The Surveyors of the Highway were Thomas Fleming, Leaf Square, Pendleton; Charles Ryder, Collyhurst Hall; Peter Watson, Store Street, Piccadilly; Robert Andrew,

Turkey-red dyer, Green Mount, Harpurhey; David Bellhouse, Nicholas Street; Edmund Buckley, iron merchant and copperas manufacturer, Mather Street, and Richard Warren, gentlemen, Leigh Place, Ardwick. There were then only three collectors of the " Highway Ley."

The deputy constable was Stephen Lavender, whose house was near the present site of the Bank of England in King Street. He succeeded the notorious Joseph Nadin, who had been deputy constable twenty years when he resigned it. Lavender had been one of the celebrated Bow Street officers, and was one of those who were ordered to arrest the Cato Street Conspirators. He afterwards traced Thistlewood to an obscure lodging, and only escaped with his life by flinging himself on the bed in which lay Thistlewood, who was in the act of firing a pistol at him. He died in 1833, having held the office twelve years, and was succeded by Joseph Saddler Thomas.

All the paid staff which Lavender had under him in 1829 were four beadles, whose names were Thomas Worthington, George Moss, Anthony Jefferson, and John Page; seven assistants, and four street-keepers. The colour of their livery was brown. Soon after I came to Manchester I well remember hearing of a riot in the neighbourhood of Ancoats, when one or two factories were set on fire. I was passing the Royal Hotel just as Lavender was coming up Mosley Street at the head of about nine or ten beadles, walking in single file, each carrying a drawn cutlass in his hand, and remember seeing them cross over from Mosley Street to Oldham Street. Of course they would be assisted in quelling the disturbance by the special constables of the district. Fifty years ago, when trade was bad and food scarce, as I have before remarked, it was the practice of the working classes to try and mend matters by rioting, attacking cotton factories, smashing the machinery, and often setting fire to them. I well remember, when a boy, going through the factory of the Messrs. Whitehead at Rawtenstall with my father, and one of the firm explaining to him how a mob had a short time previously broken into the factory and destroyed a large quantity of the machinery. In 1829 the factories of Mr. Thomas Harbottle, Mr. James Guest, and Messrs. Twiss were gutted, and that of Messrs. Parker was burnt down.

The boroughreeve for 1829 was David Bannerman, who then lived in Mosley Street, and the two constables were Robert Ogden and John Bentley. Mr. Ogden was a cotton spinner, and lived next door to Mr. Houldsworth, the M.P., in Portland Place, and Mr. Bentley, who was out of business, lived just round the corner in Piccadilly. Besides the beadles I have named, other paid officials in connection with the town's business were: One keeper of each of the four lock-ups in Swan Street, Knot Mill, London Road, and Kirby Street; two clerks, one office-keeper, one comptroller, one cashier, two inspectors of nuisances, and five collectors of gas rents—viz., James Booth, Isaac Mawson, George Pratt, William Gleave, and Evan Mellor, the four last of whom also collected the police rate.

Our interests at night used to be committed to the care of a number of men, some of whom were advanced in

years, known as watchmen, but who were nick-named
"Charleys." They wore broad-brimmed hats having a
yellow band round each, and brown topcoats. Little
wooden huts known as watch-boxes, just large enough to
allow one man to sit in, were provided for them, and were
placed in quiet corners in each district. I remember there
was one near to our back gates in Cromford Court. It used
to be said that young fellows returning home late occasionally upset a watchman in his box by overturning it. Their
practice, as they went their rounds, was to bawl out the
hour of the night and the kind of weather which prevailed ;
as, for instance, "Past twelve, fine starry night." In this
case they would emphasise the word "past" by elongating
the sound of the vowel, and clip the "twelve" rather short.
It was a very comfortable thing if you happened to be
awake in the night to know how matters were going on
outside in these respects.

I have not been able to ascertain the exact number of
watchmen employed in Manchester in 1829, but have
ascertained that in 1815 there were fifty-three and ten
supernumeraries, the wages of the watchmen being as
follows : From November to February inclusive, thirteen
shillings per week for ten hours from 8 p.m. to 6 a.m. ; for
March, April, September, and October, eleven-and-sixpence
per week, hours from 9 till 5 ; for the four summer months,
ten shillings per week, hours from 10 till 4. There were
two police officers at that time, Samuel Foxcroft and
Jonathan Hern. In 1825 the number of watchmen was
seventy-four and nine supernumeraries, whose wages had by
this time been increased five shillings per week.

As already stated in an earlier chapter, fifty years ago Manchester possessed no police court of its own, the only one being in Salford at the New Bailey, which was presided over for many years by John Frederick Foster, a barrister, who was generally respected, and filled the office so as to win universal applause. His salary was £1,000 per annum, which was provided by a magisterial rate levied on the inhabitants of the two towns of Manchester and Salford. He was assisted by six unpaid magistrates, one of whom was Mr. Isaac Blackburne, the distributor of stamps ; and another was the Rev. C. W. Ethelstone, one of the Fellows of the Old Church.

Besides those already mentioned Manchester possessed several other officers who were employed in the government of the town. These were for the most part tradesmen and other men of business. There were, for instance, two "mise leyers" and one "mise gatherer." There were twenty-four "market lookers for fish and flesh," amongst them being Thomas Yates, of the Star Hotel ; Stephen Lavender, and Thomas Skinner Noton. There were nine "inspectors of white meats," amongst them being Mr. George Crossley, the governor of the Blue-coat School. There were eleven "officers to prevent engrossing, regrating, and forestalling," amongst them being Henry Charles Lacy, the great coach proprietor and landlord of the Royal Hotel. The two officers "for tasting wholesome ale and beer" were William Eland, the box-office keeper at the theatre, who lived in Brazenose Street ; and Alexander Bower, a drysalter, living at the Oaks, Fallowfield. Mr. Joshua Ryle, a woollen draper in Old Millgate was, the "market looker for the assize of bread." There were seven "bye-law men," and about the same number for "muzzling mastiff dogs and bitches," amongst whom were George Southam, the grocer, and father of the late eminent surgeon of that name, and Richard Thelwell, the silver-smith in St. Ann's Square, each person being appointed to a certain district. There were officers "to prevent the cutting and gashing of raw hides," and "searchers and sealers of leather," the same two gentlemen filling both offices, James Travis and John Baggs, and each being a boot and shoe maker. There were officers "for distributing the rent-charge of Collyhurst."

The most surprising of these appointments was that of "scavenger," which was filled by a number of most respect-able inhabitants. Amongst them were Mr. Thomas Sowler, who was appointed to St. Ann's Square and back streets; Mr. Robert Duck, agent for the Sun Fire Office, to Market Street; and Mr. Henry Charles Lacy to Shudehill, High Street, and back streets. There were about fifteen of these officials. The last of these offices was that of "pounder," which was filled by Robert Burton. All these appoint-ments were made by the Lord of the Manor at his court leet, which was held in a room over the Shambles in Brown Street, the present site of the Post Office.

CHAPTER XXI.

GAS, WATER, AND HACKNEY COACHES.

THERE are not many things which remind us more of the great changes which have taken place in our daily surroundings than the price of GAS. Fifty years ago its price in Manchester was twelve shillings per thousand cubic feet, to-day it is three shillings for gas of nearly double its illuminating power. When the Peace of Amiens was celebrated in 1802, the front of Boulton and Watt's manufactory was brilliantly lighted up with gas, when all Birmingham poured forth to view the spectacle, and strangers carried to every part of the country an account of what they had seen. The news was spread everywhere by the newspapers, with instructions how to prepare the gas, and coal was distilled in tobacco-pipes at the fireside all over the kingdom. A successful instance of such experimenting I can well remember when a very little boy some years after. Three years after the illumination by gas of Boulton and Watt's manufactory, Mr. Murdoch, a Cornish engineer, visited this neighbourhood, and was engaged by Messrs. Phillips and Lee to light up their factory in Chapel Street, Salford. Their example was soon followed by other persons, one of the earliest places thus

lighted being the Police Office situated in Police Street, at
the lower end of King Street. It is said that the first private
house lighted with gas here was that of Mr. James Leech,
who lived in a large house in Springfield Lane, Salford.
The first gasworks were erected in Water Street in 1817,
and the first Gas Act was obtained in 1824. The merit of
originating the gasworks of Manchester upon the present
basis, so that from the first they became the property of
the ratepayers and the profits were appropriated to the
improvement of the town, is due to the late George
William Wood, formerly M.P. for the southern division of
the county, and Mr. Thomas Fleming, sen., through whose
united efforts this great boon was secured. Fifty years ago
gas was supplied in two ways—by meter and by burner.
If supplied by meter the price was, as I have said, twelve
shillings per thousand feet. Places of worship, manu-
factories, inns, and places where the time of burning it was
irregular were supplied by meter only; but shops and
places where the gas was burnt at stated and regular
intervals were supplied and charged according to the
number and kind of burners used. The burners were
supplied by the Commissioners, and were of two kinds,
Cockspurs and Argands. A scale of prices was issued
embracing three particulars—the number of jets, the height
of the flame, and the hour of extinguishing the gas. The
hours for extinguishing the gas were eight, nine, ten, eleven,
or twelve o'clock, and twelve for all on Saturday evenings.
No extra charge was made if the light was extinguished
within fifteen minutes of the time contracted for; but if the
gas was burnt at any other time, the consumer, if discovered,

was fined. All rents by burners were to be paid in advance. The department was managed by thirty directors, who were chosen from the body of Police Commissioners, ten of whom retired annually, when ten others were appointed in their stead. Their principal staff consisted of a secretary, John Thorpe, jun.; a superintendent of No. 1 Station, Jacob Davies; a general superintendent, John Outhett; an inspector, James Crompton; an office clerk, James Drew; and five collectors. Fifty years ago the gas receipts for the year were £20,000, and the payment from the gas profits to the Improvement Committee was under £7,000. The receipts for 1879 were £320,000, and the payment to the Improvement Committee £52,000. These figures are amazing, and most strikingly indicate the difference between the Manchester of fifty years ago and that of to-day.

WATER.—Manchester was not so fortunate in the case of its water supply as with that of gas. In the first instance it was not taken up by the Police Commissioners, but was left to the enterprise of others. The Manchester and Salford Waterworks Company was established in 1808, and fifty years ago the supply of both towns was in their hands, at which time the daily consumption was about 1,400,000 gallons. The company had small reservoirs at Gorton, Beswick, Bradford, and Audenshaw, and their office, which I well remember, was a few doors higher up than the Albion Hotel, Piccadilly, and next door to the bookshop of Mr. William Ellerby. At first the water was supplied in stone pipes, for which iron ones were substituted in 1817, the stone ones being very liable to burst. But the name "stone pipe water" continued long after, for I well recollect that this was the name generally used to describe the company's water fifty years ago. It was then only turned on for about three or four hours each day. In Market Street it was turned on generally at noon, and was received into a large stone cistern, which stood in the yard of the premises where I was, at the bottom of which a smaller vessel of porous stone was cemented, which served as a filter. The peculiar noise produced by the water driving the air out of the pipe before it came on I seem as if I could hear now, while my thoughts are carried back to those times.

HACKNEY COACHES.—Fifty years ago cabs were not known in Manchester, and were not introduced into the town till ten years after. The first vehicle of this kind was built by Mr. W. H. Beeston, of Tib Street, for Mr. William White, of Spear Street, who began plying with it from the Piccadilly stand in 1839. Mr. White is probably the oldest coach and cab proprietor in Manchester, and fifty years ago lived in Rook Street. The vehicles known as hackney coaches, which have been supplanted by cabs, were larger and much heavier, and were drawn by two horses, though in the later period of their history smaller ones were constructed, which were drawn by one horse only. It appears that there was an attempt to establish hackney coaches here as early as 1750, but the extremities of the town being comparatively so near together, and within easy walking distance, the inhabitants did not encourage the attempt, still preferring the favourite sedan chair when they wished to ride. In 1750 we find there were two hackney coaches which stood in St. Ann's

Square. In 1810 hackney coaches were finally established in Manchester, and in 1815 as many as twenty coaches, but not more, were allowed to ply for hire in Manchester and Salford, or within four miles. The coaches were to stand in the centre of St. Ann's Square, and at the top of Market Street, between Marsden Square, and High Street; the fare being eighteenpence a mile if charged by distance. It was at the discretion of the driver to charge either by time or distance. If by time, the fare was eighteenpence for any time not exceeding half an hour. Fifty years ago the number of coaches allowed had increased to fifty, which were distributed as follows: Fourteen in a line along the middle of St. Ann's Square, ten in a line along the middle of the higher end of Market Street, from the end of Palace Street towards High Street, and the remainder in a line along the south side of Piccadilly. The year after the railway to Liverpool was opened the committee added six coaches to those previously allowed, which were to ply opposite the railway office in Liverpool Road, and at the junction of Oxford Street and Lower Mosley Street. Very stringent regulations existed as to the provision of check-strings, and as to the omission of the driver to hold the same when driving. The fares were the same as those just quoted as existing in 1815, with the exception that provision was made for coaches drawn by one horse, the fares for which were a shilling a mile.

CHAPTER XXII.

MEDICAL AND OTHER CHARITABLE INSTITUTIONS.

IT is to the efforts of Mr. Charles White, assisted by a few other gentlemen, that the establishment of the first Manchester infirmary is due. In 1752 a house in Garden Street, Shudehill, was taken for the purpose, Mr. Joseph Massey undertaking to pay all the expenses of the first year, and Mr. Charles White volunteering his services as a medical man. Mr. White, it is well known, was an eminent surgeon, who resided in a large and handsome house which stood on the site of the old Town Hall, having formerly been a pupil of the celebrated John Hunter. The house was opened as an infirmary on the 24th of June, and, by the end of the year, seventy-five in-patients had been received and 249 out-patients had been treated; the first year's expense, which was defrayed by Mr. Massey, being £405. The success of the undertaking was so marked that a public meeting was called, at which a resolution was passed to erect a building capable of holding eighty patients.

At this time there were but few houses between Market Street Lane and the village of Ardwick. Somewhere about where the Infirmary esplanade now is was a large and long pit, known as " Daubholes," behind which was " Daubholes Field." Most people are sufficiently acquainted with the traditions of Manchester as to know that it was in this pit that "scolds" were formerly dipped by means of the ducking stool. The field and pond were the property of the lord of the manor, Sir Oswald Mosley, who liberally gave a lease of the land for a term of 990 years for the purpose of erecting an infirmary on it, when the pond became the once well-known " Infirmary pond," but is now a thing of the past. The first stone of the new Infirmary was laid on the 20th of May, 1754, by Mr. Miles Bower, according to one account; but, according to Dr. Renaud, by Mr. Massey, who became its first president. The total cost of the building and its furniture was about £4,000. The money was freely contributed by the inhabitants, and amongst other contributions were the proceeds of the first night's performance at the new theatre in Marsden Street. In 1760 a musical entertainment was given in the grounds of the Infirmary, the proceeds of which were given to its funds. The Infirmary was finished and opened in 1755. To Manchester belongs the honour of founding the second lunatic asylum in the English provinces, which was built as a wing to the Infirmary, having a lower elevation, between that building and Portland Street, at a cost (including furnishing) of £1,500, and was finished in 1766. In 1787 and 1790 considerable additions were made at the back of the Infirmary, so that out-patients could be admitted daily instead of on Monday only as heretofore. In 1792 still further additions were made, and it became necessary to appeal to the public for funds. This was done through the

medium of a Hospital Sunday in all the churches and
chapels in Manchester, when £4,000 was thus collected,
the largest amount being taken at the Independent Chapel
in Mosley Street, the pulpit then being filled by the
Rev. T. Kennedy, and the collection amounting to £220.
In 1783 an "air balloon" ascended from the Infirmary
grounds, which alighted at Cromford, in Derbyshire. The
admittance to the grounds was one shilling, the proceeds
going to the Infirmary funds.

The erection thus described was standing exactly in the
same state fifty years ago. It was a plain brick building,
which, with the lunatic hospital, extended in the direction
of Portland Street, having the large pond in front extending
the whole length, railed off from the street with plain iron
palisading. The baths, which were built about 1781, were
on the right of the entrance gates, and fifty years ago were
under the superintendence of Mr. William Galor.* At that
time the president of the Infirmary was the Earl of Stamford
and Warrington, and the treasurer Mr. Thomas Entwistle,
whilst of deputy-treasurers there were no less than twenty-
seven. The physicians to the institution were, Drs. John
Mitchell, Edmund Lyon, Edward Garbutt, J. L. Bardsley,
Davenport Hulme, and W. C. Henry. The surgeons
were, W. Simmons, John Thorpe, J. A. Ransome, James
Ainsworth, Robert Thorpe, and W. J. Wilson. The visiting
apothecaries were John Cook and Daniel Lynch, both of
them druggists, but, having been in business before the
Apothecaries Act of 1815, still retained the privilege of

---

* An account of them has been given on page 9.

visiting patients.   Mr. H. T. Worthington was the house apothecary, and Mr. W. E. Guest house surgeon.   The collector was Mr. James Molineux, who was a friend of my master, and had been overtaken by some of the disasters of 1826.   The matron was Mrs. Sarah Loftus, and the secretary, Mr. H. Neild,. who afterwards became the manager of the Savings Bank.   The treasurer of the adjoining institution was Mr. Thomas Hoyle, and the other officers were those of the Infirmary.   Connected with the Infirmary was also the Board of Health, or House of Recovery (for sick and fever patients), in Aytoun Street, which was opened in 1797.   Its president in 1829 was the first Sir Robert Peel, its vice-president Mr. R. J. Norreys, and the medical officers were those of the Infirmary.   In 1818 an amateur performance took place at the Theatre Royal, for the benefit of the asylum, when the proceeds amounted to £300.

What is now known as ST. MARY'S HOSPITAL was then called the Lying-in Hospital, and was situated on the bank of the Irwell opposite the front of New Bailey Prison in Stanley Street, Salford.   It was first established in 1790, and was removed to Stanley Street in 1796, where it stood fifty years ago, but was some time afterwards removed to North Parade, St. Mary's.   Its president was the Earl of Grosvenor, and its vice-presidents Sir Robert Peel, Sir Oswald Mosley, the Rev. Dr. Calvert, warden of the Collegiate Church, and Mr. Joseph Yates, iron merchant, of Portland Street.   The treasurer was Mr. Hugh Hornby Birley, with twelve deputy-treasurers, amongst whom were Mr. Benjamin Joule and Mr. J. Ollivant.   Dr. Hull was the physician, and Messrs. John and Robert Thorpe and Dr. Agnew the

" surgeons-extraordinary." The surgeons for the out-
districts were Messrs. James Lowe, Thomas Fawdington,
and John Roberton. Connected with the institution was
a large medical committee, and a still larger ladies'
committee, the former consisting of the medical officers
already named, and in addition Dr. Freckleton, Messrs.
Hudson, Radford, Kinder Wood, Ollier, Ainsworth,
Ransome, Brigham, Barton, Jordan, Dudley, Bamber, and
Turner. Of these medical men all have passed away
except Dr. Radford, who at an advanced age, is still an
active member of the medical staff of the same hospital,
under an altered name and under altered circumstances.
The ladies' committee consisted of Mesdames Agnew,
Boutflower, Bower, Barton, T. Brooks, Samuel Brooks,
Elsdale, Hoyle, Hall, Henson, Lomas, Marris, Marsden,
Nunn, King, Place, Roylance, T. Rothwell, Tate,
T. Townsend, Tweddell, Wadkin, and Misses Ainsworth
and Hadfield.

There are few charitable institutions of which Manchester
may be prouder than of its EYE INSTITUTION, now located
in such capital and convenient premises in St. John's Street.
It may be fairly said to be at the head of all similar
provincial institutions. Fifty years ago its domicile was
of a more humble character. It was first established in
1815, and occupied premises at No. 35, Faulkner Street.
In 1829 Mr. Nicholas Thomason was the secretary and collector, and became the governor of the institution, which had
been removed to Princess Street. Its president for many
years was Sir Thomas Stanley, Bart. (his son becoming
Lord Stanley of Alderley), and amongst its vice-presidents

were William Grant and John Leaf. Its committee consisted of Thomas Norris, J. Chippendale, Adam Dugdale, Daniel Grant, W. J. Wilson, Daniel Lynch, J. Brackenbury, George Grundy, John Ollivant, William Hutchinson, and the Revs. Moses Randall and R. Basnett. Dr. Hull was the consulting physician. Messrs. Samuel Barton and John Windsor were the surgeons, and Messrs. R. T. Hunt and J. E. Gordon assistant surgeons.

The LOCK HOSPITAL was opened in 1819. Fifty years ago it was located in Bond Street; its president was Mr. David Holt, and its medical officers were Dr. Hull, and Messrs. Jordan and Brigham. The house surgeon was Mr. Lewis Henry Nathan.

In addition to these medical charities there were also Dispensaries for Salford and Pendleton at 23, Broken Bank; for Chorlton Row (now Chorlton-upon-Medlock) at 236, Oxford Road; and for Ardwick and Ancoats at 181, Great Ancoats Street. The president of the Salford Dispensary was Mr. William Garnett of Lark Hill (situated in what is now Peel Park), who so often unsuccessfully opposed Joseph Brotherton as a candidate for parliamentary honours. The medical staff included Messrs. Thomas Brownbill, George Gardom, John Boutflower, and Dr. Harland; Mr. Boutflower being still engaged in practice, and Dr. Harland also surviving. The president of the Ancoats Dispensary was Mr. George Murray, the cotton spinner, of Ancoats Hall; and amongst its medical officers were included Dr. James Phillips Kay, whose house was then in King Street; Messrs. Thomas Turner, Joseph A. Ransome, and Ashton M. Heath.

THE FEMALE PENITENTIARY was then situated in Rusholme Road, next to Buck's livery stables, Mr. Edward Lloyd, the barrister, of King Street, being its treasurer. The same plan existed then as now of having two secretaries, one a minister of the Established Church and the other a minister of a nonconforming church, the secretaries fifty years ago being the Rev. William Marsden and the Rev. John Birt. The matron was Mrs. Elizabeth Price, who was shortly succeeded by Mrs. Lydia Colebeck.

THE MANCHESTER AUXILIARY OF THE BRITISH AND FOREIGN BIBLE SOCIETY was established in 1810, its depository fifty years ago being in King Street, in a house next to the Town Hall, at the lower end, which also contained the offices of Higson, Bagshaw, and Higson, and of Edward Bent, solicitors. Its patron was the Bishop of Chester, and its president Sir Oswald Mosley. Amongst the vice-presidents were the Rev. John Clowes, of the Collegiate Church ; the Rev. John Clowes, of St. John's Church ; the Rev. Melville Horne, Messrs. William Townend and James Wood. The treasurer was Mr. William Fox. The life governors were John Burton, Peter Marsland, Jonathan Peel, Joseph Smith, and Samuel Stocks ; and the governors Samuel Fletcher and E. Norris. Amongst the committee were the Revs. Wm. Huntingdon, William Nunn, Hugh Stowell, J. A. Coombs, R. S. M'All ; Messrs. Benjamin Braidley, George Hadfield, and Thomas Harbottle. The honorary secretaries were the Revs. John Hollist and William Roby. At that time the society did not employ any paid secretary or agent. The annual meeting of the society in 1829 was held in the Manor

Court Room, Brown Street, Sir Oswald Mosley, the lord of the manor and president of the society, being in the chair. The Rev. Andrew Brandram, one of the general secretaries, attended as a deputation from the parent society, the other speakers being the Revs. William Lord (Wesleyan), John Birt, W. Thistlethwaite, G. S. Bull of Bierley, A. Hepworth (St. Luke's, Chorlton Row), J. A. Coombs, and R. S. M'All; Messrs. J. S. Bramall, Samuel Fletcher, and John Burton, calico-printer (of Daniel Burton and Sons). The report stated that the parent institution, during its twenty-four years' existence, had expended more than a million and a half of money, had distributed upwards of five millions and a half copies of the Bible and Testament in not less than a hundred and five different languages and dialects, in fifty-eight of which the Bible had never been before printed, and that thirty-eight new translations were then in progress. The number of donors and subscribers in 1828 was 193, whose bene-factions and subscriptions amounted to £324. Amongst the subscribers are found the names of Miss Byrom, of Quay Street; Messrs. Benjamin Braidley; Samuel Brooks, the banker, Market Street; Isaac Crewdson; J. and T. Fildes, Shudehill; Samuel Fletcher; G. R. Chappell; George Hadfield, solicitor; J. H. Heron; Dr. Hull; Benjamin Joule, the brewer; Dr. Lignum (so-called, proprietor of the "Antiscorbutic Drops"); J. M'Clure and J. M'Clure jun.; Mottershead and Brown, druggists; W. Newall, grocer, owner of Newall's Buildings; John Ollivant, silversmith, Exchange Street; Michael Peacock, Deansgate; Thomas and Richard Potter (father and uncle

of the late Sir John Potter and Mr. T. B. Potter, M.P.);
Charles Rider, Collyhurst Hall; Samuel Prince, grocer,
Market Street; R. Scarr, St. Ann's Square; E. Thompson,
bookseller, Market Street; J. Wadkin, Pendleton; Wood
and Westhead, High Street; the Revs. W. Nunn; J. A.
Coombs; J. Clowes, fellow of the Collegiate Church;
J. Clowes, St. John's; William Roby, Hugh Stowell, and
Melville Horne. The latter gentleman, who, as I have
said, was one of the vice-presidents of the Bible Society,
was a popular preacher and was the immediate predecessor
of the Rev. Hugh Stowell at St. Stephen's, Salford. He
was the author of some controversial tracts as to the
circulation of the Douay version of the Bible by the Bible
Society. He died at Ashbourne, in Derbyshire, in 1841,
in the eightieth year of his age.

THE Manchester Branch of the SOCIETY FOR PROMOTING
CHRISTIAN KNOWLEDGE was instituted in 1814, and fifty
years ago had its quarters at the depository of the Bible
Society in King Street. It was not without its friends. Its
patrons were the (present) Earl of Wilton, the Bishop of
Chester, and Lord Kenyon. Its president was the
Rev. Dr. Calvert, warden of the Collegiate Church; its
treasurer was Mr. Thomas Hardman; and its secretaries
were the Rev. Henry Fielding, chaplain to the House of
Correction, and afterwards clerk in orders at the Old
Church; the Rev. Peter Hordern, librarian of the Chetham
College; and Mr. Charles Smith, of Cheetwood. The
RELIGIOUS TRACT SOCIEEY was established here in 1812,
and the WESLEYAN TRACT SOCIETY in 1822.

THE HUMANE SOCIETY was originally established in 1791, under the patronage of and mainly through the public-spirited exertions of Mr. Thomas Butterworth Bayley, once chairman of the quarter sessions. In the same year the STRANGERS' FRIEND SOCIETY was established under the auspices and by the aid of the Rev. Dr. Adam Clarke, who was at that time stationed in Manchester. Although it was principally supported by Wesleyan Methodists, it was eminently catholic in its operations, inasmuch as its benefits were extended to persons of every other denomination, or of no denomination, who were relieved according to no other standard than the measure of their distress and the capability of its funds. The SAMARITAN SOCIETY, established in 1824, was an institution of a similar nature, whose meetings were held weekly, on the Friday evening, in the vestry of Gravel Lane Chapel. The PHILANTHROPIC SOCIETY, established in 1811, was another benevolent institution, which fifty years ago used to hold its meetings at Hayward's Hotel, in Bridge Street, having for its secretary Mr. Robert Walmsley, of Red Bank. It shortly after changed its quarters to the Dog and Patridge, Ducie Place, when Mr. Daniel Grant became its president, and Mr. Edward Loyd, the banker, its treasurer. The SOCIETY FOR THE ENCOURAGEMENT OF FAITHFUL FEMALE SERVANTS was founded in 1816, as a free registry office. Its object was to reward those servants of subscribers who had lived for a certain time in their service with annual premiums. Its office fifty years ago was in Chapel Walks, having been removed there from King Street, and its conductress was Mrs. Mary Owen.

THE COMMERCIAL CLERKS' SOCIETY was èstablished in 1802, and was a provident institution, established for the benefit of tradesmen and clerks, who by the payment of an entrance fee of from three to five guineas, according to age, and an annual payment of one guinea, with the aid of honorary contributions, made provision for sickness and old age, as well as for their wives and children.

In enumerating the charitable institutions of Manchester which existed fifty years ago, the free public schools ought not to be omitted. At the head of these was the FREE GRAMMAR SCHOOL in Long Millgate. Of this the Rev. Jeremiah Smith, D.D., was high master; the Rev. Nicholas Germon, high master's assistant; the Rev. Robinson Elsdale, second master; the Rev. John Johnson, second master's assistant; and the Rev. John Dallas, master of the lower school. Of the BLUE COAT SCHOOL, Mr. George Crossley was governor; the Rev. Peter Hordern, curate of St. Mark's, Cheetham Hill, librarian; Mr. William Mullis, assistant librarian; and the Rev. W. Bootle Guest, master of the school. The LADIES' JUBILEE SCHOOL in New Bridge Street, Strangeways, had its origin in 1806, in the benevolence of several ladies. In 1809 a house was procured in Broughton Lane, which contained ten girls; and in 1810 a building was erected on a plot of land given by Lord Ducie in New Bridge Street, by public subscription, in commemoration of the fiftieth year of George the Third's reign. The new building was capable of accommodating thirty-two girls, which was the number in the house fifty years ago. In 1832 a splendid legacy of nearly £11,000 from the late Mrs. Frances Hall enabled

the committee to enlarge the building so as to accommo-
date forty girls. At the time I speak of the matron of the
school was Mrs. Ann Alcock. At a suitable age the girls
are put out as domestic servants, the applications for them
far exceeding the supply. The COLLEGIATE CHURCH
CHARITY SCHOOL was also for girls only, and was situated
in Fennel Street. It contained sixty girls, the mistress
being Miss Mary Beard. The MANCHESTER SCHOOL FOR
THE DEAF AND DUMB was opened in February, 1825,
and fifty years ago was situated in Stanley Street, Salford,
near the Lying-in Hospital. Its superintendent was
Mr. William Vaughan, and its honorary Secretary
Mr. William Bateman; Dr. Davenport Hulme, and
Mr. Thomas Turner, being its medical officers. It then
contained fourteen inmates.

THE NATIONAL SCHOOLS on Dr. Bell's system were two,
one in Salford, founded in 1812, and one in Granby Row,
opened in 1813. The Granby Row School contained
440 scholars, Mr. William Johnson being master, and his
wife mistress. I remember Mr. Johnson very well. He
was a good-looking man, gentlemanly in his manners,
and was a member of the Oddfellows' Society. The
LANCASTERIAN SCHOOL was in Marshall Street, Oldham
Road, and had 1,000 scholars, with Mr. John Perkins,
superintendent, and Mrs. Hannah Brown, mistress. There
were three Infants' Schools—one in Buxton Street, London
Road, with John Halliwell, master; one in King Street,
Salford, Thomas Merry being master; and one in Saville
Street, Chorlton Row, with James Bartley, master.

There were also the New Jerusalem Free Day School in

Irwell Street, Joseph Moss, master; St. Mark's Charity, Cheetham Hill, with forty scholars, and John Lee, master; St. Mary's Charity, 64, Water Street, for girls, having fifty scholars, Elizabeth Tudor, mistress; St. John's Charity, Gartside Street, for girls, Mary Harrison, mistress; St. Paul's Charity, Turner Street; Friends' Female Sewing School, for girls, Hannah Campion, mistress; Catholic Free School, 13, Lloyd Street, Patrick J. Murphy, master, and Susannah Fox, mistress; and, lastly, the Unitarian Free School, Back Mosley Street, the Rev. Edward Hawks, master. The Workhouse School, in Strangeways, contained about fifty scholars. In all these schools a gratuitous education was given fifty years ago, and show the efforts made in that day to educate the poor.

CHAPTER XXIII.

LITERARY, SCIENTIFIC, AND OTHER SOCIETIES.

NO provincial society of the same nature has acquired a fame so extensive and well-deserved as the MANCHESTER LITERARY AND PHILOSOPHICAL, or which has reflected so much credit on the place of its birth. It was originated in 1781, and has always been famous on account of its interesting memoirs, which have been translated into the French and German languages. Amongst the deceased contributors to these have been Dr. Watson, Bishop of Llandaff; Dr. Thomas Percival; Mr. Charles White, the eminent physician and surgeon of Manchester; the Rev. Dr. Barnes; Mr. Thomas Henry, F.R.S.; Dr. John Ferrier; the Rev. Gilbert Wakefield; Dr. James Currie; Mr. John Gough; and Dr. Dalton, F.R.S.

Previous to the winter of 1781 the Society had for some time existed as an occasional assemblage at private houses; but in the winter of that year it became organized as a public body. Its first promoters were Dr. Thomas Percival, Mr. Thomas Henry, and Mr. Charles White. Dr. Percival became its first joint-president in conjunction with Mr. James Massey, who, it will be remembered, was so instrumental in establishing the Infirmary. On the death of Mr. Massey, Dr. Percival became sole president. He was elected a Fellow of the Royal Society before he was twenty years of age, being, it is said, the youngest member ever introduced into that learned corporation. He assisted in establishing "The Manchester Academy for the Education of Protestant Dissenting Ministers," afterwards known as the Manchester College. The building erected for the Academy was at the lower end of Mosley Street, that part being then called Dawson Street, standing back from the street and leaving a flagged space fenced with iron palisadings, and was in existence fifty years ago. Mr. Charles White, the eminent surgeon, was one of the first vice-presidents of the Society, and remained such several years. He was elected a Fellow of the Royal Society in 1761, and, as before stated, it was to his exertions, associated with those of Mr. Massey, that the establishment of the Infirmary is due. He was born in Manchester, and continued to practice till he was eighty-four years of age. He died in 1813, shortly after he had ceased to practice. Mr. Thomas Henry, who also assisted in founding the Society, becoming one of its first joint-secretaries, was a Fellow of the Royal Society, and became a very eminent chemist. He was apprenticed to a surgeon-apothecary at Wrexham. After filling the situation of assistant to Mr. Malbon, a visiting apothecary at Oxford, he settled at Knutsford, at which place he remained five years, and then removed to Manchester, where he succeeded to the business of a respectable apothecary in King Street. He died in 1816, aged eighty-two, and as late as 1815 his name appears in the directory as an apothecary at 40, King Street. He was the originator of that popular medicine known as Henry's Calcined Magnesia. In 1771 he communicated to the Royal College of Physicians of London an improved method of preparing magnesia, which was published in their Transactions. When he presented this communication nothing could have been further from his thoughts than engaging in the preparation of the article. When the measure was urged upon him by friends, he did not relinquish his scruples until he had been assured by such men as Sir John Pringle, Sir Clifton Wintringham, and Dr. Warren that as to the college they saw no objection, and that for the public advantage and his own it was highly desirable. The article was then manufactured in East Street, Bale Street, and is so still.

Fifty years ago the president of the Society was John Dalton, F.R.S. (not then doctor), and the vice-presidents were Dr. Edward Holme, F.R.S.; Dr. William Henry, F.R.S., son of Thomas Henry; Peter Ewart, cotton spinner, of East Street; and George William Wood, afterwards M.P. The treasurer was Benjamin Heywood, the banker; the secretaries, Peter Clare and the Rev. John James Tayler, minister of Mosley Street Unitarian Chapel; and the librarian John Davies. Dalton became a member of the Literary and Philosophical Society in 1794. The first paper which he read before the Society after joining it related to that disease of the eyes from which he suffered, known as colour-blindness. The paper was entitled " Extraordinary Facts relating to the Vision of Colours, with observations, by Mr. John Dalton," and was read on the 31st of October, 1794. Dalton originally was a teacher of mathematics at Kendal, and was induced to remove to Manchester to accept the office of Professor of Mathematics and Natural Philosophy at the New College, Mosley Street. He resided within the college for about six years, till it was removed to York. On withdrawing from it he began to teach mathematics and natural philosophy privately at his residence in Faulkner Street, but shortly after removed to the house of John Cockbain, a member of the Society of Friends, having the use of the lower rooms in the building of the Society in George Street for the purpose of study and instruction. After living some time with Cockbain, Dalton went to live with the Rev. William Johns, immediately opposite his rooms. Johns had a good boys' school, and it was here that Dalton was living fifty years ago. A few years afterwards the whole line of private houses of which Johns' was one was sold for warehouse purposes, when Dalton, being ejected, took a house in Faulkner Street for his undivided occupancy. He was elected a Fellow of the Royal Society in 1822, and received the Oxford degree of Doctor of Civil Law in 1833. He died on the 27th of July, 1844, in the seventy-eighth year of his age. Who will say that his longevity was not due, at least in some degree, to the very wise practice, which he religiously observed, of on one afternoon in every week, laying aside all mental toil and indulging in physical recreation? A choice party of friends met every Thursday afternoon at Tattersall's bowling green on the way to Stretford, amongst whom none enjoyed a game at bowls better than the worthy Doctor.

Amongst the deceased contributors of papers to the Literary and Philosophical Society was Mr. John Gough. He resided at Kendal, and was a most intimate friend of Dalton's. After his death, the Doctor said of him that "he might justly be deemed a prodigy in scientific attainments. Deprived of sight in infancy by smallpox, he lived to an advanced age under one of the greatest misfortunes which can fall to the lot of man. By the liberality of his father he received a good classical and mathematical education. He excelled in astronomy, optics, pneumatics, chemistry, natural history in general, and botany in particular. Mr. Gough was as much gratified with imparting his stores of knowledge as I was in receiving them. My use to him was chiefly in reading, writing, and making calculations and diagrams, and in participating with him in the pleasure resulting from successful investigations. But as Mr. Gough was above receiving any pecuniary recompense, the balance of advantage was greatly in my favour." Dr. Dalton's most intimate friend, in the latter period of his life, was Peter Clare, the senior secretary of the Society, of whom mention has been made in a previous chapter.

Dr. Edward Holme, the senior vice-president, was an eminent physician residing at the higher end of King Street; he, Mr. Thomas Radford, Mr. Thomas Turner, and Mr. James Ainsworth, surgeons, living not far from each other, in that street fifty years ago. Dr. Holme was elected a member of the Literary and Philosophical Society on the same evening on which Dalton was, viz., on the 25th of April, 1794.

Dr. William Henry, who fifty years ago was another vice-president of the Society, as before stated, was the son of Thomas Henry, already mentioned. He lived to become eminent as a chemist, and when a comparatively young man delivered several courses of lectures on Chemistry in Manchester. These lectures were illustrated by very expensive apparatus, and contained experiments of a highly-interesting character. When coal gas was applied to the purpose of illumination, he was one of the first to determine its constitution, to point out the best mode of analysis, and to suggest the most effective methods of obviating the inconveniences to which, in its early application, it was liable. In 1835 Lord Brougham came down from London to give an address at the old Mechanics' Institution in Cooper Street, to which only members of the institution were admitted. I well remember paying five shillings as a quarter's subscription, so that I might hear him. On that occasion, speaking of Dr. Henry, his lordship said : " I met an old and worthy friend of mine, a man of great ability and learning, your townsman, Dr. Henry. We were fellow-collegians, and learned chemisty together—though, God wot, he learned a great deal more than I did."

Mr. John Davies, who was the librarian of the institution fifty years ago, I well remember as a plain, unassuming, though intelligent-looking man, well versed in the scientific discoveries of the age. He delivered a lecture at the Mechanics' Institution, which was afterwards published in pamphlet form, and which contained a review of the principal scientific discoveries of that day.

THE NATURAL HISTORY SOCIETY fifty years ago had its rooms at the top of King Street, near to Mr. Thomas Turner's and Mr. James Ainsworth's, the surgeons, the rooms being kept by Mrs. Susan Steemson. It was established in 1821, and in 1829 possessed a museum of considerable value and variety. Its patrons then were the Earl of Wilton and Sir Oswald Mosley; the president was Dr. Holme, before mentioned; and its vice-presidents Dr. Henry, Mr. John Moore, and Messrs. Ransome and Ainsworth, surgeons; the secretaries were Messrs. Thomas Turner and Peter Barrow, surgeons; the treasurers, Edward Lloyd and Thomas Fleming; and the curators, Robert Hindley, John Beever, John Owen, and the Rev. R. H. Whitelock. The museum was removed to Peter Street in 1835.

THE BOTANICAL AND HORTICULTURAL SOCIETY was established in 1827, and the gardens were opened in 1831. Previously, its exhibitions were held at the Town Hall, and its secretaries were John Milner Marris, of Marris, Son, and Jacksons, Cannon Street; and James Benson, cloth merchant, Brown Street. When the gardens were opened, the first officers of the Society were as follows:—Patrons, the Earl of Stamford and Warrington, the Earl of Wilton, Lord Suffield, and T. J. Trafford; president, Sir Oswald Mosley; treasurer, Richard Potter, afterwards M.P.; honorary secretary, the Rev. P. Hordern, librarian of the Blue Coat School; acting secretary, Mr. John Holt Stanway, accountant, of Marsden Street; and curator, William Mowbray. The council-room of the Society was then at 9, Marsden Street.

A FLORAL AND HORTICULTURAL SOCIETY had been recently established, and was in a flourishing condition fifty years ago. There was also an AGRICULTURAL SOCIETY, which was one of the earliest institutions of the kind established in England, having been founded in 1767. It comprehended an area of thirty miles round Manchester, and at that time held its meetings at the Royal Hotel.

THE SOCIETY FOR THE PROSECUTION OF FELONS AND RECEIVERS OF STOLEN GOODS was also in active operation fifty years ago, its trustees being Oswald Milne, the solicitor; James Hall, dyer, of Ordsall; and Thomas Hoyle, calico printer. Its president was William Woolley, and its vice-president George Whyatt, dyer, of Openshaw. The committee met on the first Monday in the months of March, June, September, and December, from seven to nine p.m., and consisted of the president and vice-president, James Hall, jun., Sunnyside; John Worrall, Ordsall; William Harrison, Old Quay; John Barge, calico printer, Broughton; and Charles Bradbury, calenderer, St. Mary's. The committee met at the Unicorn Inn, which was then kept by Joseph Challender. This was the building which by its projection caused the entrance to Smithy Door from the Market Place to be so narrow and dangerous. It was here, too, that the once celebrated John Shaw's Club was held, which has been referred to previously. Shaw occupied the house, it is said, upwards of fifty-eight years, and died in 1796 at the age of eighty-three. He was an eccentric man, and used to turn out all his customers at eight o'clock every evening, occasionally using the whip, it is said, if any were obstinate, though the hint was generally sufficient.　There used to be a portrait of him in oil at the Thatched House Tavern, which I have seen many years ago, and which is now, I understand, at the Mitre Hotel, Cathedral Yard.

The Pine Street School of Medicine and Surgery was in a flourishing condition fifty years ago.　It was founded by the late Mr. Thomas Turner.　Mr. Jordan had begun a course of lectures on Anatomy in 1814, and in 1822 Mr. Turner began to lecture on the same subject in the rooms of the Literary and Philosophical Society.　In 1824 Mr. Turner attempted to combine the exertions of individual teachers in one complete system of medical instruction, and in the following year the Pine Street School was fully organized, when he delivered there a course of lectures on Anatomy.　The other lecturers were Dr. James L. Bardsley, on the Principles and Practice of Physic and Materia Medica; Mr. Ransome, on Surgery; Dr. Dalton, on Chemistry; Mr. Kinder Wood, on Midwifery; and Mr. Thomson, on Botany.　Fifty years ago Mr. Turner had retired from his position as lecturer on Anatomy, which was jointly filled by Mr. Guest and Mr. Ransome.　About the same time a second School of Medicine was started in Mount Street by Mr. Jordan, who obtained the co-operation of several of his professional friends, he continuing his lectures on Anatomy, whilst Dr. Freckleton lectured on the Practice of Medicine and Materia Medica; Mr. John Davies, the librarian of the Literary and Philosophical Society, on Chemistry; Mr. Radford (still living and active), on Midwifery; Mr. Fawdington and Mr. Boutflower (the latter also still in practice), on Surgery; and Mr. Blundstone giving Anatomical Demonstrations.

It is just about fifty years since the ROYAL MANCHESTER INSTITUTION was opened. Its first secretary was Mr. Geo. F. Bury, a solicitor, son of Mr. John Bury, timber merchant, of Salford, who was one of the mainsprings of its original organisation. The Institution was deprived of his services by a shocking and fatal coach accident, a few years afterwards. The original aim of the promoters was a very modest one, their first intention being to purchase premises in King Street and re-model them. The premises fixed upon were those occupied by Mr. William Howe, a well-known auctioneer and wine merchant, near Four Yards, and which nearly fifty years ago were occupied by Mr. John Morris, the auctioneer. It was intended to form a junction between this institution and the Natural History Society, and a public meeting was held in the Exchange Dining-room, at which a resolution was passed expressing "a hope that arrangements in every respect satisfactory may be made for the accommodation of its valuable collections in the apartments of the house purchased for the Institution, and that the two societies may ever be distinguished by a cordial and zealous co-operation for the furtherance of their common object." A numerous and influential committee was appointed by the meeting, amongst whom were Sir Oswald Mosley, Dr. J. D. Hulme, Dr. Edward Holme, Dr. William Henry, Messrs. E. J. Lloyd, the barrister, Robert Hindley, George W. Wood, William Garnett, David Holt, H. H. Birley, R. H. Greg, J. A. Ransome, W. Townend, Jonathan Dawson, Francis Phillips, James

Beardoe, and Robert Christie.   Such was the success of
the meeting that the sober views of the projectors were
overturned.   There was some difference of opinion at first,
but the tide of popular feeling set in so strongly that it was
resolved to build a hall in Mosley Street, which was
commenced in 1825.   Four architectural plans were
produced, from which the Council selected the model of an
erection by Mr. Barry, of London, which was to cost from
£18,000 to £20,000.   At the close of 1831 the total cost
of land and buildings amounted to £26,070.   About
£32,000 had been received, which left a balance of nearly
£6,000 for the purchase of works of art.

Fifty years ago the MECHANICS' INSTITUTION, which was
erected in 1824, stood at the lower end of Cooper Street,
and cost £7,000.   The building is still standing, and it is
said was the first erected for the purpose in England.   In
1829 the Secretary was Mr. Thomas Hopkins, who was
succeeded by Mr. S. E. Cottam, and the librarian
Mr. Abraham Bennett, who was succeeded by Mr. William
Turner.   I well remember Mr. Day, a succeeding secretary,
under whose able and energetic management the institution
greatly prospered.   The very interesting and popular
exhibitions which used to be held for many weeks at
Christmas, every year, are worthy of being remembered.
Lord Brougham's visit to the institution, for which purpose
he made a special journey from London, has been
mentioned previously.

Owing to some dissatisfaction which arose as to the
management of the first institution, in 1829 a rival, styled
the New Mechanics' Institution, was started in Brazenose

Street, and was afterwards removed to Pool Street, Lloyd Street. Its president was Mr. Detrosier, its treasurer Mr. Thomas Potter, its secretaries Messrs. Keighley and Bond, and its librarian Mr. John Taylor Christie. It was at first in contemplation to erect a large hall for the purpose, but although the plan was advocated by Mr. Joseph Hume, M.P., who presided at a public dinner for its promotion, it was not sufficiently supported to succeed, and was abandoned. The ATHENÆUM was not built till 1835.

The present CONCERT HALL at that time was in course of erection, the first concert given in it being in 1831. The old Concert Room as before intimated, was in Fountain Street, a little lower than York Street. The first stone was laid by Mr. Edward Greaves, of Culcheth, on the 24th of August, 1775. A so-called musical festival was held in the room on the 21st of September, 1785. In a description of Manchester written one hundred years ago it is stated that "the Concert Room is esteemed to be one of the best in England, for the convenient disposition of the seats, the elegance of its lustres, and organ. The retiring room and backstairs for the performers, the judicious elevation of the orchestra to produce the happiest effect which music so powerfully commands, and the genteel company at the concerts on public nights, are undeniable proofs that this species of entertainment was planned with judgment, and is conducted with the utmost decency, prudence, and integrity."

THE ASSEMBLY ROOMS were in a plain brick building at the corner of Charlotte Street and Mosley Street, opposite to Dr. M'All's chapel, and were opened in 1792. To their use at the last Manchester festival reference will be made in a future chapter.

THE EXCHANGE of fifty years ago was a very different kind of building from the large and handsome erection which now adorns the lower end of Market Street. It had been enlarged three or four times, and at the time we speak of was comparatively very small. It had its well-known semi-circular front, the enlargement having always been effected at the back, in the direction of St. Ann's Square. It was then as built originally, and had never been enlarged. Its first stone was laid in 1806 by Mr. George Phillips, a member of the firm of Thomas Phillips and Co., merchants, of Bridge Street, whose house was at Sedgley. It was erected with a capital of £32,000, derived from four hundred shares of £80 each. Previously the Exchange used to stand at the other side of the Market Place, and was built in 1729 at the expense of Sir Oswald Mosley. Its front was ornamented by four columns surmounted by a pinnacle, a representation of which is given in Casson and Berry's well-known map of Manchester. The lower part of the first Exchange was intended for the merchants and chapmen to transact their business in, but it is said they generally preferred the Market Place in front of it for that purpose, and that butchers' stalls were occasionally set up in the Exchange on market days. The upper storey was intended for a sessions room and manor court, and was sometimes used for concerts and public exhibitions.

THE CHAMBER OF COMMERCE fifty years ago was in Exchange Buildings, in Crow Alley, behind the Exchange, at which time Mr. George William Wood was its president, and Mr. George Evans Aubrey, secretary. It was first established in 1820.

Of Public Libraries in Manchester in 1829 there were seven. The next in importance to the one connected with Chetham College was the Portico. This building was begun in 1802 and opened in 1806, and cost £7,000, which was taken up in four hundred shares. The chairman of the committee was then Dr. Edward Holme; the treasurer, Mr. Frederick Maude; the secretary and librarian, the Rev. William Whitelegg, minister of the Unitarian Chapel, Platt; and the assistant librarian, Mr. Simon Williamson. The oldest library after the College one, is the Manchester Circulating Library, having for its librarian at the time of which we speak a lady, in the person of Mrs. Blinkhorn. It was opened in 1765 in Exchange Buildings, and was afterwards removed into a room in the Exchange, for which the committee fifty years ago only paid a rental of £30. The next in importance was the New Circulating Library, which was opened in 1792, and at one time was located in Pool Fold, but in 1829 was in Fountain Street, when John Tonge was its librarian. Another library was afterwards opened which was known fifty years ago as the New Library, then situated in St. Ann's Street, and had for its librarian William Barrow. Besides these there were the library of the Mechanics' Institution and the Law Library, situated in Marsden Street, the secretary of which was Mr. James Chapman, the first coroner of Manchester.

Markets.—Fifty years ago there was no Cross Lane Cattle Market, but that market was then held on Wednesday, in Smithfield, Shudehill, which on other days was occupied

by traders in a variety of commodities.   Of course the area
thus occupied was nothing like so large as now.   From
5,000 to 10,000 head of cattle were weekly sold there.
The principal places for the sale of garden produce besides
Smithfield were the markets in Smithy Door and the Market
Place.   There were several butchers' shambles in the town,
the principal one being at the corner of Bridge Street and
Deansgate, adjoining which was a small market for fruits
and flowers.   Another was under the Manor Court Room,
on the present site of the Post Office in Brown Street.   A
third was in London Road, which was opened in 1824.
The Butter Market, which had been held in Smithy Door,
was removed to the Brown Street market.   The Fish
Market, which has been lately pulled down to make way
for a more convenient structure, was erected fifty years ago,
having been built on the site of some butchers' shambles.
The Hay Market was then held in Great Bridgewater
Street, and had been removed from Market Street in 1804,
and the Potato Market was held at Smithfield.   The
present Corn Exchange in Hanging Ditch was not then
erected, but the Corn Market was held in a court yard
connected with the Spread Eagle Inn, which is opposite the
present Corn Exchange.   This hostelry is one of the oldest
in the town, and in 1745 was used by the Duke of Perth
and many of the officers of the prince's army.   When the inn
was partly rebuilt in 1838, a signet ring and other old
valuables were found.   Bamford in his " Life of a Radical,"
narrates that at the time of the Peterloo riot, Hunt stayed
there, and was grossly insulted by some commercial
travellers who were in the house.

The market tolls were at that time the property of Sir Oswald Mosley, the lord of the manor. The manor of Manchester had remained in the Mosley family more than 230 years, having been originally purchased from John Lacye mercer, of London, in 1596, for £3,500, by Sir Nicholas Mosley. After being Sheriff and Lord Mayor of London, he came to reside in this neighbourhood, building the old hall known as Hough End (generally pronounced Ouse end), near Chorlton-cum-Hardy, still in a fine state of preservation, and occupied by Mr. Lomax as a farmhouse. In 1808 a negotiation was set on foot by a town's meeting for the purchase of the manor. For this property and its privileges Sir Oswald asked £90,000, and the deputation appointed to treat with him offered him £70,000. The difference was adjusted, but unfortunately another town's meeting undid all that had been done, and the negotiation came to nothing. In 1845 the Town Council were glad to become the purchasers for £200,000.

CHAPTER XXIV.

NEWSPAPERS.

IN few things is there a greater contrast between the Manchester of fifty years ago and that of to-day than in relation to the Press. Then, no daily paper was pushed under the door before we were downstairs in a morning, containing not only an account of what has occurred in Manchester, but the news of the world of the preceding day, spread out before us with amazing exactness. The London morning papers contained an account of the debates in Parliament of the previous evening as now, but did not arrive here till the following morning. So that, for instance, the debates of Monday night were not read in Manchester till Wednesday. An attempt was made by Mr. Charles Murdo Young, the spirited proprietor of the *Evening Sun*, to improve upon this, but it was to so slight an extent that it seems to us now to be hardly worth the trouble he took. He gave in his evening edition an account of what took place in Parliament down to half-past five o'clock, by having relays of boys on horseback who, every quarter of an hour or less, carried a report of the debates from the House to the *Sun* office; and in this way they were printed and despatched by the mails going north at six o'clock. But in those days, though the hour of the meeting of Parliament has not been changed, the debates began earlier, inasmuch as so much valuable time was not taken up at the commencement by long, numerous, and complicated questions being put to the Ministers, as is now the case. As to foreign news, what the newspapers contained was generally weeks, if not months, old. There was then neither telegraph, railway, nor ocean steamship.

The Manchester newspapers, of which there were eight, were all weekly, six being published on Saturday—viz., the *Chronicle*, the *Courier*, the *Gazette*, the *Guardian*, the *Advertiser*, and the *Times*, whilst the *Herald* was published on Thursday by the proprietor of the *Courier*, and the *Mercury* on Tuesday by the proprietors of the *Guardian*. Those were the days, as before observed, in which the Chancellor of the Exchequer used all his ingenuity in discovering, not how many taxes he could remit, but in how many ways he could put his hand into the pocket of the British taxpayer. Hence the newspaper was taxed all round—the paper on which it was printed, the advertisements it contained, and finally the newspaper itself. Every newspaper had a large red stamp imprinted on it, bearing the words " duty fourpence ;" and as the price of the newspaper was threepence, the full charge for each Manchester one was sevenpence. In 1836 the duty was reduced to a penny, and the price of the newspaper to fourpence.

The oldest of the eight newspapers which I have mentioned was the *Manchester Mercury*, which was first published in 1752, by Joseph Harrop, at the sign of the

Printing Press, in the Market Place; opposite the clock side of the old Exchange. The day of publication was Tuesday, which does not seem to have been altered, although the title was slightly altered after the eighth issue, when it became *Harrop's Manchester Mercury and General Advertiser.* It ceased to be published on the 28th of December, 1830, after an existence of seventy-nine years. In 1764, to encourage the sale of his newspaper, Mr. Harrop gave in weekly numbers " a new History of England," which he tells his readers at the close cost him a hundred guineas. He died in 1804, having when a youth served his apprenticeship as a letterpress printer with Mr. Henry Whitworth, who published the first Manchester newspaper in 1730, entitled *Whitworth's Manchester Gazette,* which was afterwards changed to the *Manchester Magazine,* the price of it being three-halfpence. Its number dated December 24, 1745, gives a circumstantial account of the movements of the rebel army under Prince Charles. How long the paper survived the rebellion is not known, but it had ceased to exist when Mr. Harrop began the *Mercury.* The first number of the *Manchester Journal,* printed by Schofield and Turnbull, made its appearance either in 1752 or 1754, but was discontinued in two or three years. One or two other equally futile attempts to establish a newspaper followed.

The first *Manchester Chronicle* or *Anderton's Universal Advertiser* was published by Thomas Anderton, at the Shakespeare's Head, near the Market Cross, but was short-lived. Another newspaper entitled *Prescott's Manchester Journal* was printed and published every Saturday by

John Prescott in Old Millgate, the price of which was twopence, and the first number of which appeared in 1771; but it, alas! shared the fate of its predecessor. Hence in 1781 *Harrop's Mercury* had entire possession of the field, when Mr. Charles Wheeler recommenced the publication of the *Manchester Chronicle;* so that of the eight newspapers published here fifty years ago, excepting the *Mercury,* which ceased to exist in December, 1830, the *Chronicle* was the oldest. It continued until the end of 1842, when it expired, as was said, " after a lingering illness." The truth was, it was pushed off the stage by its more spirited and more liberal contemporaries, notwithstanding that it had at one time the lion's share of advertisements.

Before coming to the establishment of the chief Manchester journals, it may be as well to notify a few other efforts to establish newspapers here. In 1792 political feeling ran very high in Manchester, when the formation of a " Church and King Club " led to the establishment of the " Manchester Constitutional Society " by the leading Liberals of the day, amongst whom were Thomas, father of the late C. J. S. Walker, mentioned in a previous chapter, George Lloyd, James Darbyshire, Thomas Cooper, a barrister, George Phillips (afterwards Sir George, mentioned previously as having laid the first stone of the late Exchange), and Thomas Kershaw. Some of the members of the new Liberal Society induced Matthew Faulkner, one of its members, to start a newspaper to advocate their principles, under the name of the *Manchester Herald,* which had not been published many months before a " Church and King" mob gathered in the Market Place opposite

Faulkner's premises, and attacked the front of the house and shop with stones and brickbats till the windows were all smashed in, and the premises otherwise injured. From thence the mob proceeded to attack the house of Mr. Thomas Walker in South Parade, mention of which has already been made. During the continuance of the riot, the deputy-constable, whose name was Unite, was present, and actually applauded the mob, saying "it will do them good to be frightened a bit," at the same time clapping some of the most active of the rioters on the back, and saying " Good lads; good lads." It is no wonder that the *Herald* did not live many months.

During the first twenty-one years of the present century, nearly twenty attempts to establish newspapers were made which proved abortive. In 1803 four such attempts were made. First, the *Telegraph* by James Edmonds and Co. ; which was succeeded by the *Mercantile Gazette and Liverpool and Manchester Daily Advertiser*. This was the first attempt to establish a daily paper out of London, and was originated by Dr. Solomon, a well-known quack doctor, and the proprietor of a very popular patent medicine known as the Balm of Gilead. The Balm succeeded but the paper did not. Next followed the *Argus*, published by Joseph Aston ; and a theatrical paper named the *Townsman*, the editor of which was James Watson, a well-known character, generally designated Jemmy Watson, and sometimes "the Doctor." In 1804 the *British Volunteer* made its appearance from the press of Mr. Harrop of the *Mercury* office. It was followed by the *Mail*, published on a Tuesday by Joseph Aston. In 1809 the same publisher brought out the *Exchange Herald*, the day of its publication being at first Saturday, which after a time was changed to Tuesday and then to Thursday. In 1814 the *Manchester Magazine* was published monthly, and continued for three years; and in 1817 a predecessor of the present *Manchester Courier* was published by Messrs. Cowdroy and Rathbone, but of opposite politics to the present one. In 1818, the *Observer* was published by Thomas Rogerson, which changed hands several times, at one time belonging to James Wroe, the well-known Radical bookseller, and was discontinued in June, 1821. The *Spectator*, printed by Mr. Thomas Wilkinson, the father of the present Mr. J. F. Wilkinson, of the Guttenberg Works, appeared first on Saturday, the 7th of November, 1818, and was succeeded by the *Recorder*, the first number of which appeared on Thursday, the 6th of May, and was printed by John Leigh in the Market Place, and edited by Joseph Macardy, who afterwards took so prominent a part in the establishment of some of the joint-stock banks here. The *Patriot*, another of Joseph Aston's papers, was issued first in August, 1819. In 1820 the *Observer* was printed by Mr. Chapman, who was fined £250 for printing a libel on Mr. Thomas Fleming. In November, 1821, the *Catholic* was issued, which was changed to the *Catholic Phœnix* in 1822, and was printed by Joseph Pratt, of Bridge Street. In the same year a second attempt was made to establish a daily newspaper here—the *Northern Express and Lancashire Daily Post*, which, though printed in Stockport, was published in Manchester for Henry Burgess, the first number appearing on the 1st of December. In 1822, the *Manchester Iris*, was started, being printed and published by Henry Smith, and was discontinued in 1823. To complete the list of these short-lived newspapers, the *Manchester Advertiser*, which was circulated gratuitously, was printed by Joseph Pratt, for Stephen Whalley, the first number appearing in July, 1825; and the *Voice of the People*, printed by John Hampson, was begun on the 1st of January, 1831, a few days after the *Mercury* had ceased to exist.

The *Manchester and Salford Advertiser* was supported by the licensed victuallers, and was begun in 1828. It was jointly owned by Mrs. Leresche and Mr. George Condy, the barrister, who was its editor and was one of the commissioners in bankruptcy. Its office was near to the present shop of Messrs. Darbyshire in Market Street, and was then removed higher up the street, and afterwards formed a conspicuous object at the corner of that street and Spring Gardens. Of the *Chronicle* mention has already been made as having enjoyed at one time the chief advertising business. Its founder was Mr. Charles Wheeler, who died in 1827, at the age of 76, Mr. John Wheeler, his son, having been taken into partnership with his father as proprietors of the *Chronicle*. I well remember John, whose face was much affected by the wind, on which account he used to ride through the streets on horseback with a veil covering his face, and won the soubriquet of the "Veiled Prophet." He was the father of the present Mr. Serjeant Wheeler, the only remaining link of a pretty numerous progeny of Manchester literary men connected with the press.

In 1829 the leading newspaper here was the *Manchester Guardian*, which was printed and published by Messrs.

Taylor and Garnett, the office being in Market Street, not far from the spot afterwards occupied by the Bank of Manchester, and now occupied by Sharp and Scott, grocers. The editor was Mr. John Edward Taylor, the senior proprietor, son of the Rev. John Taylor, a Unitarian minister, who was born at Ilminster, in Somersetshire, in 1791. He was originally intended for the medical profession, but for some reason this design was frustrated, and he was placed with a manufacturer in Manchester as an apprentice. It is said that his services were so highly valued that his indentures were given to him before his apprenticeship had terminated. In 1815 his name appears in the directory as a fustian manufacturer, and in that for 1820 as a cotton merchant. His father, about the year 1800, having joined the Society of Friends, became the manager of their school, in Jackson's Row. He resided in Islington Street, Salford, his son during the time he was in business residing next door to him, afterwards removing to the Crescent, Salford, where he lived in 1829. He early manifested a capacity for public business, and when about nineteen years of age, became secretary to the Lancasterian School. In following years he took an active part in those political discussions which then greatly agitated the public mind, and which paved the way for the beneficial changes which have taken place during the last fifty years. Cowdroy's *Manchester Gazette* was at that time the only organ of the Liberal party, and to it Mr. John Edward Taylor contributed freely, furnishing accounts of and comments on the various political transactions then passing.

It is said to be " an ill wind which blows nobody good;"

and but for one of these proverbial ill winds, we might
have been at this day without our daily *Guardian*. The
fact was that Mr. Taylor became involved in a law suit and
was prosecuted for libel, and it was this circumstance which
principally led to the establishment of the *Guardian*.
Political feeling, as we have seen, ran high in Manchester
and Salford, when in 1818 a meeting of Police Commissioners was held in Salford, at which Mr. Taylor's name
was proposed as a commissioner. This was opposed by
Mr. John Greenwood, a counterpane manufacturer, who
used some very strong language, although good Joseph
Brotherton, who was present, counselled moderation.
Mr. Taylor felt that he had been publicly insulted, and
addressed a stinging letter to Mr. Greenwood, which formed
the ground of action. The grand jury at the Salford
Quarter Sessions found a true bill against him. The trial
was removed to the King's Bench, and took place at
Lancaster, on the 29th of March, 1819. Mr. Taylor undertook his defence in person, conducting it with great ability,
and was allowed to call witnesses in justification of his
statements, it being, it is said, the only instance on record
up to that time of a defendant being allowed to do so.
Baron Wood was the judge, and Scarlett (afterwards
Lord Abinger) the prosecuting counsel; both treated him
most contemptuously. Joseph Brotherton was his first
witness, and his quietly given evidence seemed to tell on
the jury. The next was Mr. Charles Rickards, father of
the late chairman of the Board of Guardians, and who lived
in Regent Road. Scarlett evidently expected the jury would
return a verdict in accordance with his desires, and this

might have been so had it not been that the foreman was a
man made of sterling metal, honest John Rylands, of Warrington, who was observed, when the jury retired, to take his
top coat up and throw it over his arm with the air of a man
determined not to give way to fear or favour, but to see the
right done. The jury were locked up, and after waiting a
considerable time the court broke up, and by-and-by the
judge went to bed. Hour after hour passed, as Taylor's
friends paced the streets near the castle ; then a noise was
heard, and the jury were marshalled to the judge's lodgings,
and were conducted to his bedroom, where he sat bolt
upright in bed, and was astonished to receive their verdict
of " Not Guilty."

In the conduct of his defence, Mr. Taylor's friends, who
had accompanied him to Lancaster, were much impressed
with his ability and boldness. In returning, one of them
said to him, " Why don't you begin a newspaper? if you
will, we will help you." It was felt how great a need
there was of a good Liberal paper. Twelve hundred
pounds were subscribed by twelve gentlemen, and in two
years more the *Manchester Guardian* was established.
Accordingly in due course the following announcement was
made : " On Saturday the 5th of May, 1821, will be
published, price sevenpence, No. 1 of a new weekly paper
to be entitled the *Manchester Guardian*, printed and
published by J. Garnett, No. 28A, Market Street, Manchester, where orders, advertisements, and communications
will be thankfully received after the 30th of April, and in
the meantime by Mr. Sowler, bookseller, St. Ann's Square ;
Messrs. Robinson and Ellis, St. Ann's Place; and by

Mr. John Ford, Market Street." In reference to this announcement it must be borne in mind that Mr. Sowler had not then started the *Courier*. The first office of the *Guardian* was near the end of New Cannon Street. It is said that Mr. Taylor was the first newspaper proprietor in Manchester who was capable of acting as editor. He died in 1844 at the age of fifty-two. It has been truly said of him that "he was at all times an active and untiring advocate of the public improvements of the town, many of which owe their origin entirely to him."

Mr. Jeremiah Garnett originally came to Manchester from the neighbourhood of Otley with Mr. Thomas Forrest, who afterwards became a bookseller. They were both letterpress printers, and Garnett obtained employment in Mr. Wheeler's printing office, and was frequently employed in reporting. He reported the Peterloo meeting for the *Chronicle*, and was a witness on the trial of Birley and others in connection with that affair. On the establishment of the *Guardian*, Mr. Taylor engaged him to assist in reporting; and, owing to the valuable aid he was able to afford in the general management of the paper, and its improved character, which made it superior to all competitors, he became a partner, and eventually editor. At first the other Manchester journalists looked on the innovator with contempt, foretelling its speedy extinction. Leaders they regarded as a foolish innovation, and thought correct reports an unnecessary expense. As to advertisements, Mr. Wheeler, who had the main share, refused to receive any after one o'clock on the Friday; having the large impression of 3,000 to work off, he must needs go to press at three o'clock; whereas Mr. Garnett received them with thanks as late on the Friday evening as any one chose to bring them. The printed matter of a *Guardian* of fifty years ago filled a sheet about half the size of the present *Guardian*, that is to say four pages, on each of which the printed matter measured 23 inches by 18. The size of the page was afterwards enlarged to 26 inches by 20. The type was much smaller than at present, and the printing was neater. The leaders varied much in length, and each had its title printed at its head in small roman capitals. The number of advertisements form a striking contrast with those in to-day's *Guardian*, especially when it is remembered that it came out only once a week. In one of the numbers for the early part of 1829, selected quite at haphazard, there were just 111 advertisements, 85 of which were on the front page. Of the total, 13 were "legal notices," eight "sales by private contract," 37 "sales by auction," 24 "to be let," and 29 others. Two of them are illustrated, one being a tailor's advertisement, exhibiting a gentleman in a splendidly-fitting suit.

The limits of these papers prevent me from doing more than name one who joined the staff of the *Guardian* at a later period of its history, and to whose admirable reporting, and to his other labours in connection with it, its success in a great measure is due. I allude to Mr. John Harland, F.S.A., who was born at Hull in 1806 and died here in 1868.

The *Manchester Times* in 1829 was published by Archibald Prentice, in the Angel Yard, Market Place, which has since been completely metamorphosed, and is now known as the Hopwood Avenue. Mr. Prentice was a hard-headed Scotchman, the son of a Lanarkshire farmer, and when a young man came to Manchester as the agent of a Glasgow firm of muslin manufacturers. In 1819 he was living in Islington Street, Salford, next door to Mr. John Edward Taylor, and in 1824 he was still in business, residing in Faulkner Street. He formed one of the earnest, active band of reformers, who were beginning to make their influence felt. Shortly after the date last mentioned he purchased *Cowdroy's Gazette*, which then had a circulation of from 1,000 to 1,500 a week, paying Cowdroy's widow £800 down, and engaging to pay her £100 a year more for eight years. Towards the end of 1827 Mr. Prentice was in difficulties, and in January, 1828, he issued a manly address in which he explained his losses and position. This brought around him many kind and sympathizing friends, who formed a joint-stock company and incorporated the *Gazette* with a new journal, which was entitled the *Manchester Times and Gazette*. Towards the close of 1828 the title of *Gazette* was dropped, and, as I have said, the *Manchester Times* was published at Angel Yard by Mr. Prentice. In a year or two the office was removed to the left-hand side of Market Street going up, and eventually to Ducie Place, now covered by the Exchange. Mr. Prentice was joined after a short time by Mr. William Cathrall, who was for many years reporting agent for the *Times*, living in Lower Byrom Street. He was a Wesleyan with whom I was well acquainted, and attended Irwell Street Chapel. Having myself a place of business in Ducie Place at the time when the office of the *Manchester Times* was there, I used to be fond of going in on the Friday evening, and seeing the papers worked off on a roller machine, turned by a solitary man. What a contrast with what is to be seen to-day in the printing office of one of the present Manchester newspapers !

About 1845 Mr. Prentice sold the *Manchester Times* to three gentlemen, two of whom had taken a very active part in the Anti-Corn-Law agitation, Henry Rawson, Henry Barry Peacock, and Abraham Walter Paulton, when Mr. Paulton became its editor. Mr. Paulton had been a medical man at Bolton, and being present during the delivery of an Anti-Corn-Law lecture one evening, he was greatly exasperated at the stupid way in which the lecturer answered the questions of some disputant after the lecture. He jumped on the platform and undertook the task of answering the man himself. He was thus led into the vortex of agitation, and became one of the most prominent and successful of Anti-Corn-Law lecturers. I remember him well, and have frequently listened to him. He died a few years ago at his house in Surrey.

Shortly after the *Times* had changed hands another newspaper was started which advocated the same principles as the *Manchester Times*, and looked for support to the same class of readers. It took the name of the *Examiner*. It was felt by the friends of reform that there was considerable waste of power in supporting two newspapers of precisely similar views, and about 1848 a union was effected and the *Manchester Examiner and Times*, published by Alexander Ireland & Co., was the result. Mr. Thomas Ballantyne had been editor of the *Examiner*, and after a while he retired, when Mr. Paulton became editor of the *Examiner and Times.* On his retirement, about 1854, the proprietors were singularly fortunate in securing the services of the present editor, who was previously a Baptist minister in Salford. The attention of the proprietors of the paper was directed to him from the fact that the Anti-Corn-Law League had offered a large sum of money as a prize for the best essay on the Corn Laws, for which Mr. Henry Dunckley was the successful competitor. Mr. H. B. Peacock had a select tailoring business in King Street, and afterwards in St. Ann's Square, but became well known in local literary, dramatic, and musical circles. His natural bias towards literature and criticism led him in middle life to surrender his business engagements and to devote himself to more congenial pursuits. He had formerly been art, literary, and dramatic critic on the *Courier*, and after the establishment of the *Examiner and Times*, he joined its staff in the same capacity. Archibald Prentice died in 1857, aged 65 ; and H. B. Peacock in 1876.

The *Manchester Courier* fifty years ago was published by Mr. Thomas Sowler, a bookseller and stationer in St. Ann's Square. His father was a letterpress printer, and in 1794 was carrying on business as such under the firm of Sowler and Russell, at 13, Hunt's Bank. They afterwards removed to the river side of Deansgate, near the Old Church end, where Mr. Russell, after Mr. Sowler's death, continued the business in partnership with Mr. Allen, and where Mrs. Russell still continued it fifty years since. Mr. Russell, it has been mentioned before, was a Wesleyan, and was the means of introducing Methodism into the village of

Cheetham Hill. Thomas Sowler, the son, when quite a young man, opened a bookseller and stationer's shop in St. Ann's Square, on the Deansgate side near the Exchange end. It will be remembered that when the prospectus of the *Guardian* was published in 1821, Mr. Sowler's name was given as one of its agents. On the 1st of January, 1825, the first number of the *Courier* was published by Mr. Sowler, his original intention being to publish it on a Thursday. The intention, however, was changed, and it continued to be published on a Saturday till it became a daily paper. It was announced in the first number that a portion of its columns was to be devoted to Science, the Fine Arts, and Belles Lettres. Its first editor was Alaric A. Watts. Mr. Thomas Sowler will be remembered as a good-looking, rather portly, well-dressed, and gentlemanly-looking man, who, being short-sighted, generally wore his spectacles in the street.

The contrast between the Manchester newspapers of to-day, and those of fifty years ago, is remarkable. A paper now rarely, if ever, contains any reference to the contents of one of its contemporaries. Each seems to ignore the existence of the rest. In former days such references were very common.

When each paper was stamped there was no difficulty in ascertaining the average weekly number of copies of each printed. In a return made rather less than fifty years since I find the number as follows :—*Guardian*, 5,144 ; *Advertiser*, 3,827 ; *Times*, 3,269 ; *Courier*, 2,635 ; *Chronicle*, 1,038.

CHAPTER XXV.

BUILDING CLUBS.

THERE were several building societies in operation fifty years ago, and all of them were held at public-houses. The first of which I have any personal knowledge, and of which I became a member whilst quite a young man, was held at the Red Lion in Church Street. I was introduced to it by Mr. Jonathan Rawson, of Cromford Court, and remember a Mr. Mellor and Mr. William Froggatt, house painter, as members of it. I have not been able to ascertain when such societies were originated, or by whom. The first that I can hear of was held at a public-house in Ancoats in 1817. The following were in existence fifty years ago: One at the house of Joshua Beatson, the Black Mare, Canal Street, Ancoats; one at the Lamb Inn, Oldham Road, kept by William Hanley; one at the Black Horse, Greek Street, Rusholme Road; and one at the Salutation Tavern, Boundary Lane, Oxford Road, which was established by the workpeople of Mr. Hugh Hornby Birley some time between 1825 and 1830. It appears that shortly after this an effort was made to establish a building society on temperance principles, which held its meetings at the Old Meal House in Nicholas

Croft, and was afterwards removed to the Lever Street Chapel, when its name was changed from the Temperance to the Manchester and Salford Building Society.

The societies at that time existing were not on the permanent system as now, but were terminating. They seem to have been in a great measure public-house clubs, but were conducted with order and decorum, as the stringency of the rules indicates. For a long time after their first establishment it never seemed to enter the heads of the managers that one of these clubs could be held anywhere else than in a public-house, or that the business could be got through without something to drink. The landlord seems to have been quite as important a person in connection with them as the secretary. I have before me the printed rules of one which was established in 1821 at the house of Thomas Nelson, the Union Inn, Horrocks, Red Bank. As the rules present a striking contrast with the rules of building societies as at present constituted, a brief description of them may be interesting. No doubt the rules of this society were a type of others.

The spirit of the times is reflected in the legal jargon and verbosity of some of the rules, which are in the form of sixteen articles of agreement "indented, made, concluded, and fully agreed upon between Thomas Nelson, innkeeper; Thomas Constantine, joiner; William Taylor, shopkeeper; Samuel Ashworth, shopkeeper; William Reid, fustian cutter; Alexander Parkinson, silk manufacturer, six of the subscribers and also trustees, who mutually, reciprocally, jointly, separately, and distinctly covenanted, declared, and agreed, etc." The last article declares that "the parties all agree amongst themselves that they shall and will in all things well and truly observe, perform, fulfil, accomplish, pay, and keep all and singular the covenants, articles, clauses, payments, conditions, and agreements, etc."

The first article provides that there shall be three trustees, to be in office six months, when the three seniors were to retire and three others were appointed, and so on, three to be changed every six months. Anyone refusing to serve was to pay a fine of five shillings, but if re-elected within thirteen months he should not be obliged to serve. The monthly meeting was to begin at seven and close at nine p.m., and if there was any dispute as to the exact time, the matter was to be settled by the majority. The monthly subscription was ten shillings per share, and the privilege of receiving an advance was sold to the highest bidder out of three times bidding. Every member receiving his money was to pay eight shillings and fourpence per share per month. The fines for non-payment of the subscription were threepence per share for the first month, sixpence for the second, a shilling for the third, two shillings for the fourth, four shillings for the fifth, and for each following month four shillings. If not paid up at the end of twelve months, the defaulter was to be excluded and forfeit all money he had paid, as well as all the benefit belonging to him in the club. Any member entitled to receive his purchase money was to give two days' notice to the treasurer, and was to pay six shillings to the trustees for their expenses; and in case they had to go more than two miles from the Market Place, he should pay reasonable expenses. The names and residences of the trustees for

the time were to be entered in a book to be kept by the
landlord, to whom application was to be made, and if he
failed to give notice to the trustees, he was to be fined ten
shillings and sixpence. Not less than four were to act, and
if any trustee should refuse to go, he was to be fined two
shillings. Great care was to be exercised as to the admission of new members, and any member relating *(sic)* any
unfavourable remark made on any person wishing to enter
was to be fined five shillings. The landlord was to give
security for the safe keeping of the box and books of the
society, and there were to be five locks and keys to the box
—three keys for the three senior trustees, and one each
for the treasurer and landlord. When the trustees were
summoned to attend to transact certain business at a time
fixed by the senior trustee, if any of them did not attend
within half-an-hour, he was fined a shilling; if not within an
hour, two shillings; and if not within an hour and a half,
three shillings. If grievances arose, the complainant was
to apply to the trustees, who were to appoint a committee
of investigation. If the complaint were unfounded, the
person making it was to pay the expenses of the committee,
and *vice-versa.* If any member refused to serve on the bye-law
committee, he was fined two shillings; if fifteen minutes
late at any of its meetings, he was fined sixpence; if
half-an-hour late, a shilling; and an hour, eighteenpence,
unless hindered by business or indisposition. The fines
were to go to the general fund. If any of the trustees or
secretary were not in the clubroom on the night of meeting
by half-past seven o'clock, he was fined sixpence; if not by
eight, a shilling; or half-past eight, five shillings. The

senior trustee was to keep good order in the club-room.   If
any officer embezzled any money, he was to repay it and be
fined two guineas, or be excluded.

If any member of the club should manifest signs of being
under the influence of drink, he should be ordered to withdraw; if he refused he was fined sixpence, and again
ordered to withdraw; if he still refused, another fine of
sixpence was imposed, and the order to withdraw repeated,
and so on till he yielded.   Any member using offensive or
indecent language, was to be called to order, and if he
should not desist, was fined a shilling.   But if any member
should fight with or strike another he was fined five shillings.
There were two drink stewards appointed whose office
lasted for three months.   They were to serve in rotation,
as their names stood on the book, or be fined two shillings.
If a drink steward was not in the clubroom by half-past
seven he was fined threepence, if not by eight, sixpence,
and if not by half-past eight two shillings and sixpence.
The secretary was to have a salary of one guinea for the
first six months, after that it was to be fixed as the members
should agree.

There is no mention in the rules of borrowing money or
entrusting it on deposit to the society.   There was no
danger of a run on the trustees, and but little temptation
was held out to the property speculator.   The societies were
economically managed, and every member took an interest
in the welfare of the society and knew how matters were
getting on.   Not only so, but the members became
acquainted with each other, and where the club was well
conducted many a pleasant evening was often spent.

CHAPTER XXVI.

MUSIC, PAGANINI, AND MALIBRAN.

IT is just about fifty years since what may be called a revival in the musical world of Manchester seems to have taken place, the evidences of which were the establishment of the Glee Club, the building of the present Concert Hall, the institution of the Manchester Choral Society, and the production and public performance of an oratorio by a Manchester musician.

The GLEE CLUB was originated in 1830, and its meetings were held in the large room behind Hayward's Hotel, in Bridge Street. Its first president was Mr. William Shore. My master, Horatio Miller, became a member of it, and took me with him on one occasion. I remember Mr. John Isherwood as one of its members; he was a stout, thick-set man, having a capital bass voice. He was a member of the choir, I believe, at St. Peter's Church. He died shortly after this, and left a son, James, also a musical man, but who, unlike his father, was thin and spare.

The Concert Hall was opened in 1831, the Concert Rooms—as they were called—having been previously in Fountain Street. The original income from the present hall was 3,000 guineas, derived from 600 subscribers of five guineas each, each of whom had two tickets to every concert, one for himself and another for a lady member of his family, for any male under age, or for any person not resident within a prescribed distance.

The Manchester CHORAL SOCIETY was founded in 1833, and held its first meeting in the Exchange Dining Room. Amongst the professors of music then resident here was Mr. Richard Cudmore, living in George Street. He composed an oratorio called "The Martyr of Antioch," which was performed at the Theatre Royal in 1832, and from which it was thought worthy to give a selection on the occasion of the last Musical Festival here.

Amongst the musical characters of Manchester in those days I may mention the following, whom I remember : David Ward Banks; Gregory, violinist; Hughes, oboe player; Henry Arnold, teacher of music; Thomas Buck, engraver and member of Old Church choir; the two Malones, who used to sing at the Catholic Chapel; J. Sheldrick, Prestwich; and Miss Barlow, singers.

Although it is not quite fifty years since Paganini visited Manchester, and since the last Musical Festival here, I may be allowed to include them in these reminiscences. Paganini visited Manchester some little time after I came here, and well do I recollect the occasion. His performance took place in the old Theatre Royal in Fountain Street, into the pit of which I obtained admission after a desperate struggle. The steps leading to it out of Fountain Street took a sharp turn to the left, presenting an ugly elbow, against which, so great was the crush, I got jammed, and had considerable difficulty in extricating myself. The house was crowded some time before the beginning of the performance, and when at last the time arrived, a tall, gaunt figure stepped to the front of the stage with fiddle in one hand and bow in the other, with his long hair turned back showing a fine forehead and an intellectual face. Nothing could exceed his awkward appearance as he stood bowing to the audience, in response to their plaudits. He seemed like a fish out of water until the uproar ceased, when a sudden change came over him as he placed his violin in position. He then seemed all at once to forget where he was, and losing the painful expression of countenance he had previously manifested, his features assumed an earnest expression of delight and his whole soul seemed absorbed in his instrument. I make no pretensions to musical criticism, and having listened to Norman-Neruda and Joachim in later days, I have often wondered as I have been charmed by their performance whether Paganini excelled them. One marvellous feat which he accomplished that night I remember was the imitation on his violin of the several noises heard in a farm-yard, such as the cackling of geese, the braying of an ass, and the grunting of a pig. In after years a blind man known as Tom Inglescent, who kept the Paganini Tavern in Great Ancoats Street, became a very clever imitator of the great violinist.

It so happened that having finished my apprenticeship, and concluded a term of service as an assistant with Mr. Horatio Miller, I left his employ on the Saturday before the last Manchester Musical Festival, and resolved to enjoy the Festival week, which began on Monday the

12th of September, 1836.   There have been only two musical festivals in Manchester, one in 1828 and one in 1836.   On the first occasion the receipts were about £15,000, leaving a profit of £5,000, which was divided amongst the charitable institutions of the town.   In this sum, however, was included a donation of £500 from the first Sir Robert Peel, and another munificent contribution from his son and successor.   On the last occasion there was no donation higher than £20, and the receipts were £17,500, which left a profit of £4,230, out of which £1,500 were paid to the Infirmary.

The Festival included a dress ball on the Monday evening at the Assembly Rooms, four morning performances of sacred music in the Old Church, three miscellaneous concerts at the old Theatre Royal in Fountain Street, on Tuesday, Wednesday, and Thursday evenings, and on Friday evening a fancy dress ball.   The Tuesday morning's performance at the Old Church included more than fifty recitatives, airs, and choruses, and began with Attwood's Coronation Anthem, which was followed by the whole of Haydn's "Creation," in three parts.   This was succeeded by a selection from Mozart's "Requiem," and Bishop's cantata, "The Seventh Day," concluded the programme.   Besides principals there were 102 instrumentalists, and 224 chorus singers, gathered from York, London, Manchester, Liverpool, and other parts of Lancashire.   The principal vocalists were Mesdames Malibran, Caradori Allan, Assandri, Bishop, Knyvett, A. Shaw, and Clara Novello (then not more than eighteen); and of gentlemen, Lablache, Braham, Bennett, Phillips, Ivanoff, and Machin.   The principal instrumental

performers were—Violin, De Beriot (Malibran's husband);
violoncello, Lindley; contra-basso, Dragonetti; cornet,
Harper; flute, Nicholson; oboe, Cooke; clarionet,
Willman; bassoon, Baumann; and horn, Platt. The
conductor was Sir George Smart; and the leader of the
band at the evening concerts was Mori, and of the
oratorios at the church F. Cramer, whilst the organist was
W. Wilkinson, of Manchester.

It was my good fortune to be present at the concerts on
Tuesday and Wednesday evenings, on which latter occasion
I heard Malibran sing the very last note she ever sang on
earth. I was also present to hear the "Messiah" on
Thursday morning, and finished up the week with the fancy
dress ball on Friday night. On the Monday there were
two full rehearsals, one at the church, at which all the
principal and other performers were present except
Malibran, and which began at nine a.m., and did not
terminate till nearly five p.m. In the evening there was a
second rehearsal at the theatre, which was not over till
eleven p.m. At the ball on Monday evening there was a
good deal of excitement caused by a report, which rapidly
spread through the room, that several gentlemen had been
eased of their purses. Deputy-constable Thomas was sent
for and scrutinized the company, but the birds had taken
wing. However, next morning, just before the oratorio of
the "Creation" was begun, when the audience were
crowding into the church, a carriage drove up, and four
well-dressed gentlemen, with two dashingly-attired ladies,
alighted and marched up the covered way to present their
tickets. Thomas saw them and proceeded to put some

rather awkward questions to them, on which the ladies left
in disgust. The gentlemen were eventually locked up, and,
on being brought before the magistrates next morning, it
was proved that they were members of the swell-mob of
London.

At the Tuesday evening concert, after an Italian song
most exquisitely given by Lablache and Malibran, I
remember being most pleased with Phillips' rendering of
"The Light of other Days," accompanied by Harper on the
cornet, which was one of the finest performances I ever
heard. The duet by Malibran and Lablache was a comic
song, which convulsed the whole audience, he trying to
imitate Malibran in a falsetto voice, whilst she retorted
upon him in a kind of bass. It was on Wednesday evening
that Malibran sang as perhaps she had never done before,
and died in the attempt. Caradori Allan and she were
appointed to sing in a duet from "Andronico," when they
seemed to rival each other in their efforts. The scene is
very vividly impressed on my memory. There was a rather
high note, in singing which one of the two indulged in a
brilliant trill, which was followed by a similar effort on the
part of the other. The effort quite electrified the audience,
and when the song was finished the applause was almost
overwhelming, and an encore demanded. Unfortunately
Malibran responded to it, and again the two went through
their parts with (if possible) increased ardour, and retired
amidst tremendous applause. In a very short time
Dr. Bardsley (uncle of the late Sir James) was called
from his seat in the pit, with Mr. Worthington the
surgeon, to see Malibran. Soon after, one of the stewards

was obliged to announce that she had become so ill
that Dr. Bardsley had deemed it necessary to bleed her
in the arm (!), and considered it would not be safe for
her to take any further part in the performance that night.
Neither was she able to take her part in the "Messiah"
at the church the next morning, although, contrary to the
wish of the committee, and, in the first instance, of her
medical advisers, she insisted on going to the church. She
had not been long in the ante-room, however, when she
was seized with hysterics, and was brought back to her
hotel, from which she never removed till her death, which
took place on the Friday week, September 23rd. She was
interred in the Collegiate Church, on Saturday, Oct. 1st,
the Roman Catholic service for the dead having been previously performed at the hotel by the Rev. James Crook,
of St. Augustine's, Granby Row. A series of contentions
regarding the removal of Malibran's remains to Brussels
began on the Wednesday following. Representations were
made by a relative of M. de Beriot to the Festival
Committee, who in reply maintained that the funeral had
been carried out in strict accordance with the instructions
given by M. de Beriot to Mr. Thomas Beale, Alderman
Willert, and Mr. Joseph Ewart. Many negotiations took
place, and eventually a suit was instituted in the Consistory
Court. At length towards the end of December a simple
and touching letter was addressed by the singer's mother to
Mr. Sharp, the senior churchwarden, which cleared away
the opposition. Feeling had run very high, and in order
to avoid anything like popular tumult, at five o'clock on a
dark December morning, the almost weird-like scene of the

exhumation of Malibran's body took place, between twelve
and thirteen weeks after its interment, and long before
people were astir the remains of the ill-fated cantatrice were
many miles removed from Manchester.

After the effort referred to of the two queens of the
festival, Braham sang " Mad Tom," accompanied on the
piano by Sir George Smart, with splendid effect, and shortly
after Lablache gave " Non piu andrai," from " Figaro." I
remember the ease with which he sang it, standing at the
front of the stage with the fingers of his right hand between
the buttons of his waistcoat, and producing such full, rich,
mellow notes, as my next neighbour remarked to me, as
though he had a musical instrument in his inside. The
song was encored, and though I have never heard the air
since I have remembered it to this day. He was, I believe,
musical preceptor to the Queen when she was Princess
Victoria. I also call to mind the beautiful playing of a
concerto on the violoncello by William Lindley, accompanied by Dragonetti on the contra-basso.

Hearing the " Messiah" on Thursday morning for the
first time in my life under such exceptionally happy circumstances, it is no wonder that its performance afforded me
the most unbounded delight. My old master, Horatio
Miller, who was a man of refined and cultivated taste, and
had lived in London nearly all his life, told me afterwards
that the performance had exceeded anything he had ever
heard, and that the exquisite character of some of the
singing had produced such an effect upon his nerves that
he was good for nothing the rest of the day. The opening
recitative and air by Braham were fine indeed. The parts

assigned to Malibran were principally taken by Caradori Allan. In the Hallelujah Chorus, Harper's trumpet added much to its effect; it was said that he was the best performer on that instrument ever heard in England.

As to the Fancy Dress Ball, I suppose no sight like it has ever been witnessed in Manchester, either before or since, and perhaps never will be again, inasmuch as now the old Theatre Royal and the Assembly Rooms are gone, it would be difficult to find the necessary space. There was no single building in Manchester which would contain a fourth part of the persons expected to attend the ball, and hence it was determined to throw into one suite of rooms the Portico, the Assembly Rooms (which were exactly opposite, in Mosley Street), and the Theatre Royal, which was behind the Assembly Rooms, in Fountain Street. Accordingly, wide covered communications were built over Mosley Street and Back Mosley Street, connecting these buildings together, in addition to which a spacious building was erected over Charlotte Street, to be used as a refreshment-room. Although so much space was provided —for it was said that the suite of apartments referred to, with the passages, formed a promenade of little less than a quarter of a mile in length—yet the rooms were crowded to suffocation. Dancing was very difficult in the Theatre, the stage and auditorium of which were made into one great ballroom; but in the two ballrooms in the Assembly Room, and especially in the Portico Newsroom, there was a good deal of dancing. The principal entrance was in Mosley Street, not Cooper Street, and the company were at once ushered into the tea-room; but as the evening advanced, locomotion was difficult, and the passages over Back Mosley Street into the Theatre were choked with people, and it took an hour to get into the supper-room, built over Charlotte Street. Many never succeeded in reaching that room at all. The lounge or drawing-room over Mosley Street was extremely elegant, fitted up with splendour and with an appearance of great comfort, with abundance of ottomans and mirrors. I believe there were nearly five thousand persons present, and one thing which greatly surprised me was the large number of fancy dresses which arrived in Manchester to be hired out, which were sent by firms in London, and no doubt from the Continent also. As the time of the ball approached, the prices, which at first were high, were greatly moderated, so that the day before I was able to hire a dress, representing a Turkish sailor, for fifteen shillings. No doubt many of the wealthy had dresses made to order, but an enormous number were hired, and there seemed to be no limit to the supply. It was the only time in my life at which I have been present at a ball, and it was an occasion not to be forgotten.

CHAPTER XXVII.

PUBLIC AMUSEMENTS.

A DESCRIPTION of what Manchester was fifty years ago would be incomplete without some notice of the public amusements of the day, which were not so numerous as now, even in proportion to the population. Neither Belle Vue nor Pomona Gardens then flourished; but instead Vauxhall or Tinker's Gardens, in the neighbourhood of Collyhurst, was the favourite resort of the class of people who patronised that sort of thing. Instead of visitors brought by cheap trips on the rails from Lincolnshire, Warwickshire, Yorkshire, Wales, and many parts of the north of England, Tinker's Gardens were supported chiefly by Manchester people and those who lived not far distant. I cannot describe them, as I never saw them till they were in ruins, when I saw the sand they contained being carted away, but they were nothing like the others mentioned either in extent or attractiveness. They were originated some time at the close of the last century by Robert Tinker, who died in 1836, at the age of seventy. An attempt was once made to establish Zoological Gardens, which were opened in a lane turning out of the Higher Broughton Road, on the right-hand side going up. They were well stocked and tastefully laid out, but not being supported as they deserved to be, were after a time closed. The animals and their cages, the plants, and fixtures were sold by auction by Mr. Fletcher, many of the animals being purchased by Mr. Jennison, the proprietor of Belle Vue Gardens, and formed the nucleus of his present collection. Neither were there such places of amusement as the casinos and music halls of the Lower Mosley Street and Peter Street types to attract the populace. I have mentioned before that the hours of business were much longer than at present, some of the warehouses not closing till very late. As for the Saturday afternoon holiday, it was not even dreamt of. Hence people had fewer opportunities of indulging their inclinations in this direction. There was no such thing as a weekly concert of any kind; for those which preceded Hallé's, conducted by the late David W. Banks, did not begin till many years after. The opportunities afforded to people outside the Concert Hall of hearing good music were few and far between.

Kersal Moor, or as it was generally pronounced by the lower orders "Karsey Moor," races were held during the Wednesday, Thursday, and Friday of Whit week, and were then as popular as the races of to-day. The managers of Sunday Schools had not the same opportunities of presenting counter attractions by means of cheap railway trips to distant places (some of them outrageously distant) as now. Still they managed to amuse and interest the young people quite as effectually. As to the railways, there is the greatest possible contrast between the Whit week in Manchester of 1830 and that of 1880, and no stronger illustration can be furnished of how the supply of a good thing creates the demand for it.

Kersal Moor races were first established a century previously to the time I speak of, and were opposed by Dr. Byrom, who wrote a pamphlet strongly condemning them. They were kept up for fifteen years and were then discontinued, but in another fifteen years were re-established. On the second attempt, though a very long and severe paper war was carried on against their renewal, they retained their hold of the public, and in 1777 the grand stand was built. It has been previously mentioned that one of the principal supporters of the races fifty years ago was Mr. Thomas Houldsworth, M.P., a cotton spinner, who lived at No. 2, Portland Place, the site of the present Queen's Hotel. He was a great favourite with the racing public, who were much elated by the victory of any one of his horses, which were always known by his jockeys wearing jackets of green and gold. Unlike the present racecourse, as I am told, the moor was as free as the air you breathe there. Under the stands were drinking-bars, which were let off to various publicans, amongst which one of the most popular was old Joseph Blears, the landlord of the Jolly Carters at Winton, near Eccles, who was a customer of ours for soda-water. It was at his house, it will be remembered, that a servant girl was foully murdered in 1826 by two brothers named M'Keand, with the view of plundering the house. They stabbed Mrs. Blears in several parts of the body, but she survived nearly twenty years. The event caused a great sensation throughout the country. I remember going to the house and inspecting the scene of the murder. The murderers were afterwards apprehended and executed at Lancaster. Just behind the grand stand was a hillock on which, in 1790, a man was hanged for a burglary committed at the house of a Mr. Cheetham, on the Chester Road. In addition to Kersal Moor races, the Earl of Wilton opened Heaton Park for races for one or two days in the autumn of every year, and they were nearly as well patronized as the former. In 1839 the Earl discontinued them.

The barbarous sport of bull-baiting was, fifty years ago, not quite extinct, for although not practised in Manchester, it was at Eccles on the occasion of the wakes, which were attended by a large number of Manchester people who could find delight in such cruelty. Akin to this was the practice of cock-fighting, which flourished here fifty years ago. The cockpit, which, as the name implies, had been originally in Cockpit Hill, behind Market Street, was then in Salford, near Greengate. Every Whit week the sport began on the Monday and usually lasted all the week. The Earl of Derby (great grandfather of the present earl) was a chief supporter of cock-fighting, and used to stay at the Albion Hotel during Whit week. Living in Market Street, I well remember him driving down to the cockpit in a carriage and four every day about twelve o'clock in that week.

It is said that the first place employed as a theatre was a temporary structure of timber at the bottom of King Street. After this a theatre was opened in Marsden Street, in 1753, and was closed in 1775. In this year application was made to Parliament for a bill to erect what was called, fifty years ago, the " Minor Theatre," at the corner of Spring Gardens and York Street, but which was originally called the Theatre Royal. As illustrating the spirit of that age, it is worth mentioning that the bill was opposed by the Bishop of London, on the ground that Manchester was a manufacturing town, and nothing could be more destructive to the political welfare of the place; whilst it was supported by the Earl of Carlisle, because Manchester, he said, had become the seat of Methodism, and he thought there was no way so effectual to eradicate " that dark, odious, and ridiculous enthusiasm as by giving the people cheerful amusements, which might counteract their methodistical melancholy!" This building was burnt down in 1789, and the following year the theatre was erected which was standing on the same spot fifty years ago, and which (then called the " Minor"), with the Royal, in Fountain Street, were the only theatres in Manchester. I remember three of the performers at the Minor whom I knew by sight off the stage, one of whom was Henry (generally called Harry) Beverley, the lessee and manager, a man above the average size, who had a comical expression of the face. Another was a rather slim, spare man, a comedian, named Sloane; and the third was a short, stiff-built man, named Preston, who was the principal tragedian, and, I believe, a great favourite with the gallery people. He afterwards kept a public-house, and we supplied him with soda-water, so that I got to know him, and found him a very decent fellow. On one occasion Sloane ascended with some noted aëronaut in a balloon, when it was announced that after his descent he would make his way to the theatre and give the audience an

account of his aërial voyage. An attempt was made at
another time, I remember, to increase the attraction of the
theatre by providing a huge mirror, or rather set of mirrors
in one immense sheet, to divide the stage from the rest of
the house.

I remember going there on one occasion to hear a
lecture on taxation by William Cobbett. He was a
fair-complexioned, roundish-built man, above the average
height, wore knee-breeches, and presented the appearance
of a respectable, well-to-do farmer. Unlike Richard Cobden
in appearance, he resembled him in the treatment of his
subject, in his free use of Saxon words, and his clear,
common-sense way of putting his case. In connection with
his name I may say here that I remember Henry Hunt,
too, of Peterloo notoriety, proceeding up Market Street,
and standing up in an open carriage drawn by four grey
horses at a walking pace, accompanied by a crowd of
working people. He was a hardy-looking, big, square-built
man, and presented a sun-browned face. I also once
caught a sight of Sir Francis Burdett, as he was turning out
of Market Street into Pool Fold, walking with one or two
other gentlemen, and followed by a small crowd. If my
memory does not deceive me, he wore knee-breeches and
top-boots. In after-days I saw and heard Feargus O'Connor
several times.

The Theatre Royal in Fountain Street was opened in
1807, under the management of Mr. Macready (I think
the late Mr. Macready's father), at a rental of £2,000 a
year, and fifty years ago was under the management of
Mr. Robert Clarke, who, as before stated, was a friend of

my master. I have previously explained that my father, being a Wesleyan minister, bound me an apprentice to a gentleman of the same religious denomination, who, during my apprenticeship, sold the business to Mr. Horatio Miller, of London, who, amongst other literary and artistic tastes, was dramatically inclined. As I remained with Mr. Miller, it was in this way I gained a knowledge of various actors, both eminent and ordinary, and have already mentioned several great performers, such as Charles Kemble, Dowton, Macready, and others, who, when in Manchester, used to visit my master, and with some of whom I have dined at the ordinary table. Amongst the regular company of the Theatre Royal was a comedian named Baker, who used to call, and who was very popular with theatrical audiences, and rather witty. I remember hearing of his once entering the bar of the White Bear, where were a number of gentlemen whom he knew. One of them, who had a silver snuff-box, after taking a pinch of snuff from it, laid it on the table, when Baker, taking it up and likewise taking a pinch, put the box into his pocket and was walking off with it. On being called back and requested to leave the box behind him, he replied that it seemed "a hard case that a poor actor was not allowed to take a box for his own bene-fit." The White Bear was then kept by the well-known Ben Oldfield, of whom it was written after his death: "This gentleman might not be inaptly styled the Peter Pindar of Lancashire; his wit was keen and brilliant, and his humour rough, but full of living nature." I remember him as a well-built, pleasant-looking, and well-dressed man.

Some years after, and before the Free Trade Hall was

built, in the days of the Anti-Corn-Law agitation, a large bazaar was held in the old Theatre Royal, in which I took an active part. A committee of nearly two hundred ladies was formed, including many who had distinguished themselves in works of charity and philanthropy in various parts of the country. It was originally intended that it should be held in the Town Hall, but it soon became apparent that the building would not be large enough. The Theatre Royal was at length fixed upon, and its whole interior changed under the superintendence of an architect. The pit was boarded over, and its sombre appearance was converted into one of great beauty and brilliance. There has been no bazaar like it either before or since. It was continued for ten working days, viz., from the Monday of one week to the Thursday of the following week, during which the greatest enthusiasm prevailed. The receipts were £8,333, which was made up to £10,000 by the proceeds of a sale of the remains by auction and by various donations of money. There were thirty-eight stalls, at one of which a sister of Richard Cobden presided. Living authors contributed many of their works, amongst whom were Campbell, Moore, Rogers, Ebenezer Elliott, the Rev. John Foster, Dr. Pye Smith, Airy (the Astronomer Royal), Dr. Elliotson, Miss Martineau, and Mrs. Marcet. A very large and very valuable collection of autographs, including those of the Queen, Prince Albert, and the Royal dukes, was disposed of by lottery. There was a large refreshment stall presided over by Mrs. Thomas Woolley, and as I supplied the soda water and lemonade, I undertook the management of that department for her.

I had the free run of the building, and never enjoyed a week and a half more. I remember getting up into the higher regions of the theatre and discovering how thunder was produced and whence the hail came.

The old building was burnt down on the 7th of May, 1844, having been in use thirty-seven years. In it the most renowned men and women in the dramatic profession appeared from time to time during its existence.

CHAPTER XXVIII.

DRESS AND CONCLUSION.

IN concluding these reminiscences it must naturally be
the case that several subjects illustrating the condition
of Manchester fifty years ago will remain unnoticed. There
are one or two matters, however, which may here be
mentioned promiscuously. And first a word on gentlemen's
dress, which differed in many respects from that of to-day.
To begin at the highest point. The hat worn by gentlemen
was always what is commonly called a "top hat," which
was covered with beaver, a gentleman's beaver hat being
an article now quite out of fashion. There were such
things as silk hats, but the silk was not so skilfully prepared
as now, and the hats then covered with silk were shabbier
and cheaper than beaver hats. The soft flexible felt hats
so much worn (especially by clergymen) at this day, a
gentleman would have been ashamed to be seen in. It is
difficult to say why so many clergymen, who should of all
men look clean and gentlemanly, delight in wearing such
shabby old felt hats. A clergyman fifty years ago looked
the gentleman. Next, under the hat you always saw the
lip and chin clean-shaved. A man who let his beard grow
would have been taken for a foreigner. So that in these

two respects many of the male portion of society, with some of the clergy at their head, have undoubtedly retrograded. Wearing a queue, which was so common at the close of the last century, had just gone out of fashion, the last person in Manchester who wore one, as I have stated previously, being Mr. Yates, of the Star Hotel, in whose family the hotel yet remains.

Loose shirt collars had not come into use, and the collar, if worn at all, was generally part of the shirt, and but comparatively few persons wore them. Instead of the light, narrow neckties now worn, large bulky neckerchiefs and stiff deep stocks were the fashion. Elderly gentlemen wore their shirts at the breast finished off by a large plaited ruffle. The coat was generally swallow-tailed and made of good broadcloth, and rarely of the cheap shoddy material now so much used. Frock coats were beginning to come into use, but the other were more general, and often made of coloured cloth, as blue or brown, in which case they were adorned with bright, metallic buttons, either gold or silver-plated. Many persons will remember the late Mr. C. J. S. Walker, the magistrate, whose blue coat, buttoned up to the chin and adorned with bright buttons, was about the last of the kind seen in Manchester. The coat collar was very much deeper and the sleeve narrower, especially at the wrists, following the shape of the arm, so that the coat could not be easily slipped on and off as now, but required a good deal of uncomfortable tugging for the purpose. The lower garment was passing through a transition state. Knee-breeches were going out and trousers were coming in, young and middle-aged men generally wearing the latter, whilst most elderly men adhered to the old fashion, with which gaiters made of the same material as the breeches were generally worn. Trousers were made much narrower than at present, so much so that they were generally strapped down under the boot. This last article of apparel was a very different thing from the convenient boot now adopted. The manufacture of india-rubber goods had not then been developed, and elastics were unknown. The boot for men then in fashion was the Wellington, the leg of which reached above the calf, and the average cost of which was twenty-seven shillings a pair. For an outside covering with elderly men, the jacket introduced by Lord Spencer and named after him was a favourite. Younger men often wore a plain cloak made of fine cloth, having a simple collar without any cape. I well remember my master having one such made of blue cloth with velvet collar and lined with red, unbuttoned in front.

I dare not venture to say anything as to the dress of the ladies, which of course has undergone endless changes since the days we speak of. I will only say that two of the most striking changes refer to the head and the feet. For first the ladies wore bonnets—and bonnets then were bonnets, though they were not so large as when John Wesley denounced those of his followers who wore " elephantine bonnets." A hat was rarely seen on a lady's head. A favourite pattern was that of the " cottage bonnet," under which many a pretty face with neatly parted hair was often admired. Secondly, the most striking feature in a lady's walking attire at that time was that boots were not worn, instead of which it was customary to see ladies in the street clad in low sandal shoes, with white stockings and comparatively short dresses.

I should like to mention another matter with respect to which a great change has taken place in Manchester during the last fifty years. I allude to the diminution of the practice of what is called swearing on the part of respectable men. When I came to Manchester as an apprentice in 1829 it was quite common for respectable gentlemen, when they came into the shop to make a purchase, unconsciously and habitually to use some of those expressions which are classed under the head of swearing. The practice was very common in ordinary conversation, but now it is a rare thing to hear what you formerly did. Amongst the lower orders I fear no such improvement has taken place, either with regard to swearing or drunkenness; for as to the latter also I think an improvement has taken place on the part of respectable people.

I have mentioned before that fifty years ago there were only twenty-three tobacconists' shops in Manchester, whilst to-day there are nearly 500. It was a rare thing then to see a respectable person smoking a pipe as he went to business in a morning, especially a young man, to say nothing of mere youths.

I can only allude to a class of subjects so vast and so interesting that a good volume might be written on them. I refer to the thousand and one scientific inventions of the past half century which have been applied in so many ways to the improvement and the manufacture of articles in use in every-day life, tending to lighten labour, make life more comfortable, and in various ways minister to our happiness. Take one very simple instance as an illustration—that of a trifling and insignificant article which, though in daily use, is thought but little of. Few people stop to bestow a moment's thought on the great convenience promoted by its use as compared with the inconvenience which attended the striking of a light fifty years ago. People who only know the lucifer match have no idea of the trouble and inconvenience of the tinder-box and flint and steel in use fifty years ago. The tinder box was a round tin box, with a loose lid fitting inside upon the tinder, which was domestically prepared by the burning of rags, in the production of which a little skill was required, and which it was requisite to keep dry. The operator took in one hand the steel, which was shaped like a small letter n of the fifteenth century, and the flint in the other, and began striking them together over the exposed tinder till a spark fell and ignited it. Sometimes the spark expired, when the operation was recommenced and continued till the tinder was ignited, when the operator gently blew the spark with his mouth and applied a match which ignited. These matches were very roughly made and were about six or eight inches long, having had both their roughly pointed ends dipped in melted brimstone. Everybody will see what a tedious and troublesome process this was as compared with the present mode of striking a light. Is it wrong, in the interests of us non-smokers, to wish that it was still as difficult to strike a light out of doors?

I well remember the first lucifer matches sold in boxes, about two or three years after I came here as an apprentice.

The maker's name was Jones, and they were a shilling a box, the box being about the same size as at present. The matches were neatly made and were broad and thin, about the thickness of a piece of cardboard. With each box was given a piece of sand-paper doubled, through which you drew the match sharply. I have on my library table a tin box for many years used for postage stamps, which more than forty-five years ago contained lucifer matches. It is about twice the size of an ordinary penny box of matches, painted inside and out, and so well made it seems but little the worse for wear, and which sold for half-a-crown when full of matches.

I might also instance the marvellous development of the indiarubber trade in the manufacture of mackintosh garments, elastic cord and webbing, and numerous articles used in surgery, nursing, and for other purposes.

There are many other changes in everyday matters which are the result not so much of scientific invention as of the application of common sense and experience; as, for instance, the improved method of removing furniture in covered vans. The old way of loading it on a lurry or in an ordinary cart, and transporting it from one part of the country to another in wet weather, was one of the most miserable undertakings one can conceive. One wonders why some such plan as the present was not adopted sooner.

There is hardly a science that can be named which has not contributed its share to the happiness and well-being of mankind during the past half century. During that time the electric telegraph has been invented; the art of the photographer has arrived at a high state of perfection;

steam ships have learnt to trust themselves beyond our rivers and coasts and have ventured on the wide ocean, and now find their way to all parts of the world; the spectroscope has almost rivalled the telescope in the marvellous character of its discoveries; and many industries have been almost revolutionized through the improvements which have been effected in them.

True, these inventions are not confined to Manchester; still they are intimately associated with these Reminiscences. One cannot but feel an interest in the future as well as the past, and wonder what sort of place Manchester will be in fifty years hence—how large it will be, and what the moral, educational, and social condition of its inhabitants will be. It may be the lot of some other observer of men and things in the year 1930 to try to interest his fellow-townsmen by REMINISCENCES OF MANCHESTER FIFTY YEARS AGO.

APPENDIX.

The following additional information, in reference to one or two gentlemen mentioned in the preceding pages, has appeared in the columns of the *Manchester City News* :—

MANCHESTER DOCTORS, page 47.—MANCUNIENSIS, F.S.A., says : "Mr. Slugg has furnished us with a great amount of interesting and reliable information respecting Manchester druggists and medical men of a past and passing generation. Brazenose Street appears to have been at one time a sort of medico-classic ground, but its fame in that respect has now almost, if not entirely, vanished. One worthy, I may mention, has been overlooked—an old bachelor surgeon of the name of Tomlinson, who was an especial favourite with the ladies, and a practitioner of general good repute. Dr. Carbutt died from an attack of paralysis, about 1833; he was clever, eccentric, and sarcastic. Speaking once of the increasing number of lecturers, he said he could not expectorate out of his window without spitting upon one of that fraternity. He was associated and on intimate terms with John Dalton, Peter Clare, John Davies, Andrew Buchan, and others of the philosophic school, but his companionship did not tend to his equanimity of temper. On one occasion, being at the same dinner table with the late Sir James Kay-Shuttleworth, then Dr. J. P. Kay, the latter being summoned to attend a distant patient, Dr. Carbutt, as soon as the door was closed, rose from his seat, and striking the table violently, exclaimed, 'Confound it, I quite forgot to tell my servant to send for me.' It is, I think, to be regretted that the five years' apprenticeship to a medical practitioner was abolished, for various and substantial reasons, which might easily be assigned. The pupil of

Mr. Ollier was Mr. Charles Juckes. Mr. Richmond, an old pupil of Mr. Windsor, settled down to practice in Stretford Road, then a new neighbourhood, after waiting some time in Gartside Street, on the departure of Mr. Hunt to join Dr. Radford, in Ridgefield. Mr. Richmond's able and exhaustive report on the sanitary condition of Hulme, in 1849, with those of Mr. Hatton for Chorlton, and Mr. Kirkham for Ardwick, which followed, was the first to attract public attention to the hygienic condition of the masses, and led to, if indeed it was not the direct cause, of the formation of the present Sanitary Association. The report of the first-named gentleman, made after the fever and choleraic visitations of 1847 and 1849, and presented to the chairman of the Chorlton Board of Guardians, I have read, and do not find it much, if at all, improved upon by more recent sanitary investigations. It contains much valuable information as to the condition of the township, and with the statistical tables and chart accompanying, shows clearly where the fever nests lay, and the physical and social influences that so greatly affected the mortality in particular localities. The late Mr. Walker Golland at one time lived in Brazenose Street, and Mr. Roberts resided in Lever Street, nearly opposite Mr. Fawdington's house."

Dr. RADFORD reminds me that I have omitted the name of Mr. WILLIAM WOOD—a medical practitioner whose reputation was very high. The fact is he had retired from practice more than fifty years ago, and his name is not to be found in the Directory either of 1829 or 1832. He was one of the surgeons of the Lying-in Hospital, and had been a pupil at the Infirmary, afterwards becoming house surgeon to that institution. On commencing practice, he was presented with a magnificent silver cup by the Trustees of the Infirmary, which he bequeathed to Dr. Radford. He used to live in King Street, and died at Didsbury, in 1852, in his 84th year, affording another instance, in addition to the many already mentioned, of the longevity of medical men who have spent the best part of their lives in the heart of Manchester.

HORATIO MILLER, page 72.—Mrs. ISABELLA BANKS communicates the following: "May I add a few words by way of addenda to

Mr. Slugg's very copious and valuable reminiscences? He remarks that Horatio Miller, of Market Street, ' was no common man,' and he is quite right in so saying. He was a man of scholarly attainments and fastidious refinement, a perfect gentleman in manner and bearing; somewhat caustic and cynical, his sarcasm was withering. But he was far from unkindly, as I know, for he overlooked and advised upon my *Ivy Leaves* before the volume went to press, though his own versification was wofully wanting in poetry; one more proof that criticism is a distinctive faculty. Mr. Slugg, perhaps, was not aware that Mr. H. Miller had gone out with either Captain Parry or Sir John Ross (or both) on one of their early Arctic expeditions. He had been, as a youth, offered an appointment as ' page ' to George the Fourth, and rejected the offer as *infra dig.* At one time I think he wrote the dramatic critiques for the *Advertiser.* At all events, he was a frequenter of the theatres. He was in the stage box of the old Theatre Royal the night when, during the performance of *The Tempest*, the wires by which Ariel (Miss Gardner) was suspended, gave way, and she fell from a considerable height face downwards on the stage; Prospero (Mr. Butler) being too inebriated to stand steadily, much less rush to her assistance. Had he been sober he might have broken her fall, caught her, in fact, as I from the upper boxes saw first one wire snap, and then the second with the extra strain. As it was, Mr. Miller disappearing from the stage-box was one of the first to reach her, there being a door communicating with the stage close to the stage-box, and, having some medical knowledge, was of use. He told us the next morning she was more frightened than hurt. I and my friends thought she must be half killed. At the last Manchester Musical Festival (during which Malibran died) there was a magnificent fancy ball to wind up with, theatre, assembly rooms, portico, all being pressed into the service, and connected with temporary galleries, and a refreshment-room built over Charlotte Street. Mr. Miller for that occasion assumed the character of a jester (probably Touchstone), having had a model of his own head and face taken for his gilt bauble. His dress was rich and appropriate—two shades of amber trimmed with gold. He looked the cynical, not to say sardonic, jester to a T, and was fully capable of sustaining the character."

JOSEPH GALE, page 98.—FELSTOX remarks : " I have always had
great pleasure myself, and known others also who have looked forward
to Mr. Slugg's interesting communications. Mr. Joseph Gale was
apprenticed to Mr. Dominic Bolongaro, who was a printseller, frame
maker, carver, and gilder, and had his place of business in Old Millgate,
on the left-hand side from the Market Place, where he also sold mathematical instruments. At this place, while Mr. Gale was there, I bought
an ivory sector, for which I paid 7s. 6d. Mr. Gale was in business as
printseller and gilder, in Market Street, near Cromford Court, and I
believe in the identical shop now occupied by Mr. Dominic Bolongaro,
son of the one Gale served his apprenticeship with. After this Mr.
Gale had a shop in King Street, where for some time he carried on the
business of printseller, carver, gilder, and picture-frame maker. This
shop was separated by an entry leading into Back King Street, from
Miss Boardman's well-known confectionery establishment—rebuilt, and
now a glass shop. Gale's old shop was taken by the late Mr. Findley,
the bootmaker, and where that business is still carried on. I should
not omit to mention that Gale had a stall in what was called the
Bazaar in Police Street, in which building there was also a diorama ;
but I suppose the place did not answer, and the whole of it was let to
Messrs. Watts, before Kendal, Milne, and Faulkner took it, and so
enormously enlarged it by adding to it the adjoining shops and warehouses, nearly rebuilding it altogether. Gale was also at one time an
auctioneer, and sold the stock of greyhounds which belonged to the
late Philip Houghton. One of the dogs, called Priam, had just won the
Waterloo Cup, and Gale sold it by auction for upwards of two hundred
guineas. Gale was once a hatter in Ducie Place, never in King Street.
This place commenced in Market Street, having on one side the
Exchange, and ended in Bank Street, opposite to the present Ducie
Buildings. Now it is part of the present Exchange. Here Gale introduced a new feature into the hatting trade. He had a barrel of beer
with cheese for his visitors, whom he hoped to make customers if not
so already. In the rage for share speculations Gale became a sharebroker, and was a cheerful member of that community ; and if he did
not die wealthy he was not alone, after the fearful panic of 1847. As

a printseller, Gale had an excellent connection, and published several engravings, one of Heaton Park Races, under the patronage of the Earl of Wilton. He also published a most excellent engraved portrait of John Wells (Wells, Cooke, and Potter). But he was better known for his sparkling wit, his humour, his drollery, which were inimitable. He was always welcome at the 'feast of reason and the flow of soul.' He was once a good singer, but his voice failed him, and I remember he once said (on being asked) that he did not feel well, and perceived that his memory was failing him. He forgot to go home at nights. Gale had no fancy for dogs, and was never considered an intemperate man. He was acceptable to the learned Condy on account of his classical inclinations and general intelligence. I remember there was a Mr. Gale about that time who, as I am told, was in business as a maker-up, callenderer, or packer. He was fond of greyhounds and coursing ; but whether he, to use the expression, 'coursed away all his substance' I know not."

[The Mr. Gale here referred to was Mr. Robert Gale, of the firm of Gale and Mayor, who lived 50 years ago in Chapel Walks, and whose works were close by in Back Pool Fold.]

Mr. D. W. BANKS, page 103.—The following is from Mr. J. HULME : "Mr. D. W. Banks was a great favourite of mine, and I believed at one time there was no one equal to him as a musician and conductor of concerts, such as those I well remember him conducting at the popular Monday evening concerts in the Old Free Trade Hall, under what I consider now to have been very great difficulties, for he had to be conductor and accompanist both in one—sometimes on the organ, and sometimes on the pianoforte, according to the nature of the piece to be performed. There was no band then, the prices of admission being so low that a band was out of the question. The best seats were only one shilling, the second seats or gallery sixpence, and all the rest threepence—truly working-class prices. Programmes were printed every week with the whole of the words of the pieces, and were sold at a penny. I have a small number of them now in my possession, including four oratorios, the 'Messiah,' the 'Creation,' 'Elijah,' and 'Israel in Egypt.' I can spend an hour very agreeably now and then looking over these old programmes, and calling to mind who sang such and such pieces, and the impression I had at the time about each of them. Mr. Banks encouraged and brought out as much as he possibly could at these concerts the local talent, which he was quick to discern, and, when found, he put to the fore. He did not entirely depend on local talent, however, but had help sometimes from the neighbouring county of Yorkshire, such as Mrs. Sunderland and others. I think it need not be recounted the number of Christmas days that Mr. D. W. Banks produced Handel's masterpiece, the "Messiah," which practice is worthily continued by an able successor, Mr. De Jong. I fully believe that the late D. W. Banks, and the popular Monday evening concerts at the old Free Trade Hall, effectually prepared the way for Mr. Charles Hallé and the now famous Thursday evening concerts at the new Free Trade Hall, and that it is a misfortune for the working classes of Manchester and Salford that the opportunity for hearing really good music at a working-class rate is lost to them through the want of a sufficiently large room at little cost and another talented and energetic conductor like Mr. David Ward Banks. An incident came under my observation when Mr. Banks was organist at St. Thomas's Church, Pendleton. When he first went to St. Thomas's, the church-wardens had only a small hired organ with six stops, which, as may be supposed, did not quite satisfy the rising ambitions of Mr. D. W. B., nor the churchwardens either, one of whom was the late Jeremiah Royle, a warm supporter of music in Manchester, and a friend of the late John Isherwood and Mr. Wilkinson, the organist, both connected with St. Peter's choir, Manchester, at the time. Efforts were accordingly made, and a new organ obtained, I think from Wren and Boston, and it was set up and announced by placard to be opened on a certain day, and that the then leading organist of the day would preside— Mr. Wilkinson. This did not suit Mr. Banks, who was now a rising young man, so he rebelled, and a new arrangement had to be made, fresh placards printed and posted, which said that the new organ would be opened on such a day, and that Mr. David Ward Banks would preside—and he did, Mr. Wilkinson coming a short time after-wards to test the instrument. On the opening day several singers came from Manchester to assist the regular choir, which consisted of a family from Pendlebury—father, son, daughter, and nephew. Miss Cordwell, the daughter, was a beautiful singer, and Mr. B. was proud of her. In the evening more assistants came, and one or two of them pushed past Miss Cordwell (who was very diminutive) to the place of honour next to the organist. Mr. B. ordered them away, and Miss C. to come to her own place."

JOHN LAW, page 201.—Mr. ROBERT WOOD, of Cheetham Hill, says: "Allow me to supplement Mr. Slugg's interesting reminiscences by a few additional particulars respecting the Law family. David Law, the father of the celebrated John or Jack Law, kept the Bowling Green Hotel, in Strangeways. This hotel was perhaps a hundred yards beyond the Ducie Arms, and together with the green ran back to the river. I believe it was kept most if not all its time by David Law and his widow and their son David. After Mrs. Law was a widow she became very celebrated for making veal pies, and it was then usually known as the Veal Pie House, and is still well remembered by several old men who, when they were boys attending the Grammar School, would often go into the country, as they then called it, to fetch a veal pie for dinner. Through the kindness of a friend I have in my possession at present a subscriber's ticket, well got up and in good preservation, which reads as follows :—

Strangeways New Bowling Green. Subscription from May the 5th to October 27, 1788, Thursdays excepted, 10s. 6d. Not transferable. No. 2.

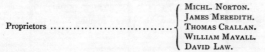

Proprietors ....
- MICHL. NORTON.
- JAMES MEREDITH.
- THOMAS CRALLAN.
- WILLIAM MAYALL.
- DAVID LAW.

This bowling green is now covered with streets and buildings ; but perhaps it would be interesting to state a few particulars relating to the gentlemen named above. Michl. Norton was the agent of Sir Oswald Mosley, and collected his rents. James Meredith was the uncle of Mr. Meredith, law stationer in King Street. Thomas Crallan was a brewer living at Ardwick, and was succeeded by his son, who became a wealthy man and left the neighbourhood more than half a century ago. William Mayall was an ironmonger in Cateaton Street. David Law, as I have before named, was the landlord. William Mayall began business as an ironmonger in Cateaton Street in the year 1745, and it was continued by him till the year 1797. It was then transferred to Hutchinson and Mallalieu till 1827, and was afterwards continued by Mallalieu and Lees to 1837, then Lees and Lister, then Lees alone, Lees' executors, and is now Leech Brothers. So that the same business has been conducted on the same premises for the last hundred and thirty-four years.

THE POST OFFICE, page 202.—Although the following refers to a date much anterior to that of the preceding Reminiscences—it will be found very interesting as giving an authentic account of the Manchester Post Office 160 years ago. It is an extract from the Fourth Annual Report of the Postmaster-General, published in 1858, and was kindly communicated to me at the last moment by Mr. W. Clarke, the Postmaster of Worthing. The Mr. Eldershaw mentioned is the same gentleman named previously on page 204. The Extract is given verbatim.

EXTRACT from a REPORT by Mr. GAY.

"As a contrast to the Manchester of the present time, with its *three* London mails every day, its almost hourly communication with Liverpool, and its two or more posts with all the surrounding towns, I beg to append this copy of a Manchester postal bill dated 1721, for which I am indebted to Mr. Eldershaw of the Manchester Post Office.

' At Manchester

'According to the last regulation, 1721.

The Post goes out

'To London, &c., or to any ⎫ Monday ⎫
  of the towns in or near ⎬ Wednesday ⎬ Morning 9 o'clock.
  the road to London ⎭ Saturday ⎭

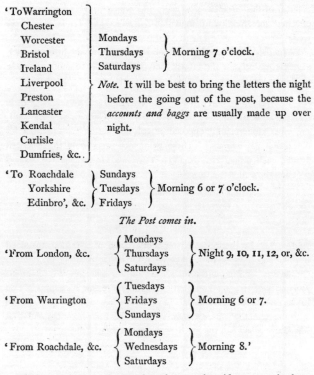

'To Warrington
Chester
Worcester
Bristol
Ireland

Mondays
Thursdays
Saturdays
} Morning 7 o'clock.

Liverpool
Preston
Lancaster
Kendal
Carlisle
Dumfries, &c.

Note. It will be best to bring the letters the night before the going out of the post, because the *accounts and baggs* are usually made up over night.

'To Roachdale
Yorkshire
Edinbro', &c.

Sundays
Tuesdays
Fridays
} Morning 6 or 7 o'clock.

The Post comes in.

'From London, &c.

Mondays
Thursdays
Saturdays
} Night 9, 10, 11, 12, or, &c.

'From Warrington

Tuesdays
Fridays
Sundays
} Morning 6 or 7.

'From Roachdale, &c.

Mondays
Wednesdays
Saturdays
} Morning 8.'

"It is amusing to observe that the post is said to come in from London three days per week at night 9, 10, 11, 12, or, &c. The beautiful uncertainty as to the hour leads one to surmise that an Inspector-General of Mails did not exist in those days.

"Then, again, the simplicity with which some clerk, having an eye to his own comfort, entreats the public to bring their letters the night before, because 'the *accounts* and *baggs* usually made up over night,' is at sad variance with the existing regulations of the Department through which letters can be posted up to within *five* minutes of the dispatch of a mail, and which provide for the receipt of letters for America up to within *ten minutes of the sailing of the packet.*

"Whether the manufacturers of Manchester would listen to such a gentle entreaty in the present day, even if it were more correctly written, is extremely doubtful."

MR. WILLIAM GARNETT.—Mr. DAVID KELLY thinks "it is scarcely accurate to say (page 252) that Mr. Garnett, of Lark Hill, 'so often unsuccessfully opposed Joseph Brotherton as a candidate for parliamentary honours.' These gentlemen were only thrice pitted against each other, viz., in 1832, 1837, and 1841. On the second occasion the poll stood thus :—

> Brotherton......................... 890
> Garnett 888
> _____
> Majority............... 2

And as Mr. Brotherton voted for himself, and Mr. Garnett abstained from voting, there was not much room for either boasting or wailing. On the first counting of the votes, the returning officer gave Mr. Garnett a majority of six, and that gentleman was addressing his supporters on his success, in the grounds at Lark Hill, when a messenger arrived with the news that there was an error in the first counting, and that Mr. Garnett had lost the election by two votes."

ERRATUM.

MR. HEAP'S GRAND-DAUGHTER.—At page 70 it is said : "I understand that Mrs. Pochin, the wife of the M.P., is the grand-daughter" of the Mr. Heap there mentioned. The author regrets to say that he has been misinformed on the subject.

OBITUARY.

No less than the following eight persons, named in the preceding pages, have departed this life since these lines first appeared in print :—

Mr. THOMAS SLAGG, mentioned on page 21, a younger brother of the late Mr. John Slagg. He had retired from business, and had resided at Lytham for many years. I knew him well, and before his leaving Manchester, was very intimate with him. He was a friendly and somewhat jovial man.

Miss GERALDINE E. JEWSBURY, the novelist, named on page 65, died on the 23rd of September, 1880.

The LADY referred to on page 82, as possessing a Bible and Prayer Book purchased at the shop of Mr. Charles Ambery. She died August 9th, 1880, aged 65 years. Whilst she lived, she took great interest in the production of these Reminiscences, and, had she been spared, would have been gratified in seeing their completion in their present shape.

Mr. THOMAS ROWORTH, bookseller, of St. Ann's Square, mentioned page 85, died January 13th, 1881, aged 65 years, having been born on the day on which the battle of Waterloo was fought. He was greatly respected by all who knew him.

Mr. EDWARD GOODALL, carpet dealer, King Street. He originally came from Heckmondwike, more than fifty years ago, and established a very extensive business, in the shop which still retains his name. He had been a teetotaler the greater part of his life, and died a bachelor, at more than eighty years of age, at his residence at Sale, having been a friend of mine for more than forty years.

Miss ELIZABETH RONCHETTI, (page 98,) eldest daughter of Mr. Joshua Ronchetti, a maker of hydrometers, &c., next door to the shop in which I was an apprentice and afterwards an assistant. After living in Salford for many years, she latterly went to reside at Southport, where she died in 1880.

The Rev. WILLIAM KIDD, incumbent of Didsbury, and formerly of St. Matthew's Church, (page 126,) was killed at Didsbury Railway Station, through incautiously stepping out of the train before it had stopped, on the 18th of December, 1880.

The Rev. DUDLEY JACKSON, rector of St. Thomas', Heaton Chapel, (page 126,) died during the year 1880.

INDEX.

—•—

Abbey, Mark, 154
Abinger, Lord, 284
Abrahams, Rev. A., 192
Academy, Manchester, 261
,,   Blackburn, 131
Accidents, Coach, 215, 218, 269
Accounts' Committee, 236
Acres Fair, 13
Acton, 133
Addison, 39
Advertiser, Manchester, 277, 282
Agnew & Zanetti, 97
Agricultural Society, 267
Ainsworth, James, 51, 249, 264, 266
,,   W. H., 171
,,   Crossley, & Sudlow, 197
,,   Sykes & Co., 30
,,   T. & D., 133
Air Balloon, 249
Airy (Ast. Royal), 314
Albion Hotel, 222, 310
Alcock, Ann, 258
Alcock, Samuel, 173
Aldis, Rev. John, 187
Alexander, 146
Allan, Caradori, 300, 302
Allen, 19, 165
Ambery, Ch., 81, 88
Amusements, Public, 307
Ancoats Chapel, 166
Anderton's Universal Advertiser, 278
Andrew, R., 236
Andrews, 75, 76
,,   Henry, 203
,,   Miss, 81
Angel Yard, 287

Ansell, 68, 184
Anti-Corn-Law Agitation, 29, 139, 289, 290, 314
Anti-Slavery Agitation, 182
Argus, 280
Arkwright, Sir R., 93
Armitage, Sir Elkanah, and family, 92, 113, 133, 139, 236
Armitage, Elijah, 132
Arnold, Henry, 298
Arrival of Mails, 211
Ashton, Rev. Jos., 178
,,   Dr. & Father, 52, 175
Ashworth, Samuel, 293
Assandri, 300
Assembly Rooms, 10, 271, 305
Assize Courts, 113
Aston, Joseph, 280, 281
,,   J. P. & Ed., 197
,,   W. P., 89
Athenæum, 271
Atherton, Rev. William, 159, 161
Atkin, Eli, 60, 69, 153, 154
Atkinson & Barker, 61
,,   & Birch, 3, 200
,,   Street, 12
,,   Thomas, 186
Atomic Theory, 107
Attmore, Rev. Charles, 159
Attorneys, 195
Attwood's Cor. Anth., 300
Aubrey, 273
Australia, 199
Author's Brother, 25
Autographs of Queen, &c., 314
Auxilium, 232

Back Square, 13
Bailey, Charles and J. E., 131
,, T. B., 256
Bake, James, 99, 112
Baker, 313
,, J. G., 165
Bakers, Buxton, 100
Ball (Dr. M'All's), 141, 143
Balloon Ascent, 312
Ballantyne, Thomas, 289
Bally, William, 109
Balm of Gilead, 280
Bamford, 274
Bancks & Co., 85
Banks, Dr., 47, 49
,, D. W., 103, 298, 308, 327
,, Isabella, 324
Bann, 118
Bannerman, 7, 10, 238
Baptist Chapels, 187
Bardsley, Dr. J. L., 47, 249, 268
,, ,, S. A., 47, 302
Barge, J. & Co., 32
,, John, 267
,, Robert, 137
Barker, Robert, 185
Barley Meal, 95
Barlow, John, 236
,, Miss, 298
,, Richard, 148, 149
Barnby, Faulkner, & Co., 224
Barnes, Robt., 162, 163, 165
Barnes', Robert, Mother, 165
,, Thos., 163
,, Rev. Dr., 171, 260
Barratt, J. & S., 95
Barrett, James, 197
Barristers, 195
Barrow, Peter, 266
,, William, 273
Barry, Ch., 126, 270
Barton, John & Henry, 85
,, S., 52
Basnett, Rev. R., 119
Bateman, W., 258
Baths, Infirmary, 9
Battle, Murder, 45
Baumann, 301

Baxter, Ed., 175
Bayley, Rev. Cornelius, 121
Bazaar, Anti-Corn-Law, 314
Bazley, Thomas, 236
Beadles, Police, 237
Beale, Thomas, 303
Bealey, Mary, 42, 149, 161
,, Richard, 42
,, ,, & Co., 41
Beard, Miss M., 258
,, Rev. J. R., 176
Beardoe, James, 270
Beardsall, Rev. F., 139
Beatson, Joseph, 292
Beaufort, J. St. L., 203
Beaumont, G., 133
Beauvoisin, Amand, 103
Beaver Hats, 316
Becker, 5
Bee Hive Restaurant, 83
Beer Houses, 113
Beef Steak Chapel, 194
Beever, J., 266
Behrens, 10
Bellhouse, 44, 236
Bennett, Abraham, 270
,, 150, 300
,, J., 148
Benson, James, 266
,, Rev. J., 151
Bent, Ed., 196
,, The Misses, 87
Bent's Literary Advertiser, 87
Bentham, 86
Bentley, J., 238
Berrie, Jno., 154
Beswick, Chas., 165
Beverley, H., 311
Bianchi, 98
Bible Society, 253
Bickham, 136
Billington, Rev. J., 38, 189
Binney, Rev. T., 140
Binyon, Alfred, 184
,, Ancestors, 93
,, Benjamin, 83, 186
,, T. and E., 93, 184, 236
,, Sisters, 186

Birch, Scholes, 173
Birchin Lane Chapel, 149
Birley, H. H., 236, 269
,, Workpeople, 292
Birt, Rev. J., 187, 254
Bishop of Chester, 117, 255
,, London, 311
Bishop's "Seventh Day," 300
Black-a-Moor's Head, 14
Blackberd, G., 64
Blackburne, Rev. Dr., 117
,, Isaac, 117, 196
Blackburn Academy, 131
Black Horse, 292
,, Mare, 292
,, Friar's Bridge, 15, 106, 148
Blackley Chapel, 179
Blaine, Hy., 71
Bland, Lady Ann, 118
Bleachers, 41
Blears, Joseph, 309
Blinkhorn, 273
Blood-letting, 58, 303
Bloor, 8, 49
Blundstone, 51-269
Boats, Passage, 223
Bob Logic's Budget, 113
Boddington, T. and H., 137
Bolongaro, D., 97
Bolton Street Chapel, 194
Bond, 271
Bonded Warehouses, 113
Bonnets, 318
Booth, G. & H., 133
,, Humphrey, 118
,, Rev. E., 124
,, S., 119
Boroughreeve (1829), 238
Botanical Gardens, 113
,, Society, 266
Boulton & Watt, 242
,, Wm., 184
Boundary Street, 12
Boutflower, 49, 268
Bower, Alexander, 240
,, Miles, 248
Bowling Green, 263
Bradburn, Rev. S., 151

Bradbury, Ch., 95, 267
,, Robert, 102
,, Rev. D., 129, 130
Bradley, 73.
,, Rev. S., 124, 130, 134
,, S. M., 130
Bradshaw, 184
,, John, 137, 186, 236
Braham, 300, 304
Braid, James, 51
Braidley, Benjamin, 20, 236, 254
Braik, Alexander, 154
Bramall, 254
Bramwell, Rev. Wm., 159
Brandram, Rev. A., 254
Brandt, 195
Breach of Promise, 200
Bread Riot, 95
Breary, William, 63
Breeches, Knee, 317
Brereton, J., 63
Brewer, John, 25, 162
,, Mary, 162
Bridge Accident, 15
,, Street Shambles, 274
Bridges, 1, 15
Bridgewater Arms, 7
,, Street Chapel, 162
Brierley James, 150, 196
,, Sam, 121
Bright, John, 29
British Volunteer, 280
Brittain, Thomas, 45
Broadhurst, Henson, & Co., 20
Brockbank, 185
Brogden, Alexander, 105
,, John, 105, 154
Bromley, Mary, 149
Brooks, Frederick, 30
,, John, 28, 236
,, Sam., 10, 28, 105, 133, 236, 254
Broome, 93
Broomhead, Rev. R., 189
Brotherton, Joseph, 30, 192, 193, 284, 332
Brougham, Lord, 222, 265
Broughton Bridge, 15

Brown, Capt., 18
,,   Dr. Henry, 143
,,   G. B., 70
,,   W. S., 66, 68
,,   Street, 258
Brownbill, Thomas, 53
Brundretts, The, 168
Buck, Thomas, 298
Buckland, Rev. G., 178
Buckley, Edward, 237
,,   Jeremiah, 200
Building Societies, 292
Bull, Rev. G. S., 254
Bullbaiting, 310
Bullock, 63, 64   [164
Bunting, Rev. Jabez, 151, 157, 160,
Bunting, Rev. William, 136, 167
,,   T. P., 166, 199
Burd, Ald., 133, 165
Burdett, Sir Francis, 312
Burdsall, Rev. J., 152
Burgess, Henry, 281
Burial Grounds, 161, 168
Burton & Sons, 34, 125
,,   John, 34, 254
,,   Rev. Dr., 34, 35, 124
Bury, F., 269
,,   J., 39
Butter Market, 274
Butterworth & Brooks, 17, 28
Bye-Law Men, 241
Byrom, Ed., 120
,,   John, 121, 147, 309
,,   House, 129
,,   Miss, 254

Calico Printers, 27
Callender, W. R., 17, 136, 137
,,   S. P., 137
,,   & Sons, 163
Calvert, Chas., 73
,,   Rev. Dr., 10, 117, 255
Campbell, 314
Campion, H., 259
Cannon Street, 19
,,   ,,   Chapel, 128, 130
Capes, 18, 101
Caracci, A., 120

Caradori Allan, 300, 302
Carbutt, Dr., 323
Card, Nat., 185
Cardwell, Hy., 200
Carlisle, Earl of, 311
Carlton, Jas., 24, 145
,,   Walker, & Lewis, 24
Carriages (First Rail), 234
Carriers (Land and Water), 223, 225
Carpenter, Rev. P. P., 180
Carter, Wm., 166
Carver, 174, 224
Casartelli, 98
Casinos, 308
Cassell, Jno., 138
Casson & Berry's Map, 272
Castle Irwell, 16
Cateaton Street, 14
Catholic Phœnix, 281
Cathrall, Wm., 280, 288
Cave, Geo., 89
Cemetery, Friends', 181
Chain Bridge, 15
Challender, Joseph, 14, 267
Chalmers, Dr., 189
Chamber of Commerce, 272
Chancery Lane Chapel, 164
Chantilly House, 6
Chapel, Ancoats, 166
,,   Baptist, 187
,,   Beef Steak, 192
,,   Birchin Lane, 149
,,   Blackley, 179
,,   Bridgewater Street, 162
,,   Cannon Street, 128, 130
,,   Chancery Lane, 164
,,   Chapel Street, 144
,,   Cheetham Hill, 168
,,   Chorlton-cum-Hardy, 167
,,   Christ Church, 192, 193
,,   Cross Street, 170
,,   Dawson's Croft, 176
,,   Dobb Lane, 178
,,   Gadsby's, 187
,,   Gorton, 178
,,   Gravel Lane, 161
,,   Grosvenor Street (Wes-
        leyan), 164

Chapel, Grosvenor Street (Independent), 131
Chapels, Independent, 10, 128
Chapel, Irwell Street, 157
    ,,   Jackson Street, Hulme, 144
    ,,   Lee Street, 146
    ,,   Monton, 179
    ,,   Mosley Street (Independent), 10, 135
    ,,   Mosley Street (Unitarian), 10, 175
    ,,   Oldham Street, 121, 136, 150, 155
    ,,   Oxford Road, 166
    ,,   Platt, 176
    ,,   Presbyterian (Lloyd Street) 188
    ,,   Quakers, 53, 181
Chapels, Roman Catholic, 189
Chapel, Rusholme Road, 143
    ,,   Stand, 180
    ,,   Swan Street, 163
Chapels, Unitarian, 10, 170
    ,,   Various, 181
    ,,   Wesleyan, 147
Chapel, Windsor Bridge, 145
Chapman, James, 197, 273, 281
Chappell, G. R., 18, 25, 165, 166
Charitable Institutions, 247
Charles, Prince, 5, 278
"Charleys," 239
Checkley, Rev. J., 178
Cheek, Rev. N., 124
Cheeryble Brothers, 36
Cheetham, James, 5, 81
    ,,   Hill, 14
    ,,   ,,   Chapel, 168
Cheetham's Murder, 310
Chemistry, Lecture on, 265
Cheshire Circuit, 150
Chester Road, 12
    ,,   Coach, 219
Chetham's Statue, 99
Chew, 200
Christie, Robert, 270
    ,,   J. T., 271
Choral Society, 297, 298
Chorlton, Rev. Wm., 171
    ,,   Row, 12

Chorlton-cum-Hardy Chapel, 167
Christ Church Chapels, 192
Chronicle, Manchester, 80, 277 279, 282, 286
Church and King Mob, 110
    ,,   ,,   Club, 279
Churches of England, 115
Church, All Saints, 124
    ,,   St. Ann's, 118
    ,,   ,, Andrew's, 127
    ,,   ,, Clement's, 123
    ,,   Collegiate, 116
    ,,   St. George's, 124
    ,,   ,,   ,,   (Hulme), 127
    ,,   ,, James, 121
    ,,   ,, John's, 120, 142
    ,,   ,, Luke's, 124
    ,,   ,, Mark's, 123
    ,,   ,, Mary's, 119
    ,,   ,, Matthew's, 126
    ,,   ,, Michael's, 122
    ,,   ,, Paul's, 119
    ,,   ,, Peter's, 122
    ,,   ,, Philip's, 126
    ,,   ,, Stephen's, 124
    ,,   ,, Thomas' (Ardwick), 118
    ,,   ,,   ,, (Pendleton), 121
    ,,   Trinity, 118
Circuit, Cheshire, 150
    ,,   First Manchester, 150
    ,,   Grosvenor Street, 167
    ,,   Oldham Street, 153
    ,,   Oxford Road, 167
Clare, Peter, 107, 143, 184, 262, 264
Clark, 2
Clarke, Dr. Adam, 151, 153, 169, 256
    ,,   Rev. James, 193
    ,,   J. B., 136
    ,,   Robert, 75, 312.
Class Meetings, 166
Clayton, 121, 147
Clegg, 129
Clergymen's dress, 316
Clock, Lit. and Phil. Society, 107
Clowes, Rev. J. (St. John's), 120, 192, 254.
Clowes, Rev. J. (Collegiate Church), 117, 118, 255.
Clunie, Rev. Dr., 145

Coach Accidents, 215, 269
,, Offices, 210
,, Defiance, 212
,, Doctor, 214
,, Lord Nelson, 219
,, Mail, 211, 212
,, Peveril of Peak, 212
,, Red Rover, 213
,, Telegraph, 212
Coaches, Stage, 209
,, Liverpool, 214
,, on May Day, 220
,, Opposition, 216
,, Sundry, 219
Coachman's Fees, 215
Coats, 317
Coates, Richard, 200
Cobbett, William, 312
Cobden, Richard, 29, 109
,, Miss, 314
Cockbain, J. H., 184, 263
Cockfighting, 310
Cock Gates, 51
,, Pit Hill, 89, 310
Cockshoot, 93
Collars, Shirt, 317
College of Physicians, 262
,, Independent, 131, 132, 138
Collinson, 185
Colour Blindness (Dalton), 262
Commercial Inn, 7
Commissioners of Police, 236
Concert Hall, 11, 113, 271, 297
Concerts, Weekly, 308
Condy, George, 74, 195, 282
Coningham, Rev. J., 171
Consistory Court, 303
Constables, 237, 238
Constantine, Thomas, 293
Cook, John, 64
,, Rev. J., 118
Cooke, 301
Cooke & Beever, 200
Coombs, Rev. J. A., 144, 254, 255
Cooper, Frederick, 102
,, I., J., & G., 22
,, Thomas, 279
Corbett, Matthew & Ed., 185, 186

Corn Exchange and Market, 274
,, Laws, 29, 139
Coroner, 113, 197
Corporation Street, 5
Cottam, S. E., 270
Courier, Manchester, 277, 281, 290, 291
Court of Requests, 7
Cowdroy & Rathbone, 281
Cowdroy's *Manchester Gazette*, 283, 288
Cowherd, Rev. William, 192
Cramer F., 301
Crewdson, Isaac, 184, 186, 254
,, Jos.,Thos., and Wilson, 184
Crighton, Thomas, 143
Crompton, Joshua, 184
Crook, Rev. James, 189, 303
Cropper, Rev. Jno., 180
Crossfield, Joseph, 185
Crossley, 181
,, James, 197
,, George, 240, 257
Cross Lane Market, 273
Cross Street Chapel, 170
Crow Alley, 272
Crowther, Mrs., 160
,, Joshua, 160, 198
,, Robert, 54
Cudmore, Richard, 103, 298
Cumber, Charles, 185
Cunliffe, R. E., 200
Cunliffes, Brooks, & Co., 4
Cupid's Alley, 12, 181
Currie, Dr., 260
Cutting, Charles, 143

Dale, 68
,, Rev. Mr., 166
,, John, 160
Dallas, John, 257
,, Rev. R., 120, 257
Dalton, Dr., 106, 184, 260, 262, 268
Damages, Heavy, 200
Danson, George, 68, 184
Darbishire, James, 173, 174, 279

Darbyshire & Co., 6
Daubholes, 248
Davies, Rev. R. M., 137, 139
,, Ald., 159
,, John, 262, 265, 268
Dawson, 120, 261
,, Jonathan, 269
Dawson Street, 261
Dawson's Croft Chapel, 176
Day, 270
Dean, Rev. A., 180
,, R. W., 79, 89
,, S., 67
Deansgate, 12
De Beriot, 301
Debates, Parliamentary, 276
Dentists, 59
Dentith, Wm., 3, 30, 70, 154
Derby, Earl of, 310
"Descent from Cross" (picture), 120
Detrosier, 271
Dickenson Street, 10
"Dictum Factum," 111
Dinner Hour, 46
Diorama, 182¹
Dispensaries, 252
Districts, Police, 235
Dixon, Elijah, 88
Dobb Lane Chapel, 178
Dockray, D., 184
Doctors, 47, 323
"Doctor, The," 280
Dog and Partridge, 256
Dolly Rexford, 112
Doncaster Races, 112
Downs, John, 161
Dowton, 75, 313
Dowty, Rev. Thos., 157
Dracup, 145
Dragonetti, 304
Dress, 316
Druggists, 60
Drummond, Peter, 24, 160
Drunkenness, 319
Drysalters, 42, 43
Ducie Bridge, 14, 15
Duck, Robt., 19, 241
Duckers, Peter, 156

Duckworth, Ellis, 99
,, & Co., 200
,, William, 175
Dugard, Rev. Geo., 127
Dugdale, Jno., 30, 31, 50
Duke of Wellington, 228
,, James, 159
Dunckley, Hy., 290
Dunn, Rev. Sam., 152
Duty on Prints, 27

Earl of Wilton, 255
Easby, John, 113
Eccles, Cririe, & Slater, 195
,, Wakes, 310
Edge, Joseph, 145
Edwards, John and James, 137
Edmondson, Thomas, 183
Eland, 240
Elastics, 318
Eldershaw, 204
Ely, Rev. John, 140, 141
Ellerby, William, 84, 139
,, W. P., 137
Elliott, Ebenezer, 314
Elliotson, Dr., 314
Elsdale, Rev. Robert, 257
"Emma," Capsizing of, 137
England, Joseph, 154
Entwistle, William, 11
Envelope, Postage, 208
Erskine, 110
Ethelstone, Rev. C. W., 117, 123, 196
Evangelical Friends, 186
Evans, T. J., 87
Eveleigh, S. & J., 184
Evening Sun, 276
Everett, Rev. James, 6, 77, 151
Ewart, Peter, 175, 262
,, Joseph, 303
Examiner and Times, 289
Exchange, 272
,, *Herald*, 281
Eye Institution, 251

Fairbairn, Sir William, 174
Fancy Dress Ball, 5, 6, 13, 301

Fares by Rail, 232
Farmer, Mrs. T., 155
Faulkner, 224, 279
   ,,   & Son, 59
   ,,   Street, 10
Fawdington, 53, 268
Felt Hats, 316
Female Penitentiary, 253
Fennel Street, 14
Fernley, George, 54
   ,,   John, 11, 166, 184
Ferrier, Dr. John, 260
"Festus," Bayley's, 90
Fielden, R., 196
Fielding, Rev. H., 255
Fildes, John, 32, 137
   ,,   Jas. & Thos., 96, 154, 254
   ,,   Thos., 96, 149
Finance Committee, 236
Finch, Rev. —, 177
Fish Market, 274
Fleming, Thos., 106, 236, 243, 266, 281
Fletcher, Burd, & Wood, 20, 133
   ,,   Mrs., 65
   ,,   J. & Co., 94
   ,,   Sam., 21, 236, 254
   ,,   ,, Son, & Co., 133
   ,,   David, 133, 139
   ,,   Auctioneer, 308
Flintoff, 185
Floral and Horticultural Society, 267
Fly Sheets, 153
Ford, John, 286
Forrest, 80, 286
Fort Bros., 29
Forth, Hy., 137, 236
Foster, Rev. Jno., 314
   ,,   J. F., 10, 195, 196, 240
Foulkes, Ed., 8, 201
Fountain Street, 21
Fowden, 185
Fowler, Rev. Joseph, 151
   ,,   H. H., M.P., 151
Fox, Geo., 181
   ,,   Susannah, 259
Freckleton, Dr., 268

Free Trade Hall, 11
Freeston, Rev. J., 179
Friar, Geo. Hy., 94
Friends' Meeting House, 181
   ,,   Cemetery, 181
   ,,   Secession of, 186
Froggatt, 292
Furniss, Micah, 100
Furniture Removing, 321

Gadsby, Rev. W., 187, 188
Gadsby's Chapel, 187
Gale, Joseph, 98, 326
Galor, Wm., 9, 249
Galloway and Bowman, 102
Garbutt, Dr., 249
Gardner, Lot, 74
Gardom, 53
Garnett, Jeremiah, 5, 11, 80, 236, 285, 286
Garnett, William, 252, 269, 332
Garside, 231
Gas, 242, 244
Gaskell, Rev. J., 193
   ,,   ,, Wm., 172
   ,,   Mrs., 172
Gasquoine, 145
Gatcliffe, Rev. John, 117, 119
Gaulter, J. W., 65, 71
   ,,   Rev. John, 65, 151
Gazette, Manchester, 277
Gearey and Horne, 101
George and Dragon, 66, 82
   ,,   Street, 10
Gentlemen's Glee Club, 297
Germon, Rev. N., 122, 257
Gibb, Wm., 93
Gibson, Rev. N. W., 118
Gillow, Rev. Henry, 38, 189, 190
"Gimcrackiana," 43, 82, 83
Gladstone, W. E., 22
Glasgow, 236
Gleave, Joseph, 2, 83
Glee Club, 297
Goadsby, Francis, 63
Goodall, Ed., 91, 144, 333
Goodier, 185
Goodwin, S., 133

Gore, Rev. W., 171
Gorton Chapel, 178
Gough, John, 260, 264
Government of Town, 235
Grafton, F. W., M.P., 136
Granby Row Chapel, 190
Grant, Daniel, 10, 35, 39, 256
  ,,   William and Bros., 35
Gravel Lane Chapel, 161
Gray, Luke, 165
Greaves, Ed., 271
  ,,   John, 196
  ,,   George, 19
  ,,   Hugh, 19, 154
Greenwood, John, 108
  ,,   ,,   284
  ,,   Turner, & Clough, 109
Greg, R. II., 175, 269
Gregory, 298
  ,,   Rev. B., 147
Gregson, J. S., 43, 82
Greswell, Ch., 51
  ,,   Rev. W. P., 51
Griffin, Rev. James, 143
Griffiths, John, 133
Grindrod, 54
  ,,   Rev. Edmund, 151
Grosvenor Place, 12
Grosvenor-st. Chapel, (Indep.), 131
  ,,   ,,   (Wesln.), 164
Grundy, C. S., 176
  ,,   George, 166
  ,,   Rev. John, 172
  ,,   & Fox, 97
Guard of Mail, 212
  ,,   Telegraph, 212
  ,,   Lord Nelson, 219
Guard's Fees, 215
Guardian, Manchester, 277, 282, 286, 291
Guardian Office, 5
Guest, W. E., 250, 268
  ,,   Rev. W. B., 257
Guest's Mill, 238
Gwyther, Rev. James, 144

Hackney Coaches, 245
Hadfield, George, 84, 137, 143, 198, 254

Hadfield, John, 30
Hadley, Bob, 218
Haigh, Job, 112
Hale & Roworth, 85
Hall, Rev. Sam, 122
  ,,   Mrs. Frances, 257
  ,,   James, 184, 267
  ,,   John, 173
  ,,   Platt, 177
  ,,   Strangeways, 134
Hallé's Concerts, 308
Halley, Rev. Dr., 129, 131
Halliwell, John, 258
Hamilton, Rev. Dr., 140
  ,,   Gavin, 54
Hampson, John, 282
  ,,   R., 132
Hanging, 310
Hanley, William, 292
Hannah, Rev. Dr., 167
Harbottle, Thomas, 136, 137, 238
Hardman, Thomas, 255
  ,,   Street, 12
Hardy, Joseph, 165
Hargreaves, R. H., 64, 67
Harland, Dr., 50
  ,,   John, 287
Harper, 301, 305
Harris, Rev. Dr., 140
Harrison, Rev. Ralph, 171
  ,,   ,,   William, 179
  ,,   Thomas, 94
  ,,   John, 154
  ,,   Mary, 259
  ,,   ,,   & Co., 100
  ,,   ,,   William, 267
Harrop, Joseph, 277
  ,,   James, 202
Hats, 316
Hatton, William, 74
Haughton, Rev. —, 178
Hawks, Rev. Ed., 259
Hawkes, Rev. William, 175
Hawkshaw, Sir John, 145
Haworth, John, 9
  ,,   Richard, 162
Haymarket, 274
Haynes, William, 236
Hayward's Hotel, 256, 297

Heap, 70, 122, 332
Hearne, Rev. Daniel, 38, 189, 190
Heaton Park Races, 310
Hedley, Atkinson & Co., 35
Heelis, Stephen, 195
Helsby, 59
Henry, Alexander, M.P., 173
   ,,   Dr., 6, 175, 249, 262, 265, 266, 269
   ,,   Thomas, 260, 261
Henry's Magnesia, 262
Henson, Robert, 158, 165
Hepworth, Rev. A., 124, 254
Herald, The, 277
Herford, Rev. Brooke, 176
Heron, J. H., 136, 254
   ,,   Sir Joseph, 136
Herschel, Sir William, 152
Hesketh, 95
Heurtley, 54
Hewley, Lady, 84
Heyhurst, 166
Heywood, Abel, 173
   ,,   Benjamin, M.P., 173, 262
   ,,   James, 173
High Street, 17
Higson, Bagshaw, & Co., 200
Hill, 7
   ,,   William & John, 92, 160
Hime & Hargreaves, 92
Hinde's Charity, 113
Hindley, Robert, 76, 266, 269
Hindmarsh, Rev. —, 194
History of England, 278
Holland, F. W., 177
Hollingworth, Rev. R., 128
Holme, Dr., 48, 173, 262, 264, 266, 269, 273
Holt, David, 7, 185, 269
   ,,   John, 133
Holy Club, 147
Hopkins, Thomas, 236, 270
Hopkinsons, The, 143
Hopper, Rev. C., 148
Hopps, Ann and John, 5, 86
Hopwood Avenue, 288
Hook, Rev. Dr., 127
Hookers-In, 43, 44

Hoole, Rev. —, 147
Hordern, Rev. Peter, 123, 255, 257, 266
Horne, Rev. Melville, 124, 255
Horrocks, 293
Horte, Rev. C. D., 178
Hospital Sunday (1792), 249
   ,,   St. Mary's, 250
   ,,   Lying In, 250
   ,,   Lock, 252
Hotel, Mitre, 268
   ,,   Spread Eagle, 274
Hough End Hall, 275
Houldsworth, Thomas, 8, 309
   ,,   Henry, 175
Howarth, Rev. D., 194
Howe, Wm., 269
Hoyle, Lucy, 93
   ,,   Thos., 184, 267
   ,,   ,,   & Son, 31, 40
Hughes, 63
   ,,   Moses, 103, 142, 298
   ,,   Thos., 132
Hull, Dr., 48
   ,,   John, 154
Hulme, 12
Hulme, Dr. D., 48, 249, 258, 269
   ,,   Otho & Sons, 35
   ,,   Joseph, M.P., 271
   ,,   J. H., 145
Humphreys, Geo., 175
Hunt, R. T., 50
   ,,   Hy., 194, 274, 312
Hunter, Thos., 137
Hunter's Lane, 128
Huntingdon, Rev. W., 120
Huskisson, 230
Hyde, Jas., 103

Ince, John, 132
Independent Chapels, 10, 128
India Rubber Goods, 318, 321
Infirmary, 9, 247
   ,,   Baths, 9, 249
Ingham & Westmacott, 61
Inglescent, Tom, 299
Insecurity of Roads, 18
Inspectors of White Meats, 240

Institutions, Charitable, 247
Institution, Mechanics', 265, 270
,, ,, New, 270
,, Royal, 269
Instrumentalists, Musical Fest., 300
Inventions, Scientific, 319
Ireland, Alex. & Co., 289
Iris, The, 281
Irwell, 14
,, Street Chapel, 157
Isherwood, 297
Ivanoff, 300

Jack, Rev. Dr., 188
Jackson, Rev. E. Dudley, 126, 333
,, ,, Thomas, 151
,, E. & J., 20
,, Stanway, 143
,, Watson, & Greg, 37
Jackson's Lane, 12
,, ,, Chapel, 144
Jacobin Mob, 171
James, Rev. John, 215
,, ,, J. A., 140
Jarrold, Dr., 49, 136
Jay, Rev. William, 140
Jennison, 308
Jesse, John, 54
Jewish Immigrants, 191
,, Synagogue, 191
Jewsbury & Whitlow, 6, 64, 65
,, Miss G., 65, 333
,, ,, M. J., 65, 134
Joachim, Herr, 298
John Dalton Street, 12
Johns, Rev. William, 107, 263
Johnson, Ann, 225
,, Fynney, 160
,, James, 198
,, Rev. John, 257
,, ,, William, 124
,, Richard, 198
,, Sam, 88
,, William, 258
,, William, 186
,, W. R., 155, 165
Johnson & Rawson, 80
Jollie, Rev. Timothy, 171
"Jolly Carters," 309

Jones, Charles, 204
,, Paul, 157
,, Samuel, 174, 179
,, W. H., 89
,, Rev. William, 157
Jordan, Joseph, 50, 268
,, Mrs., 75
Joule, Benjamin, and Family, 99, 133, 254
Jubilee (George III.), 257

Kay, Alex., 173, 198
,, Dr. J. P., 55, 136
,, John Robinson, 1
,, Samuel, 173
,, Thomas, 1
,, & Darbyshire, 200
Kean (Elder), 222
Keeling, Rev. William, 121
Keighley, 271
Kelly, David, 88, 332
Kemble, Charles, 75, 313
,, John, 156
Kennedy, John, 175
,, Rev. —, 134
Kenworthy & Co., 223
,, Peter, 150
Kenyon, Lord, 255
Kersall Moor, 308
Kershaw, James, M.P., 9, 17, 133, 139
,, Thomas, 279
Kidd, Rev. W., 126, 333
Kidson, Joseph, 7
Kinchin, Ch., 147
King, Ald., 183
,, John, 101, 184
,, Street, 13
,, ,, Lower, 12
King's Birthday, 220
Kirkpatrick, Rev. Cleland, 157
Knowles, John, 4, 211
,, Thomas, 203
Knutsford, 261
Knyvett, Mrs., 300

Lablache, 300, 302, 304
Labreys, The, 94, 185, 236
Lacey, Hy. Ch., 2, 210, 240, 241

Lacye, Sir John, 275
Ladies' Dress, 318
Lamb, James, 137, 139
　,,　W. H., 60
　,,　Inn, 292
Lamp Committee, 236
Lancaster, 284, 285
　,,　John, 96
Land, Price of, 68
Lane (Architect), 182
　,,　Hunters, 128
Lathom, John, 136
Lavender, Stephen, 237, 240
Law, John, 7, 200, 329
Lawyers, 195
Lee, Daniel, & Co., 11, 19
　,,　John, 259
　,,　W. & R., 131
　,,　Street Chapel, 146
Leech, James, 243
Lees, Jonathan, 132
Leese, Joseph, 17
　,,　Kershaw, & Callender, 17
Legal Hundred, 159
Legh, of Lyme, 34
L'Hirondelle Coach, 218
Leigh, John, 81, 281
　,,　Silas, 180
Leresche, Mrs., 74, 282
Lessey, John, 66
　,,　Rev. Theoph., 68
Letter Carriers, 204
Letters, Double, 206
　,,　Delivery of, 207
Lewis, Edward, 133
Liberals, Manchester, 110, 279
Libraries, Public, 273
Library, Free, 113
Liefchild, Rev. Dr., 140
"Light of other Days," 302
Light, Striking a, 320
Lignum, Dr., 57, 254
Lindley, William, 301, 304
Lingard, Rev. Joshua, 127
Literary and Philosophical Society, 48, 173, 260
Liverpool Coaches, 214
Livingstone, 132

Lloyd, Ed. Jeremiah, 195, 269
　,,　George, 279
　,,　Rev. E. B., 215
　,,　Street Chapel, 188
Lock Hospital, 252
Loftus, Sarah, 250
Logerian System of Music, 103
Lomas, Rev. John, 152
　,,　Jno. and Geo., 165
Lomax, 275
London, Bishop of, 311
Longevity, 8, 120
Lord, Rev. Wm., 254
Lovatt, 3
Love and Barton, 85
　,,　Benj., 85
Loyd, Rev. Lewis, 178
　,,　Ed., 256, 266
Lubbock, Sir John, 123
Lucifer Matches, 320
Lunatic Asylum, 248
Lying-in Hospital, 250
Lynch, Daniel, 6, 60, 249
Lyndhurst, Lord, 96
Lyons, Dr., 49, 249

M'All, Rev. R. S., 10, 11, 134, 136, 254
　,,　　,,　Death of, 141
　,,　　,,　and Long Sermons, 141, 143
M'Connell, Henry and John, 175
Macardy, Joseph, 281
Macfadyen, Rev. J. A., 131
Machin, 300
Mackie, Ivie, 173
Mackintosh Garments, 321
Maclure, 18, 145, 164, 254, 266
Macready, 75, 312
Mad Tom, 304
Maddocks, Rev —., 189
Maden, Mrs., 56
Magistrates, 196, 240
Mail, The, 280
Mail Coaches, 211, 212
Mails, English and Foreign, 207
Makinson, John, 198
Malbon, 261

Malibran, 300
,, Death of, 303
Mallory, Rev. J. H., 117
Malones, The, 298
Manchester Negatively, 113
,, Academy, 261
,, First Election, 122
,, *Chronicle*, 278
,, *Courier*, 277, 281, 290
,, *Examiner & Times*, 289
,, *Guardian*, 277, 282, 286, 291
,, *Journal*, 278
,, *Magazine*, 278, 281
,, *Times*, 287, 288, 289
,, ,, *and Gazette*, 288
,, *and Salford Advertiser*, 74, 282
Manor Court Room, 7, 274
,, of Manchester, 275
Map of Manchester, 272
Marcet, Mrs., 314
"Marienbourn" (Tune), 155
Markets, 273
Market, Corn, 274
,, Cross Lane, 273
,, Fish, 274
,, Hay, 274
,, Lookers, 240
,, Manchester (1829), 1
,, Potato, 274
,, Smithfield, 273
,, Smithy Door, 274
,, Street, 2
,, ,, Improvement, 5
,, Tolls, 274
Marris, Son, & Jackson, 20
,, J. M., 266
,, Francis, 164, 165
Marsden Square, 19
,, John, 165
,, Rev. Geo., 122, 151, 164
,, ,, Wm., 122
Marsland John, 166
,, Joseph, 74
,, Henry and Samuel, 173
Martindale, Rev. Miles, 151
Martineau, Miss, 314

"Martyr of Antioch," 298
Mason, John, 166
Massey, James, 260
,, Joseph, 247, 248
Matches, 320
Matley, S., & Son, 40
Maude, Fr., 273
May Day and Coaches, 220
Meanley, Rev. —, 178
Mechanics' Institution, 265, 270
Medical Institutions, 247
Meeting House, Friends', 181
Melland, 143
Mellor, 292
Mendel, Emmanuel, 4, 191, 236
Mercantile Gazette, 280
Mercury, The, 277, 279
Meredith, Charles, 93
Merone, Joseph, 97
Merrick, Josiah, 185
Merry, Thomas, 258
"Messiah," Handel's, 301, 304
Methodism, Origin of, 147
,, and the Theatre, 311
Methodist, First Preaching-room, 148
Methodist, First Society, 148
Middleton, Robert, 64
Midwood, Joseph, 137
M'Kerrow, Dr., 188, 189
M'Keand, 309
Miller, Horatio, 30, 72, 73, 76, 92, 297, 299, 304, 313, 323, 324
,, Rev. Wm. Ed., 152
Millward, 155
Milnes, The, 196, 197
Mise Layers, 240
Mitchell, Dr., 47, 49, 249
Mitre Hotel, 14, 268
Mob, Church and King, 110, 280
Moffatt, Rev. Robert, 132
Molineaux, James, 250
Monton Chapel, 179
Moore, 314
,, John, 266
Mordacque, M., 102
Mori, 301
Morris, 5

Morris, Alex., 185
  ,, James, 154
  ,, John, 159, 269
  ,, Wm., 102
Mosley Arms, 7
  ,, Street, 9, 10
  ,, ,, Independent Chapel, 10, 135
  ,, ,, Unitarian Chapel, 10, 175
  ,, John, 150
  ,, Sir Oswald, 266, 269, 272, 275
  ,, Sir N., 275
Moss Side, 12
  ,, Fletcher, 95
  ,, Joseph, 259
Mottershead, John, 62
  ,, Rev. Joseph, 62, 171
  ,, & Brown, 62, 254
Mountcastle, 6
Mowbray, 266
Mozart's "Requiem," 300
Mulberry Street, 38
Mullis, Wm., 257
Murdoch, 242
Murphy, P. J., 259
Murray, 150
Music, 297, 308
  ,, Halls, 308
  ,, Sacred, 190
Musical Festival, 298, 300, 306

Nadin, Joe, 86, 237
  ,, T. & J., 196
Napier, John, 164, 165, 168
Nash, Ishmael, 184
Natural History Society, 266, 269
Neckties, 24, 317
Needham, J. C., 49, 104
  ,, Robt., 104
Neild, Ald., 184, 236
  ,, Hy., 185
  ,, Isaac, 185
Nelson, Lord, The, 217
Neruda, N., 298
Newall, Wm., 3, 96, 136, 254
Newall's Buildings, 3

New Brown Street, 5, 21
Newcome, Rev. Hy., 128, 170
Newspapers, 276
  ,, London, 204
  ,, and Post Office, 204
  ,, Tax on, 277
Newton, Rev. John, 129
  ,, ,, Robert, 151, 155, 160
"Nicholas Nickleby," 36
Nicholls Humphrey, 118
Nicholson, 301
Nield, Henry, 250
Nodal, James, Aaron, & John, 185
Norris, 133
  ,, James, 195
Northern Express, 281
Northumbrian Engine, 229
Norwich Union Office, 7
Nosworthy, Frederick, 183
Notable Persons, 105
Noton, T. S., 240
Novello, Clara, 300
Numbering of Streets, 2
Nunn, Rev. William, 123, 254
Nuttall, John, 225

Observer, The, 86, 281
O'Connor, 312
Odd Fellows' Society, 258
Oddie, James, 150
Officers, Municipal, 240, 241
Officials, Curious, 235
  ,, Police, 238
Ogden, Robert, 9
Old Bridge, 14
  ,, Church, 116, 300
  ,, Coachman, 216
  ,, Meal House, 292
  ,, Quay Company, 40
Oldfield Lane Doctor, 55
Oldfield Ben, 313
Oldham, Adam, 149
  ,, Street Chapel, 121, 136, 150, 155
  ,, Street Chapel Orchestra, 155
Olivant, 254
Oliver, 150

Opposition Coaches, 216
"Original, The," 111
Otley, 286
Overstone, Lord, 174, 179
Owen, Rev. Henry, 122
„ John, 200, 266
„ Mrs., 256
Owens, John, 141, 142, 174
Oxford Road, 10, 11
„ „ Chapel, 166

Paganini, 298
„ Tavern, 299
Palace Inn, 4
Palmer, John, 190
„ Thomas, 102
Paris, Prosper, 102
Parish Clerk, 118
Parker Street, 10
Parkinson, Alex., 293
„ Rev. Dr., 127
Parks, Public, 113
Parliament Street, 12
Parry, James, 39
„ Jno., 143
„ Thomas, 118
Parsons, Rev. James, 140
Passage Boats, 223
Patrick, James, 89
Patriot, The, 281
Paulton, Abraham Walter, 289
Paving Committee, 236
Peacock, H. B., 72, 289, 290
„ George, 159
„ Michael, 254
„ Richard, 178
„ Coach Office, 4, 211
Pearson, Benjamin, 184
Pedley, Rev. James, 121
Peduzzi, Antony and James, 97, 98
Peel, Sir Robert, 32, 37
„ Yates, & Co., 32
„ Williams, & Peel, 102
„ Park, 103
Peel's Act, 126, 127
„ Warehouse, 33
Penketh's 'Bus, 108
Percival, Dr., 260

Perkins, Geo., 101
„ John, 258
Perth, Duke of, 274
Peter Street, 10, 11
Peterloo Meeting, 286
"Peveril of Peak," 213, 216
Pharmacopœia, 57
Philanthropic Society, 256
Philips, J. and N. & Co., 22
„ Mark, M.P., 22, 180, 236
„ Robert, 180
„ R. N., M.P., 173, 180
Phillips, Aldcroft, 200
„ George, 272, 279, 300, 302
„ Francis, 269
„ and Lee, 242
Photography, 321
Physicians, 47
„ to Infirmary, 249
Piccadilly, 8
Piccope, Rev. J., 119
Pickford's, 10, 223, 226
„ Van Office, 19
Pigot, James, 79, 236
Pilkington, George, 99, 100
Pipe, Rev. John, 151
Pitt, J. W., 102
Places of Worship, 115
Plate Glass Windows, 6
Platt, 301
„ Chapel, 176
Pochin, 332
Police Commissioners, 236
„ Court, 113
„ Districts, 235
Pollard, Wm., 154
Pool Fold, 5
Pope, Henry, 137
„ Samuel, Q.C., 137
Porter, S. T., 133
Portico, 10, 177, 273, 305
Portland Place, 8
„ Street, 10
Post Office, 202, 203, 204, 205, 330
„ Old, 108
„ and Newspapers, 204
Postage, Penny, 208
Posting, 221

Potato Famine, 190
   „   Market, 274
Pot Shrigley, 34
Potter, C. & E., 35, 175
Potter, Richard, 11, 20, 134, 173, 266
   „   Sir John, 20, 173
   „   Thos., 20, 173, 179, 271
   „   „   (Solicitor), 199
   „   „   & Richd., 20, 254
   „   T. B., 20, 173
Potters & Norris, 20
Pounder, 241
Powers, John, 132
Powell, Robt., 132
Pownall, John, 4
Pratt, Joseph, 89, 281
Prentice, Archibald, 287, 288, 290
Presbyterian Chapel, 188
Prescott, John, 279
Prescott's Journal, 278
Preston, Geo., 311
Pretty, 212
Price, Bulkeley, 231
   „   Murder of, 19
Priddie, Rev. James, 145
Priestley, 129
Prince Charles, 5, 278
   „   Samuel, 2, 96, 255
Princess Victoria, 304
Pringle, Sir John, 262
Prints, Duty on, 27
Printed Velvets, 37
Procter, Daniel, 137
"Prophet, Veiled," 282

Quaife, Rev. Barzillai, 137
Quakers' Chapel, 53, 181
Quarter Sessions, 284
Queen's Visit, 103
Queues, 13, 317

Races, 308, 310
Radford, Dr., 49, 251, 264, 268, 323
Raffles, Rev. Dr., 140, 141
Railway Carriages, 234
   „   Furness, 105
   „   M. and L., Opening, 227
Raleigh, 184

Ramsbottom, 109
Ramsden, Fredk., 24
Ramsey, Charles, 37
   „   Joseph, 137
Randall, Rev. M., 117
Ransome, J. A,, 51, 184, 231, 249, 266, 268, 269
Ransome & Co., 65
Rawson, Benjamin, 70
   „   Henry, 289
   „   Jonathan, 292
Rea, Joshua, 165
Recorder, The, 281
Redfern, James, 155
Red Lion, 292
   „   Rover, 4, 71, 213
Refreshment Stall, Anti-Corn-Law Bazaar, 314
Reform Bill, 222
Regent Road Toll Bar, 15
Reid, William, 293
Reiss, Leopold, 175
Religious Tract Society, 84, 255
Renn & Boston, 102
Restaurant, Bee Hive, 83
Rexford, Dolly, 112
Reynolds, Charles, 204
Richardson, Joe, 111
   „   Joseph, 102
   „   John, 87
   „   & Roebuck, 96
Richmond, T. G., 323, 324
Rickards, 284
Ridehalgh, Mrs., 57
Rider, C., 236, 255
Rigg, Rev. Dr., 152
   „   John, 151
Rimmington, Rev. Richard, 117
Ring o' Bells, 14
Riots, 34, 237
   „   Bread, 95
Rippon, C. W., 151
Robberds, Rev. J. G., 172
Roberton, John, 50, 136
Roberts, Ben, 53
   „   John, 8, 53, 81, 154, 158
   „   Richard, 136
   „   Thomas, 62, 137

Roberts, Dale & Co., 63, 68
Robins, Mills, & Co., 223
Robinson, George, 184
    ,,   John (Accountant), 185
    ,,   ,, (Draper), 185
    ,,   Robert, 87
    ,,   Thomas, 173
    ,,   & Ellis, 285
Roby, Rev. Wm., 130, 131, 255
    ,,   ,,   Death, 134
Rogers, 314
Rogerson, Thos., 281
Roman Catholic Chapels, 189
Ronchetti, Joshua, 98
    ,,   Miss, 333
Rookes, The, 184
Rose, Micah, 154
Rothschild, 191
Rothsay Castle, 225
Rothwell, 185
Rowarth, Thomas, 85, 333
Rowbotham, J. F., 168
Royal Hotel, 2, 267
    ,,   ,,   Coach Office, 211
    ,,   Institution, 10, 269
Royle, John, 82
Ruffles, 317
Rules of Building Society, 293-296
Rumney, Alderman, 133
Rusholme Road Chapel, 143
Russell, 84, 168, 290
Rutter, J. S., 196
Rylands, John, 22, 285
    ,,   and Sons, 23
Rymer, 133

Salisbury, Marquis of, 231
Salutation Tavern, 292
Samaritan Society, 256
Sandal Shoes, 319
Sandbach, Daniel, 162
    ,,   John, 166
Sergeant, Rev. Osw., 127
    ,,   Milne & Co., 196
Sargent, Rev. Geo., 215
Satterfield & Co., 91
Satterthwaite, S. & M., 184, 185
Saturday Half Holiday, 46, 113, 308

Saul, Edward, 74
Savings Bank, 19
Scarlett, 284
Scarr, R., 255
Scarr, Petty, and Swain, 101
Scavingers, 241
Schofield & Turnbull, 278
    ,,   Rev. James, 55, 193
Scholes, Tetlow, & Co., 20
School, Blue Coat, 257
    ,,   Catholic, 259
    ,,   Collegiate Church Charity, 258
    ,,   Deaf and Dumb, 258
    ,,   Friends' Female, 259
    ,,   Grammar, 257
    ,,   Granby Row, 258
    ,,   Ladies' Jubilee, 257
    ,,   Lancasterian, 258
    ,,   of Medicine, 268
    ,,   National, 258
    ,,   New Jerusalem, 258
    ,,   St. John's, 259
    ,,   St. Mark's, 259
    ,,   Unitarian, 259
    ,,   Workhouse, 259
Schuster, Leo, 10, 175
Scientific Inventions, 319, 321
Scott, Jerry, 214
    ,,   Joe, 44
Searchers of Leather, 241
Secession, Quakers', 186
Seddon, 111
Seddon, Rev. —, 171
Sedgwick & Co., 155
Sedgwick's Court, 77
Sever, Charles, 89
Severn Warehouse, 224
Sewell, 162
"Shakespeare's Head," 278
Shambles, 7, 12, 274
Sharp, 303
    ,,   Alderman, 137
Sharpe, Roberts, & Co., 93
Shaw, Mrs., 300
    ,,   Rev. E. B., 126
Shaw's, John, 14, 267
Shaving, 316

Sheldon, Stephen & Hugh, 133
Sheldrick, 298
Sherwood, Rev. Joseph, 189
Shimwell, Isaac, 133
    ,,   Thomas, 137
Shirt Ruffles, 317
Shude Hill Pits, 163
Shuttleworth-Kay, Sir J., 136
    ,,   U., 55
Shuttleworth, John, 174
Sidebotham, 133, 139
Sigley, 64
Silkstone, Wm., 166
Simmons, W., 249
Simms, Geo., 88
Simon, Rev. Ed., 144
Simpson, Geo., 185
    ,,   L., 65
Slaggs, The, 21, 333
Slater, 196
Sloane, Jno., 311
Slugg, Rev. Thos., 159, 164
Smart, Sir Geo., 301
Smith, Hill, & Co., 92
    ,,   Charles, 255
    ,,   Rev. Dr., 118, 122, 257
    ,,   ,, Joseph, 132, 134
    ,,   ,, John, 190
    ,,   J. B., M.P., 173
    ,,   Dr. Pye, 314
Smithfield Market, 273
Smithson, Rev. J. H., 194
Smithy Door, 13, 274
Smock Frocks, 225
Smoking, 319
Snell, Bryce, & Co., 223
Smyth, Rev. Edward, 123, 124
Society, Agricultural, 267
    ,,   Bible, 253
    ,,   Botanical, 266
    ,,   Building, 292
    ,,   Christian Knowledge, 255
    ,,   Commercial Clerks, 257
    ,,   Female Servants, 256
    ,,   Floral & Horticultural, 267
    ,,   of Friends, 283
    ,,   Humane, 256   [260
    ,,   Literary and Philosophical,

Society, Natural History, 265, 269
    ,,   Philanthropic, 256
    ,,   Prosecution of Felons, 267
    ,,   Samaritan, 256
    ,,   Stranger's Friend, 256
    ,,   Tract, 255
Soda Water, 71
Soldiers, Accident to, 15
Solomon's Balm of Gilead, 280
Solicitors, 195
Somerset Street, 22
Southam, Geo., 96
Southport Coach, 220
Sowler, Thomas, 84, 241, 285, 290,
    ,,   and Russell, 290   [291
Spectator, The 281
Spectroscope, 322
Spread Eagle, 274
Squance, Rev. T., 159
St. Andrew's Lane, 130
St. Ann's Street, 13
St. Mary's Hospital, 250
St. Mary's Church Spire, 119
St. Peter's Field, 11
Stage Coaches, 209
Staines, Thomas, 62
    ,,   and Mottershead, 62
Stamford and Warrington, Earl of, 266
Stand Chapel, 180
Stanway, J. H., 266
Star Coach Office, 12
    ,,   Yard, 12
Stations, Wayside, 233
Stead, Rev. Abraham, 152
Steamships, 322
Steemson, Mrs. S., 266
Stephens, Rev. John, 151, 164
    ,,   ,, W. R., 151
Stevenson, Isaac, 184
Stevens, Rev. W., 187
Stoby, William, 101
Stocks, John, 69
    ,,   & Dentith, 64, 70
    ,,   Samuel, 155, 165
Stockdale *versus* Hansard, 26
Storey, John, 186
Stowell, Rev. Hugh, 124, 255

Strangeways, 14
Stretford Road, 12, 15
Strettles, Rev. T. B., 193
Strines Printing Co., 38
Strutt, W. & J., 174
Stubbs, J. S., 101
Sudlow, William, 103
Suffield, 266
Sumner, Dr. J. B., 117
,, Rev. John, 167
,, Thomas, 204
Sun Fire Office, 19
Sunday School, First, 96
,, ,, in Whit-week, 308
,, ,, Scholars in Peel Park, 103
Surgeons, 47
Swan Coach Office, 4, 210
,, Street Chapel, 163
Swain, Charles, 73, 87
,, and Dewhurst, 87
Swearing, 319
Swedenborg, 192
Swell Mob, 301
Swindells, John, 89
,, Thomas, 155
Syddall, Thomas, 171
Synagogue, 191

Talbot Inn, 7
Tattersall's Bowling Green, 263
Taylor (Coachman), 217
,, & Garnett, 5, 283
., Rev. George, 145
,, ,, John, 283
,, ,, John J., 10, 175, 262
,, ,, James, 178
,, Edward, 55
,, John, 186
,, John Ed., 173, 186, 236, 283
,, ,, ,, Lawsuit, 284
,, Peter, 184
,, Thos. H., 62
,, William, 293
Tax on Newspapers, 277
Telegraph, 280, 321
Temperance Building Society, 293
Thatched House Tavern, 268

Theatre, First, 310
,, Minor, 311
,, Royal, 11, 298, 300, 305, 312, 314
Thistlewaite, John, 185
,, Rev. Wm., 254
Thistlewood, 236
Thomas, J. S., 237, 301
Thomason, Nicholas, 251
Thompstone, —, 71
Thompson, Ald. Joseph, 141, 142
,, E., 255
,, Geo., 183
,, Jas. (spinner), 185
,, Joseph, senr., 139, 144
,, M'Kay & Co., 224
Thompson's, Jas., Wedding, 144
,, Boarding House, 110
Thomson, —, 268
,, Eb. & Sons, 78
,, Jas. & Jos., 79
Thornley Brow, 128
Thorpe, Jno. & Robt., 51, 249
,, Ellen and Anne, 69
., Issachar, 69
Tickets, Railway, 233
Times, London. 288
,, *Manchester*, 277, 287, 289
Tinder Box, 320
Tinker's Gardens, 307
Tippoo Sahib's violin, 152
Tobacco, Use of, 319
Tobacconists, 3
Toll Bars, 15
,, Lane, 13
Tonics, Use of, 58
Touchet, J., 173
Town Clerk, 113
,, Government, 235
Townend, Thomas, 165
,, William, 269
Townley, Rev. J., 159
Townsend, James, 66
Townsman, The 280
Trafford, T. J., 266
Trains, Liverpool, 232
Trapps, Rev. M., 190
Trousers, 317

Trueman's Warehouse, 108
Tudor, Elizabeth, 259
Turner, R., Junr., & Co., 33
,,   Thomas, 8, 48, 52, 258, 264. 266, 268
Turner, Rev. W., 172
,,   Wm., 34. 270
,,   W. A., 173
Turner's, Miss, Abduction, 34
Twiss' Mill, 238

Unicorn Inn, 14, 267
Union Inn, 293
Unitarian Chapels, 10, 170
Unite, Constable, 280
Upcraft, Rev. Thomas, 187

Various Chapels, 181
Varley, 100
,,   Edward, 101
Vaughan, George, 64
,,   William, 258
Velvets, Printed, 37
Vembergue, Eugene, 103
Victoria, Princess, 304
,,   Street and Bridge, 13
"Victory" Coach, 219
"*Voice of the People*," The, 282

Wadkin, 185, 255
Wagons, 225
Wakefield, Rev. Gilbert, 260
,,   Edward Gibbon, 34
Walker, C. J. S., 110, 317
,,   John, 195
,,   Thomas, 110, 279, 280
Warburton, 136
Ward, Dr., 47, 49
,,   Joseph, 145
,,   Miss, 54
,,   and Andrews, 103
Wardle, Mark, 89
Warehouses, Manchester, 16
Warhurst, Rev. C., 128, 129
Warre, Thomas de la, 116
Warren, Dr., 262
,,   Richard, 237
,,   Samuel and Edward, 3, 70

Warren, Rev. Dr., 3, 70, 96
"Warrington" (Tune), 179
Watch Committee, 236
Watchmen, 239
Water, 244
Waterhouse, Henry, 143, 185
Waterworks, 7, 244
Watkins, Alderman, 43
,,   Abs., 20, 174
,,   Sir Edward, 20
Watkinson, Henry, 64
Watmough, 216, 218
Watson, Bishop, 260
,,   Jemmy, 280
,,   Peter, 236
,,   Rev. R., 164, 167
Watts, Alaric A., 291
,,   S. & J., 21, 130
Waybills, 214
Weatherald, Webster, & Co., 4, 210
Weatherley, 4, 80
Webb & Simms, 88
Wesley, Chas., 148
,,   John, 53, 147, 150, 182
,,   ,,   on Bonnets, 318
Wesleyan Tract Society, 255
,,   Missionary Society, 136
,,   Chapels, 147
Westhead, Edward, 18, 165
,,   Jno., 165
,,   J. Procter, 18
Westmacott, 61
Wetherell, Sir Charles, 97
Whaite, Henry, 93
Whalley, Stephen, 281
Whatton, 231
Wheeler, Chas. & John, 282, 286
,,   Serjeant, 282
Wheelton, 25, 26
,,   Brewer, & Buckland, 25
White Bear, 313
White, Charles, 247, 260
,,   Henry Kirke, 124
,,   Ned, 217
,,   Rev. Jas., 124
,,   Wm., 185, 231
Whitehead, John & Sons, 39
,,   Messrs., 238

Whitehead, Rev. —, 178
"Whitehead, The" (vessel), 40
Whitelegge, Rev: Wm., 177, 178, 273
Whitelock, Rev.R. H., 123, 202, 226
Whitworth, Doctors, 56
,, Sir Joseph, 137
Whitworth's *Manchester Gazette*, 278
Wholesale Firms, 17
Whyatt, George, 267
Wigan, Rev. J., 128
Wilkins, Charles, 73
Wilkinson, James, 155
,, Thomas, 89, 281
,, Wm., 301
Willat, 202
Willert, 303
Williams, Lewis, 133
Williamson Professor, 199
,, S., 273
Willis, William, 88
Willman, 301
Willock, R. P., 203
Wilson, Edward, 204
,, George, 29, 109
,, Sam., 132
,, William, 70
,, W. J., 49, 51, 249
Wilton, Earl of, 230, 255, 266, 310
Wimpory, Jonathan, 101
Windmill Tavern, 99
Windows, Plate Glass, 6
Windsor, John, 49, 51, 184, 186
,, Bridge Chapel, 145
Winter, Gilbert, 236
,, Dr., 145
Wintringham, Sir Charles, 262
Wood, Baron, 284
,, Bateson, 151, 199
,, Charles, 199
,, James, 11, 18, 165, 166
,, Rev. James, 151, 199

Wood, John, 164
,, Kinder, 268
,, George William, 106, 175, 243, 262, 269, 272
,, Rev. Robert, 157, 199
,, Rose, 200
,, William, 323
,, & Wales, 17
,, & Westhead, 17, 255
,, & Wright, 136
Woodall, R., 69
Woodhead, Godfrey, 185
Woodward, William, 136
Woolley, James, 67
,, Mrs. Thomas, 314
,, William, 267
Wordsworth, Rev. W., 118
Worrall, John, 267
Worship, Places of, 115
Worsley, 177
Worthington, —, 302
,, Rev. J., 172
,, H. T., 250
,, John, 186
,, Thomas, 10, 18
Wotton, Philip, 119
Wray, Rev. C. D., 117, 118
Wright & Lee, 19
,, Ralph, 196
,, Thomas P. P., 133
Wroe, James, 86, 281
Wylde, 76

Yates, Mrs., 13
,, Thomas, 13, 240, 317
Young, Chas. Murdo, 222, 276
Young Men's Mutual Improvement Society, 139

Zanetti, Vincent, & Vittore, 97
,, & Agnew, 97
Zoological Gardens, 307, 308

JAMES F. WILKINSON, PRINTER, THE GUTTENBERG WORKS, PENDLETON ;
AND AT 34, OXFORD STREET, MANCHESTER.